BATTLEFIELDS
OF THE SECOND WORLD WAR

BATTLEFIELDS
OF THE SECOND WORLD WAR

Richard Holmes

The author wishes to thank Mark Fielder, Hamish Beeston, Georgina Harvey, Laura Humphreys, Julian Hudson and David Wilson, all of whom worked on the BBC television series that this book accompanies, for their contributions to his understanding of the battles described in it. He owes a particular debt to Hugh Bicheno, a friend for more than 35 years, for his invaluable assistance in getting the typescript ready on time. And his wife Lizzie and daughters Jessica and Corinna have enabled him to sustain this battle, and so many others.

This book is published to accompany the television series
Battlefields, produced by United Productions and first broadcast on BBC2 in 2001
Series producer: Mark Fielder
Directors: Hamish Beeston, Georgina Harvey and David Wilson

Published by BBC Worldwide Limited,
Woodlands, 80 Wood Lane, London W12 0TT

First published 2001
© Richard Holmes 2001
The moral right of the author has been asserted

Maps on page 47 and pages 194–5 based on originals © I.C.B. Dear and Oxford University Press 1995, from *The Oxford Companion to the Second World War,* edited by I.C.B. Dear, consultant editor M.R.D. Foot (1995), by permission of Oxford University Press.

ISBN 0 563 53782 5

Commissioning editor: Sally Potter
Project editor: Sarah Lavelle
Copy editor: Christine King
Designer: Linda Blakemore
Picture researcher: Bea Thomas
Cartographer: Olive Pearson

Set in Times New Roman and Gill Sans by BBC Worldwide
Printed and bound in Great Britain by Butler & Tanner Limited, Frome and London
Colour separations by Radstock Reproductions Limited, Midsomer Norton
Jacket printed by Lawrence-Allen, Weston-super-Mare

CONTENTS

INTRODUCTION

I am a child of the Second World War, conceived between the end of the German war in early May and the Japanese surrender on 14 August 1945. Although the war shaped the world I grew up in, somehow I always took it – and Allied victory in it – for granted. And somehow I never listened as intently as I might have done to men, who struck me as very old in the 1950s and 1960s but most of whom would have been younger then than I am now, when they talked about the baking heat of the Western Desert or the freezing skies over Berlin, the Apennines in winter or Normandy hedgerows in summer. It took me all too long to recognize what my colleague John Keegan told me when I was a very junior lecturer at Sandhurst, that talking to veterans was the best way of learning my craft as a military historian. If I left it almost too late for the First World War, happily I did not do so for the Second.

On Remembrance Day each year men and women who are now, alas, genuinely elderly gather before the Cenotaph in Whitehall, and at hundreds of war memorials in town and country, often in blazers and berets, most of them wearing campaign medals awarded for service in the Second World War. As time thins their ranks, this book and the BBC television series it accompanies come to thank them and to honour those who gave their lives for the freedom they won for us all. In the pages that follow I shall be looking mainly at the British role in the western Allies' war against Germany and Italy, focused around four areas where terrain or circumstances determined that there must be a trial of strength. My approach is, inevitably, selective, for this is a study of four specific campaigns. Choosing them was not easy, and my decision was shaped partly by practical considerations. For instance, both Burma and the North Atlantic were on our shortlist, but the former failed to make the final cut because of the sheer logistical and political problems of filming there,

OPPOSITE, TOP Veterans attending the Remembrance Day commemoration in London's Whitehall remember their comrades.
OPPOSITE A local tribute: a Remembrance Day ceremony at the war memorial in Esher, Surrey.

while the latter is the subject of an imminent documentary series, and it would have been unwise to wish to plough the same furrow at precisely the same time. All four campaigns – in North Africa, Italy, north-west Europe and in the skies over Germany itself – made their contribution to the defeat of Germany although, as we shall see, the scale of this contribution was not without controversy, then or now. This introductory chapter seeks to explain my own approach to the war that has overshadowed my own life, and to help place the book's constituent parts in their proper context.

At the end of *The Western Front* I suggested that hindsight permitted us to see how the Great War might have been avoided, or at least how Britain could have stayed out of it, but that 'the threat to Britain seemed real enough to them in 1914, and a sense of national honour tugged their conscience harder than it does ours today'. Twenty-five years after the outbreak of that war, with few illusions about how right and proper it was to die for one's country, once again a British Expeditionary Force (BEF) crossed the Channel to form up on the left flank of the French Army. This was at the start of what might perhaps be seen as part of a longer European war, which, arguably, began with German victory over France in the Franco-Prussian War of 1870–1 and ended not in 1945, but with the removal of the Inner German Border a generation later. While I agree with Paul Fussell, author of the important book *The Great War and Modern Memory*, that the Great War began 'the drift of modern history [which] domesticates the fantastic and normalizes the unspeakable', its sequel completed the journey and remains the yardstick against which mankind's recurrent forays to the darkest frontiers of the soul are measured. It was, in the starkest terms, the greatest event of world history, whose burden of human casualties and physical destruction dwarfed even the carnage and damage inflicted by the First World War.

As they deployed past the cemeteries and memorials of Flanders, older members of the BEF could not fail to note that the front line had not advanced much from where they left it in 1918 and, young or old, there was little enthusiasm for having to do it all over again. In *Quartered Safe Out Here,* a penetrating account of his own war in Burma, George MacDonald Fraser comments that his generation, having seen just how badly the nation had rewarded the men who fought 'the war to end war', had few illusions. But although the belief that the Great War had been a ghastly blunder was widespread – and, as G. D. Sheffield persuasively observes in his chapter in *A Time to Kill*, the Somme remained a metaphor for military failure – the sense that the sacrifices of the previous generation must be redeemed was also pervasive. To this was added the accurate judgement that if responsibility for the outbreak of war in 1914 was diffuse, blame for the renewal of conflict in 1939 could be more narrowly attributed: it was forced upon peoples who wished to live in peace by a criminal gang led by Adolf Hitler. He had been voted into power in Germany in 1933 and was bent on war, if not in 1939 certainly a year or two later, allied with similarly reckless regimes in other countries. What nobody fully anticipated was that the war would consume the prestige and energies of all the European powers to such an extent that after centuries of being the driving force of international affairs they would become minor players in the postwar world.

Mahatma Gandhi once said that European civilization would be a good idea, a quip that today's advocates of a culturally chauvinist Europe might care to remember in the light of the price paid the last time rhetoric like theirs was bandied about. In the countries fought over, every living being risked sudden death and everything made by man might be destroyed. And unlike the Great War, in which only 5 per cent of about 13 million deaths were civilian, more than 60 per cent of the 50–60 million who died during the Second World War were technically non-combatants. Yet despite the appalling cost, there is no doubt that fighting this war to the bitter end was imperative in a way that the protracted agony of its predecessor was not. The boil needed to be lanced, and pus was still oozing as the twentieth century closed, with 'ethnic cleansing' in the Balkans, racist thugs and war memorial daubers in the streets, and nests of Holocaust deniers on the Internet.

These manifestations of evil are today marginal as far as Western Europe and North America are concerned, but in 1940–5 they dominated the mainland of Europe. Afterwards eastern Europe fell under scarcely preferable Soviet tyranny for nearly half a century, but in the west ancestral enemies came together in free association to put an end to continental self-destruction. The war also gave the principles of personal liberty a momentum they might otherwise not have acquired, to counterbalance the remorseless increase of state power that was both the cause and the consequence of both world wars. The further away we get from the bloodbath of 1939–45, the easier it is to forget that the battle against tyranny is never won. For millions still living, the war was the defining period of

Hitler and Mussolini in Rome during Hitler's state visit, May 1938.

their lives against which later years of lesser intensity are weighed and sometimes found wanting. Despite common experiences of hardship, so often made worse by political ineptitude, military blunders and bureaucratic small-mindedness, they knew that human freedom was at stake.

Of the aggressor states, Fascist Italy was born of horrendous losses during the Great War (an aspect of that conflict so inadequately recognized by most Anglo-American historians). Little of the territorial compensation that had been secretly promised by the French and British in 1915 was confirmed in the 1919–20 peace settlement that generally bears the name of Versailles (although it was in fact the associated treaty of St Germain en Laye which gave a variety of Austrian possessions to Italy). The squabbling of the Italian political class paved the way for the charismatic ex-socialist Benito Mussolini to become Prime Minister in 1922 and to assume dictatorial powers in 1925. His ambition was to forge a sense of nationhood in what was still a collection of culturally and even linguistically disparate regions, around the dream of a new Roman Empire. He was widely admired for bringing order to Italy – the cliché of the period being that he made the trains run on time – until he employed poison gas and aerial bombardment of defenceless villages to conquer Abyssinia in 1935–6. The League of Nations, set up to maintain the international order established at Versailles, could do nothing to stop a man who preferred intimidation to negotiation. He pressed on with an expansionist policy in the Mediterranean that included intervention in the Spanish Civil War in 1936–9 and the annexation of Albania in April 1939.

Italy lacked the raw materials for war, but this was seemingly resolved by the Pact of Steel with Nazi Germany, signed in May 1939. But the human element was also deficient and the main result of the pact was, as we shall see, to draw the Germans into areas peripheral to their own geopolitical ambitions. These were the destruction of the Versailles settlement and a reversal of the verdict of the Great War – largely complete after the fall of France in 1940. This was to clear the way for the conquest of a land empire in the east.

Oceans of ink have been spilt debating how the rise of Hitler might have been prevented and how the resurgence of Germany might have been contained, but most would agree that, like Mussolini, he was what we would now call a degenerate gambler, certain to push his luck too far. After he became Chancellor in 1933, Germany became thoroughly remilitarized in spirit, even if the pace and extent of actual rearmament lagged.

Defeat in 1914–18 was attributed to betrayal by a Judeo-Communist conspiracy, an all-purpose scapegoat that bridged the gulf between his street-fighting followers and the military and moneyed interests with whom real power resided. Economic revival was rapid and profoundly intoxicating, and in its shadow his escalating persecution of the Jews provoked shamefully little protest either at home or abroad. Until 1939 Hitler was even able to claim the moral high ground for his aggressive diplomacy by citing the principle of reunification of peoples, one of the themes of the Fourteen Points proclaimed at Versailles by US President Woodrow Wilson as the basis for a New World Order.

The immediate cause of war in 1939 was Hitler's occupation of those parts of Czechoslovakia that had not been handed over to him at Munich six months previously by France and Britain. Their respective prime ministers reluctantly accepted that appeasement had failed and formally guaranteed Polish sovereignty, something they could do little practical to assure but an important gesture nonetheless. At the same time half-hearted diplomatic overtures were made to Soviet dictator Josef Stalin, but he also wished to recover territory lost at Versailles and was aware, thanks to agents well placed within them, that the French and British governments regarded a war between his empire and the German as akin to killing two birds with one stone. Instead, in late August 1939 Soviet and German foreign ministers Vyacheslav Molotov and Joachim von Ribbentrop signed a Non-Aggression Pact. A week later the Wehrmacht (the collective name for the German armed forces on land, sea and in the air) advanced into Poland, crushing all organized resistance in three weeks, during the last of which the Red Army also invaded to share the spoils.

Hitler was not greatly inconvenienced when France and Britain declared war on 3 September, because he knew their strategy envisaged another long war in which their armies would gather strength over a period of years behind France's strong border fortifications, while wearing down German strength with a naval blockade and aerial bombardment. He had not planned for a major war so soon, but while the Allies were further alienating Stalin by their active support for Finnish resistance to Soviet invasion in 1939–40, Hitler moved to cover his northern flank by invading Denmark and Norway and then, on 10 May 1940, struck through

OPPOSITE A German machine-gun detachment in action on the road to Warsaw, 15 September 1939.

Holland and Belgium. In six weeks France had capitulated, Italy had joined the war on the German side and the BEF was driven across the Channel, abandoning all its heavy arms and equipment, but mercifully extracting most of its soldiers, mainly through Dunkirk but also, after further fighting in Normandy, through Cherbourg, Brest and St-Nazaire.

Hitler expected Britain to sue for peace after being expelled from the mainland of Europe, and was stunned by the defiance voiced by the new Prime Minister, Winston Churchill. The German General Staff had made no provision for an operation across the Channel, and rather desultory preparations for an invasion – which some German historians argue were never taken seriously even by the planners – hinged on winning air superiority to neutralize the Royal Navy and thus gain at least temporary control of the Channel. This was not achieved, but the small number of U-boats then in service sank about a third of Britain's merchant fleet during their first 'happy time' in 1940–1 and seemed likely to force submission, so Hitler felt free to turn his attention to the east.

On 22 June 1941, in alliance with Finland, Romania and Hungary, the Germans attacked along the entire Soviet frontier in Operation Barbarossa to begin a war waged with the utmost ruthlessness by both sides. For our purposes it suffices to say that while reinforcements drawn from the Manchurian front checked the German advance short of its objectives during the winter of 1941–2, it was not until the following winter and the battle of Stalingrad, ending in February 1943, that the German tide was turned back. Even then it ebbed slowly, and it was only after the failure of the German offensive at Kursk in July 1943 that it was clear that it would not flow anew.

Before that, the first significant defeats inflicted on the Wehrmacht were by British and Commonwealth forces. By air, the Battle of Britain had demonstrated the limitations of the Luftwaffe, while the first outright defeat of a part – albeit a small one – of the German army was by Eighth Army at Alamein in Egypt in September–November 1942. Less dramatically, by shutting down the overseas trade of the Axis powers, by threatening the coasts of occupied Europe and by a bomber offensive that began to inflict serious damage from mid-1942, Britain drew down significantly on enemy manpower and resources. This helped to tip the balance on the Eastern Front – for example by tempting Hitler to attack towards the oilfields of the Caucasus, thereby creating the vulnerability exploited so well by the Red Army at Stalingrad. These were not

A German infantry NCO, hand-grenade tucked into his boot, during the invasion of Russia, June 1941.

inconsiderable achievements: before the war began Greater Germany had the second largest economy in the world and then, by conquest and alliances, such greatly increased capacity that it took the combined efforts of the British and Soviet empires just to hold the line until the USA came to tip the balance.

British naval power was the linchpin for the campaigns considered in this book, and the threat to it by the U-boats of the Kriegsmarine (German navy) cannot be said to have positively receded until the second quarter of 1943. On the other side of the globe, the island empire of Japan lost a similar struggle and was defeated by the application of barely a quarter of US military power, mostly naval, and would have been even

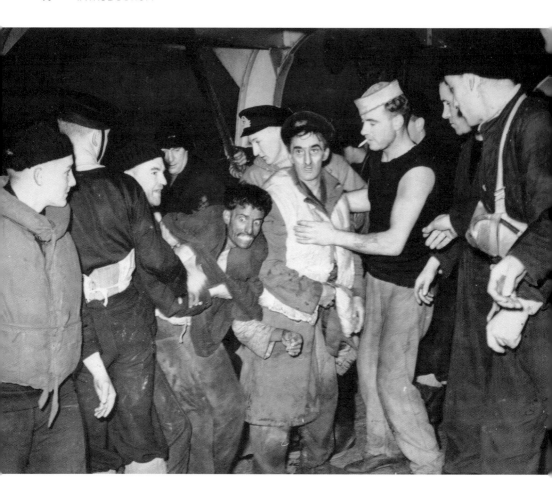

if no other country had contributed to its defeat. But the war in Europe was no less dependent on the outcome of the contest for naval supremacy, and US Pacific Commander Admiral Chester Nimitz's book on the Second World War judged it to be properly *The Great Sea War*. Although this might seem to slight the role of other services, it was an accurate strategic appreciation: without the Atlantic pipeline Britain would have been forced to capitulate, and without Britain it would have been impossible to project US power into Europe within a tolerable time scale.

ABOVE The Battle of the Atlantic: survivors from a merchant vessel, one hysterical and the other numbed, are helped aboard a destroyer, November 1940.
OPPOSITE Columns of oily smoke rise from an American tanker torpedoed by a German U-Boat, October 1942.

By 1941 Britain had exhausted the wealth built up over centuries, to buy priceless time and hope. In his recent book *1940: Myth and Reality* Clive Ponting maintains that Britain had been engulfed in 'financial disaster' by the end of 1940 and had been reduced to 'outright dependency' on the United States, suggesting that this was the reality, and talk of the nation's finest hour the myth. I see cost and gain as more directly linked, with the undoubted achievements of 1940 set alongside a cost that was indeed crippling. But of course the truth is more complex, and in many respects the war merely exposed the consequences of a decline in economic dynamism by that time at least half a century old. Chronic under-investment, managerial complacency and resistance to innovation on the shop floor were all symptomatic of a society convinced that any change must be for the worse. But if the old order finally succumbed, nothing in its life became it like the leaving of it. All the stubbornness, pride and decency of the British found expression in the words of one who rallied a nation facing probable defeat and certain ruin: 'Let us therefore brace ourselves to our duties and so bear ourselves that if the British Empire and its Commonwealth last for a thousand years men will still say – this was their finest hour.'

And it was. Britain's interest, narrowly defined, would clearly have been better served by dropping out of the war after the fall of France – but she fought on, 'by ourselves alone, but not for ourselves alone', mortgaging the future to do so. Britain became deeply indebted not only to the USA but also to the Dominions and to the government of India, despite the generous terms of their support, and there could be no return to being the hub around which a worldwide association of states revolved. The Empire had run its course well before 1939 and, if the humiliating fall of Singapore in 1942 witnessed a loss of face from which there could be no recovery, the independence of India, jewel of the imperial crown, was actually delayed rather than hastened by the war. The cost-effectiveness of empire was always dubious – the Americans had decided to relinquish formal dominion over the Philippines, the 'white man's burden' Kipling once praised them for taking up, well before the Japanese came to underline the vulnerability of overseas possessions.

The world wars were unquestionably the catalysts of far-reaching social change, not least in enabling governments to lay claim to areas of people's lives, indeed their very minds, that not even the most absolute of rulers in previous times had presumed to control. But the wars also promoted a general popular revulsion against aggressive nationalism, the erosion of unthinking deference to authority, and a profound mood of 'never again' that was not satisfied by the creation of multinational bureaucracies and which limited the ability of governments to embark upon major armed adventures in a more subtle and permanent way. In his book on the Vietnam War, *The Grunts*, Charles Anderson identified this as the reason why even those Americans of my generation who wanted to go there were psychologically ill-equipped for the war in Vietnam: 'In their zeal to relieve their offspring of the painful parts of life, the grunts' parents created a generation shielded from much of what has steeled every previous generation – the realization that a certain amount of adversity not necessarily deserved will be encountered in the course of one's life.'

Those of us born in that great celebration of life and renewed hope inadequately described as the baby boom were indeed cosseted by our parents, but they also left us in no doubt that the world in which we grew up was delivered by the caesarean section of war – even if, like me, not all of us wanted to hear much about the operation. Chief among those in attendance were Franklin Roosevelt and Winston Churchill, two patricians whose mutual admiration rode over fundamental differences in the interests of their nations. Neither was without faults, but it was astoundingly fortunate that the often ill-governed English-speaking peoples produced two such inspiring and personally compatible leaders at such a critical time.

There is no doubt that they conspired to engage a reluctant USA in the war, to the point that Roosevelt risked impeachment had the details become known. Safe behind oceanic moats, American 'splendid isolation' had seen military spending concentrated on the navy while the army withered on the vine. The 'draft' – the mechanism of conscription created in January 1940 – was kept in being by one vote in the House of Representatives a mere four months before America entered the war. As far as support for Britain went, Roosevelt could persuade Congress to accept the destroyers-for-bases swap of July 1940 (which promised Britain fifty old destroyers in return for bases in the British West Indies) and the Lend-Lease Bill (which enabled America to provide war material to nations fighting Germany, Italy and, later, Japan) that became law in March 1941 only by arguing that they would help keep America out of the war. When Hitler invaded the USSR the isolationism of the left wing of his coalition waned, but Roosevelt still had to walk a fine line. The need for finesse vanished when the Japanese attacked the US Navy base at Pearl Harbor on 7 December 1941 and Hitler declared war in solidarity, but the ways and means of the Anglo-US alliance remained to be worked out. Churchill's broad-brush definition of the underlying differences remains true:

> …the American mind runs naturally to broad, sweeping, logical conclusions on the largest scale… They feel that once the foundation has been planned on true and comprehensive lines all other stages will follow naturally and almost inevitably. The British mind does not work quite in this way. We do not think that logic and clear-cut principles are necessarily the sole keys to what

ought to be done in swiftly changing and indefinable situations. In war particularly we assign a larger importance to opportunism and improvisation, seeking rather to live and conquer in accordance with unfolding events than to aspire to dominate it often by fundamental decisions.

As we shall see, the Italian campaign owed much to Churchill's 'opportunism and improvisation', but it also reflected long-term geopolitical considerations which the Americans either disregarded or distrusted – only to adopt them with belated urgency during the Cold War. Perhaps a more fundamental source of friction was that the British had the utmost difficulty in adjusting to US resources exponentially greater than their own, while the Americans in turn were impatient with a British caution born as much of bitter experience as of limited means. But the great divide between the Americans and all the other combatants was that they knew with utter certainty that time was on their side and that the war was making them more prosperous and powerful, whereas for their enemies and their allies it brought at worst ruin, at best austerity and a sharp decline in their international standing.

If the British had trouble adjusting to American power, it paled beside the self-delusion of the Germans and the Japanese militarists, who fatally discounted how rapidly the US economy would be mobilized for war and believed that as self-defined warrior cultures they were naturally superior to what they saw as a luxury-loving matriarchy. Like the British, the tiny prewar US officer corps was no match for the German, but it was singularly unhistorical of the Axis to overlook the fact that US society had always been remarkably violent. During the Battle of the Bulge in late 1944, a German officer called upon what he thought were 'British gentlemen' surrounded at Bastogne to surrender, to which the reply came: 'We ain't British, we ain't gentlemen and we ain't surrendering' – an anecdote that bears thinking about. By European standards the American way of war was extremely wasteful of all save lives, even though those sent to the infantry were coldly judged by the US conscription authorities to be of least social value. The result was the overwhelming application of machine power that the stunned Germans dubbed *Materialschlacht*. Although, as we will see later, such distinguished scholars as Martin van Creveld and Colonel T. N. Dupuy have drawn our attention to the ability of the German army to consistently outfight Allied formations of a similar size and to generate fighting power in a more efficient manner than the British or Americans, ultimately the German rapier was no match for the American bludgeon.

The combat deaths of the Great War weigh far more heavily upon our historical perception than the much larger number of men and women randomly cut down in the prime of their lives by the world-wide influenza epidemic of 1918–20. Twenty years later, human ingenuity had begun to bring contagion and infection under control while simultaneously refining the means that men could employ to visit death and destruction upon each other. However, although this was the first war in which the scythe of septicaemia was blunted by penicillin, non-battle casualties – from disease, accident or simple exposure – often exceeded battle casualties. In Burma in 1942, for instance, 120 men were evacuated sick for every one evacuated wounded.

And if technology could help healing, it also promoted destruction. The 'sadistic ingenuity' urged upon his troops by Field Marshal Albert Kesselring, the German commander in Italy, was already evident in such devices as the *schuh* mine, designed to maim and not to kill. A dead man required only burial, whereas a mutilated soldier was a drain on resources at every stage of his painful withdrawal from the front line to his home, where his arrival could be expected to damage the morale of at least one family while imposing a long-term cost on society. A dreadful calculation, but one consistent with the logic of total war, as defined a century earlier by the Prussian officer Carl von Clausewitz in *On War*: 'If one side uses force without compunction, undeterred by the bloodshed it involves, while the other refrains, the first will gain the upper hand. That side will force the other to follow suit; each will drive its opponent to extremes, and the only limiting factors are the counterpoises inherent in war.'

That for over a century the Germans had been the most serious students and practitioners of war is unarguable but, before decrying the beastliness of the Boche, let us consider who said the following: 'The essence of war is violence; moderation in war is folly'; and: 'War is cruelty. There is no use trying to reform it; the crueller it is, the sooner it will be over.' The answers are John Hampden during the English Civil War and William Sherman during the American. War is, and at all times has been, hell for those directly involved. These have always included, to a greater or lesser extent, civilians unfortunate enough to live where combatants chose to do battle. For all the postwar polemics and popular agitation on the subject, aerial bombardment simply extended the boundaries of the battlefield; it did not make its realities any harsher.

There was nothing new about a besieged fortress, be it Britain, Japan or Germany, being bombed or starved into submission, but the permanent Holocaust exhibition at the Imperial War Museum is a reminder that the signature of this war was the millions who were put to death for no military purpose whatever in factories of cold-blooded murder. While the so-called Final Solution probably could have been implemented only in the context of the sole total war ever fought among great powers, it was nonetheless the clearest expression of what the Nazi regime stood for and the reason why few today will argue that peace, with or without honour, was ever an option when dealing with it. Although one of the victors in 1945 was a mass murderer quite on a par with Hitler, it is a measure of how far Europe had sunk into barbarism that Stalin was judged to be the lesser of two evils. Gerard Manley Hopkins' abyss was plumbed to its uttermost depth:

> *No worst, there is none. Pitched past pitch of grief,*
> *More pangs will, schooled to forepangs wilder wring.*
> *Comforter, where, where is your comforting?*

When the peoples of a given area persistently disturb the peace, outside forces move in to restore order. The view of Europe from the USA then was akin to our view of the Balkans today. Based on protective ditches far wider than the English Channel, which as Sir Francis Bacon predicted had long permitted Britain to take as much or as little of war as it chose, Pax Americana has another half century to run before matching the span of its predecessor – but the manner of its emergence was uncannily similar. While the mainland powers tore themselves apart during the French Revolutionary and Napoleonic wars, Britain grew prosperous and sent its money to do most of the fighting, until the time came to intervene directly in the decisive theatre.

This was precisely the strategy adopted by the USA during the Second World War and it is as well to bear these continuities firmly in

OPPOSITE The propaganda war: a poster advertises the well-made British film *Desert Victory*.

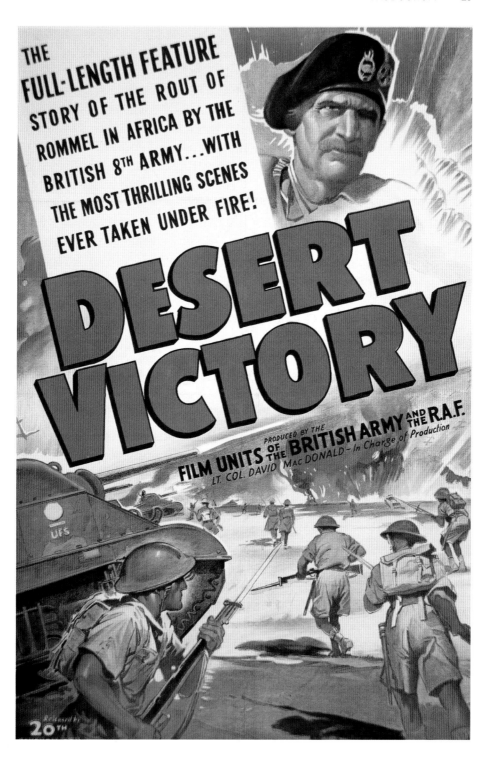

mind, because Anglo-US rivalry is thought to have played an important role in two of the campaigns we shall consider. I am not convinced of this and believe the friction was more the product of individuals wrapping swollen egos in their national colours. High responsibility can bring out the worst as well as the best in people and, although one slips into the verbal trap of referring to 'ordinary men and women', few leaders have exceptional virtues, while their vices are drearily familiar.

The writing of history is not playing tricks on the dead, but rather the uncovering of the tricks they played while alive. It is easy to be drawn into controversies created by the carping memoirs of circumstantially important men, often written as though it matters not who won or lost but how you place the blame. One has to steer between the Scylla of uncritically accepting an often carefully moulded mask and the Charybdis of tearing it down as though what lay behind was the 'real' person. In life the two are inseparable and there are very few areas of human endeavour in which the talents of the actor or even the showman are not rewarded. Politics is particularly attractive to facile dissemblers, and in peacetime armed forces the talents of the politician lead to advancement more certainly than those of the warrior. Nor is it always the case that great moments necessarily call forth great leaders: a system that rewards safe mediocrity in peacetime will tend to produce indifferent leadership in war, although the shock of defeat usually promotes radical change.

The British tend, more than most, to deprecate openly ambitious people and to discount the manner in which their ambition willy-nilly moves the pile. In *The 8:15 to War*, Peter Roach of the Desert Rats (7th Armoured Division) commented on the arrival from the staff of a new colonel who needed a field command as a step to further promotion, 'who knew the value of a record, who knew that promotion didn't just come by doing a first-class job, but by letting everyone know you were doing a first-class job'. The unnamed officer quickly obtained better facilities and equipment but this 'was not geared to advance the regiment, the army, the allies, and so end the war. This was a by-product of advancing the man.' But if, as Roach concedes, the officer was doing right by his men, what did his motives matter? We should not underestimate the military consequences of the envious levelling that was fast becoming a defining feature of British society.

For a military historian, Clausewitz's aphorism – 'War is nothing but the continuation of politics with the admixture of other means' –

represents a difficult challenge. Those who conduct wars are rightly held to a higher standard than those who govern in peacetime, yet they are produced by the same formal and informal institutions. We use the words 'government' and 'administration' almost interchangeably because at any given moment the business of government consists largely of the struggle among officials to maintain and increase their share of the budget, and this is exacerbated when financial constraints are jettisoned in time of war. The strength of any ruler rests, in great measure, on his ability to play interests off against each other within the bureaucracy and thereby enhance his role as arbiter, from whence comes the aphorism that politics is the art of the possible. Expanding the bounds of the possible is what separates significant leaders from caretakers, because bureaucracies are above all devoted to continuity and will stubbornly resist change.

The armed forces exist to cope with discontinuities, but when not doing so they are constrained by the normal rules of the public administration game, in which somebody's gain is always somebody else's loss, and this 'zero sum' mentality makes the rational use of resources a chimera and inter-agency rivalry a certainty. The harmfulness of the competition it engenders becomes more apparent in wartime, but it is a constant at all times. Negotiation goes on at all levels in the armed forces and, as in any other organization, an officer who fails to 'sell' his orders will often find them quietly sabotaged. General Sir David Fraser attributed the problems of Eighth Army in the desert to the absence of 'a directing intelligence and will'. Field Marshal Lord Carver, a participant in as well as a shrewd historian of the Desert War, replied: 'There was no lack of intention at the summit to impose a directing intelligence and will: the problem was that it soon became dissipated as it descended the channel of command, partly, but not entirely, because the machine was not capable of providing the results demanded of it.' What Carver described as 'the inherent deficiencies in organization, training and command which meant that the army's full power was never fully developed' accurately reflected the institutional matrix that formed it.

Poor leadership was, nonetheless, a significant problem and the attrition of the 'best and the brightest' during the Great War lay heavily upon the conduct of its sequel. The crowded village war memorials of Britain testify to the mauling of the yeoman class, one result of obstinately persisting in the voluntary principle while raising mass armies between 1914 and 1916. As a result the nation probably suffered a higher loss than any other among the most public-spirited of the entire male population. But if the human substance was gone, the social trappings remained and for Churchill and his kind, in many ways, the war was about affirming the place of their class in Britain as well as Britain's place in the world. That class led from the front and paid an appalling price for the privilege, but modern weapons made traditional martial virtue look a lot like suicidal stupidity and this sometimes undermined trust between officers and men. Further factors tending to make British generalship tentative were soul-deep survivor guilt and determination never again to risk casualties on a Western Front scale. The late Field Marshal Lord Harding, badly wounded as a divisional commander after Alamein while sitting on a tank trying to direct the fire of his medium guns, passionately assured me that commanders of his generation consciously strove not to follow the example of their often invisible Great War predecessors, and it showed.

Very few of these constraints acted upon US political and military leaders bursting to assert their nation's right to take the central place on the world stage that had long awaited it, backed by an economy with a tremendous 'bounce' capacity as a result of slow recovery from the Great Depression and massive investment in energy infrastructure during the 1930s. To make up for lost time, Roosevelt virtually encouraged adversarial empire building by the chiefs of the armed forces and on occasion this cost the Allies heavily. Perhaps the most notorious example was the refusal by Admiral Ernest King, commander of the US Navy, to organize convoys or even to demand that lights be doused along the Atlantic seaboard during what the U-boat crews called the 'second happy time' in 1942, until he got an increased allocation of shipyard output and authority over land-based naval patrol aircraft. Field Marshal Sir John Dill, the senior British liaison officer in Washington, commented that the 'violence of inter-service rivalry in the United States these days has to be seen to be believed and is an appreciable handicap to their war effort'.

Although Roosevelt was the titular Commander in Chief of the US armed forces, he exercised considerably less direct authority over them than Churchill did over his. No British commander would have dared to lecture Churchill the way the imperious General Douglas MacArthur,

OPPOSITE Roosevelt and Churchill meet the press during the Casablanca conference in January 1943. It was here that Roosevelt announced the Allied policy of Unconditional Surrender.

commander of land forces in the Pacific, addressed his President, but then again none of them was remotely likely to stand against him in an election with the full support of his domestic political opponents. Both because he was not one to get bogged down in detail and because he was by nature incurably devious, Roosevelt seldom issued clear-cut orders or let anyone know what he was thinking. His formidable wife Eleanor went so far as to state: 'The President never *thinks*! He *decides*.' But, having decided, at times he forced even his closest collaborators to guess what his intentions were, driving them to a quite different kind of despair than the one Churchill's tendency to 'meddle' drove his. US Army Chief of Staff General George Marshall on occasion first learned of military commitments Roosevelt had made through Dill, who had himself found out about them informally.

Roosevelt's penchant for pre-emptive public announcements was never more starkly illustrated than when, at the end of the Allied conference at Casablanca in January 1943, he announced: 'Prime Minister Churchill and I have determined that we will accept nothing less than the unconditional surrender of Germany, Italy and Japan.' Churchill could only pretend that he had been consulted and agreed, although privately his views were the same as those of US Lieutenant General George S. Patton: 'If the Hun ever needed anything to put a burr under his saddle, that's it. Now he'll fight like the goddamned devil. It will take much longer, cost us far more lives, and let the Russians take more territory.' So it did, to the point that some detect the hand of Soviet agents in influencing the decision. But this is to discount how intensely vengeful Roosevelt felt towards the Germans, and Henry Morgenthau, his Secretary of the Treasury, drew up a plan to destroy their economy so thoroughly that it would never recover. Roosevelt himself told Morgenthau: 'We either have to castrate the German people or you have to treat them in such a way so they can't just go on reproducing people who want to continue the way they have in the past.'

Although important Soviet agents were entrenched in the Roosevelt administration and worked tirelessly to undermine his relationship with Churchill, their task was facilitated by a widespread American belief that they had been tricked into the Great War by British propaganda and disinformation, and by the ambivalence an emerging world power must feel for its predecessor. Admiral King revealed the chip on his shoulder when he snarled: 'Britannia may have ruled the waves for three hundred years, but she doesn't any more.' If to this we add the fact that both parties were enveloped in selective self-righteousness, it may be reckoned remarkable that they did not, as Hitler confidently expected, turn on each other. Fortunately the common sense and fellow feeling of those on the ground matched that of Roosevelt and Churchill, as expressed by US Lieutenant General Lucian Truscott: 'British and American soldiers invariably got on well together, and it was only among the higher echelons that friction developed between the Allies. All in all, British and Americans held each other in mutual respect; they were worthy Allies who fought well together.'

Behind the lines Britain had a taste of what it was like to be an occupied country during the build-up to the invasion of Europe, with British soldiers feeling emasculated by their own low prestige and pay *vis à vis* US and Canadian troops. Once they were serving together overseas this source of tension was reduced, but it never disappeared entirely save at the fighting front itself. Away from it, the needling and brawling that took place between British and US troops should not be taken out of context. In the Mediterranean theatre, relations between the British Eighth and First Armies were also pugnacious, while in countless bar-room battles US and British infantrymen might well find themselves fighting shoulder to shoulder against their common enemies – sailors, airmen and what the American soldier-cartoonist Bill Mauldin called 'garritroopers': men close enough to the front not to need to wear ties, but not so close as to actually get shot. That is the nature of armies and fighting men will fight – just add alcohol and stand back.

However irritating to latter-day sensibilities, Truscott used the word 'British' to include troops from independent Australia, Canada, New Zealand and even South Africa, where much of the white population regarded the British as their ancestral enemy. All, and outstandingly New Zealand which mobilized more fully than any other Allied nation save Britain, made significant and unselfish contributions to the European war and rocked the Allied boat very little, although resentment at Churchill's high-handedness was to have long-term repercussions. Ties of blood and tribal loyalty brought English-speaking volunteers from all over the world to serve what they still regarded as the mother country, and even subject peoples, in particular the all-volunteer Indian Army, fought, often magnificently, for their imperial masters in a war far from their homelands. Commonwealth and Empire troops outnumbered British for much of the

Desert War, and A. E. Housman's elegy for an earlier generation is equally apt:

They braced their belts about them,
They crossed in ships the sea,
They sought and found six feet of ground,
And there they died for me.

The principal source of friction at the highest levels arose from the US belief that Churchill and his service chiefs wanted the Germans and the Russians to destroy each other before stepping in to pick up the pieces – on the face of it an unremarkable aspiration although not something likely to leap off the pages of the documentary record. But from there it was a small step to suspecting that the British were not averse to spending American lives in preference to their own, which goes to the heart of understanding the battles for Cassino: were Clark and Alexander incompatible personalities, or were they obeying politically inadmissible instructions from their masters? It is easy to skewer Clark's vanity, less easy to dismiss his suspicions.

Relations with other allies were even more fraught, particularly with Chinese Nationalist leader Chiang Kai-shek. He was described to Roosevelt as 'a vacillating, tricky, undependable old scoundrel who never keeps his word' by US Lieutenant General 'Vinegar Joe' Stilwell, who had the unenviable task of acting as Chiang's Allied chief of staff and whose comments on his British allies were no less swingeing. Chiang, in turn, is credited with the quip (about monocles affected by British India officials) that these were so that they should not see more than they could understand. If the contribution from the French Empire was more ambivalent than the British, this merely reflected the bitter realities of an occupied and divided nation, complicated by the uniquely awkward Free French leader General Charles de Gaulle. Others were treated with less consideration, in particular the Poles but also the French and British imperial contingents. Being a junior ally is an unrewarding role, and a major problem the British had while fighting the war and in writing about it since is that they too inexorably became a lesser partner as it ground to a close.

OPPOSITE An Australian member of the Tobruk garrison attending to some personal laundry, 1941.

The most prickly subject of all has been the tip of the iceberg represented by the tens of thousands from countries conquered by the Germans who volunteered to serve in the Waffen SS which, elite combat force though it was, shared too many facilities and personnel with the Nazi programmes of mass extermination for its members to claim ignorance. When mocked for reversing his life-long enmity to Communism when Germany invaded the USSR, Churchill replied that if Hitler invaded hell he would speak more kindly of the devil, but for many the choice was not so straightforward. The result was that elements of an ideologically driven European civil war were superimposed upon a traditional struggle among nations, which in some countries continued well beyond the surrender of Germany.

Those of us who have never faced such a desperate choice cannot know how we would have responded. Pre-war the 'useful fools' of the west flocked to the USSR or to Germany according to their ideological predispositions, and returned with glowing accounts of how much more progressive, dynamic and humane the dictatorships were than the depressed liberal democracies. Although the full horror of the Nazi regime did not develop until after the war began, it should have been apparent well beforehand that Stalin's murderous social engineering randomly killed the able, the talented and the intelligent across the entire range of peoples enclosed by the Soviet empire, so that the survivors should never know why or when their turn might come. From August 1939 until June 1941 he was the ally of Hitler, so the Communist parties of Europe were 'stood down' and along with other leftists denounced the war. But once the panzers rolled across the frontier he recast himself as the leader of the Slavic against the Germanic peoples in 'The Great Patriotic War', and Churchill was not alone in finding his new role easier to live with than his earlier pose as the leader of international socialism.

Those under German occupation, however, had to wrestle with the instinct to identify with the person who holds your life in his hands and to share his fear and hatred of outside forces. As a result, vicious civil wars were fought during the greater war in Yugoslavia and after it in Greece, while terrible reprisals marred the liberations of France, Italy, Holland and Belgium. And the details that have slowly emerged of the collaboration of authorities in the occupied Channel Islands can leave little doubt what the English Channel alone spared the British from discovering about their own society and people.

Ideology aside, had Hitler not invaded the USSR it is impossible to estimate how long the suffering of the conquered mainland would have continued. If sea power was all-important for the Anglo-US war effort, the fact that the eastern front absorbed the greater part of Germany's energies was no less so for the development of land operations in the west. At the time of the Normandy invasion there were fifty-nine German divisions in north-west Europe and twenty-eight in Italy – but 165, most them of higher quality, in the east. Panzer divisions were more evenly apportioned, but the ones in the west were generally there to recover from being ground down in the titanic struggle with the Red Army. This is not to belittle the Allies' achievement in breaking through concentrations of determined defenders on very constricted battlefields, only to underline that if the bulk of the Wehrmacht had not been committed elsewhere, the landings in Italy and Normandy would have been far more costly and might have failed altogether.

The hippopotamus in the drawing room of any discussion of the war is the performance of the Wehrmacht. In *A Genius for War*, Trevor Dupuy summarized his extensive statistical research in the following unflinching verdict:

> On a man for man basis the German ground soldiers consistently inflicted casualties at about a 50 per cent higher rate than they incurred from the opposing British and American troops under all circumstances. This was true when they were attacking and when they were defending, when they had local numerical superiority and when, as was usually the case, they were outnumbered, when they had local air superiority and when they did not, when they won and when they lost.

There is a danger of regarding them as the supermen their crazed leader told them they were, but the unpalatable fact remains that the German professional system was dedicated to sending the best men to the front, while the US managerial approach was no less dedicated to precisely the opposite. Although British practice was nearer the German than the US model, the cult of the amateur still held sway and the army remained what Shelford Bidwell and Dominick Graham in *Fire-Power* called 'a number of loosely co-ordinated social groups which mirror the views of the society from which they derive their attitudes to military problems'.

In *Fighting Power*, Martin van Creveld put his finger on the central paradox that the authoritarian Germans had far greater confidence in their subordinates, and vice versa, than the democratic Americans or the British: 'To generate independence, freedom had to be granted. To train men toward responsibility, authority had to be delegated. To create trust, reliability and long standing acquaintanceship had to be assured.' As a result of embracing these concepts the Wehrmacht, fighting for a regime devoted to the concept of innate Aryan superiority, employed training, organization and leadership that could turn almost any group of men, regardless of national origin, into soldiers capable of holding their own against the best the Allies could throw at them.

By contrast, Allied training not only of conscripts but also of junior infantry officers, most notoriously in the US Army, was deficient to the point of negligence, while seriously inadequate equipment remained in production throughout the war, in part because of the Not Invented Here factor which bedevilled progress in most countries. The weapon that finally won air superiority in 1944 was the long-range US-designed P-51 Mustang equipped with the British Rolls Royce Merlin engine, which the RAF had been flying since 1942. Not only did British factories continue to produce the Spitfire long after requirements had shifted from a short-range interceptor to a bomber escort and ground attack fighter capable of roaming the skies of Europe, but the US Army Air Force (USAAF) was also slow to appreciate how superior the Mustang was. Allied soldiers were also sent into battle with weapons grossly inferior to their German equivalents because, despite careful examination of captured specimens, vested interests hiding behind the mask of national prestige vied with institutional conservatism in preventing the simple expedient of copying them.

Partly for these reasons but mainly because it is the nature of mass warfare, the Allied armies were not swords, with all the implications of elegant dexterity the word implies, but battering rams in which the sharpness of the point became progressively less significant as the weight behind it steadily increased. Even when that point became splintered and blunted, the rams continued to deliver crushing blows from the condensed energies of whole peoples at war. The Allied armies had about ten people in support for every one in the line, whereas in the Wehrmacht the proportion was more balanced and support units repeatedly demonstrated the ability to become combat troops at the shrill of the *feldwebel*'s whistle.

But this is to count only those physically in the theatre. Properly calculated, on the Allied side there were hundreds in support, many of them women, for every man at the sharp end, and the 'tail' compensated for deficiencies in the 'teeth'. By contrast the Axis failed to integrate their war efforts or to mobilize women adequately, and so their soldiers had to carry what proved to be an impossible burden.

To illustrate this, let us track the trajectory of a notional shell fired at Alamein. The raw materials were mined in Colorado, sent by train to Halifax, Nova Scotia, shipped on a Norwegian freighter, in a convoy with an Australian commodore and escorted part of the way by US and Canadian warships, with Free Polish and Royal Navy escorts taking over in mid-ocean, and air cover provided by US Liberators out of Iceland and Coastal Command flying-boats based in Northern Ireland. Manufactured in a Glasgow factory, the shell was loaded in another convoy that sailed a triangular course through friendly Brazilian waters to Cape Town, from there up the east coast of Africa escorted by South African and Free Dutch warships with air cover flown by Rhodesians, and was unloaded at Port Said by dockyard workers protected by Gurkhas. From an ammunition dump guarded by New Zealand anti-aircraft gunners it was delivered to a part-Algerian Free French battery in a Detroit-built truck driven by a Senegalese and fired from a field gun built in a factory in Ontario.

Meanwhile the other side would have been weakened in a thousand ways: to illustrate this let us follow the trajectory of a shell that did not kill one of my readers, or his father or grandfather, at Alamein. It may not have been manufactured because raw materials were in limited supply thanks to the British naval blockade, or because RAF bombing killed the worker who might have assembled it. Once made, it might not have reached a Mediterranean port because partisans working with advisers from the Special Operations Executive (SOE) derailed the train carrying it. Once it was loaded, British cryptologists may have deciphered the sailing orders for the ship, permitting a Malta-based submarine or torpedo bomber to sink it. Once the shell was landed in North Africa, the truck carrying it to the front might have been blown up by the Special Air Service (SAS) or may have simply broken down for lack of spare parts, and if it reached the front the dump where it was stored may have been identified by photo reconnaissance and destroyed by the shell whose path we tracked in the preceding paragraph. Once fired, it may have missed because the gun-barrel was overdue for replacement thanks to any of the above elements of logistical attrition. And if it failed to explode, it could be because a slave labourer on the assembly line back in Germany had risked her life to sabotage the fuse.

This does not pretend to be a comprehensive list of all the ways in which the shell in question might have failed to diminish my readership, but it helps to put the role of battlefield command in perspective. After the Great War, the German military subscribed to the 'stab in the back' theory, claiming that if only the home front had held up they would have won. After the Second World War their alibi was that their defeat was either the fault of Hitler, the man who gave them the weapons and men with which they overran Europe, or the product of 'mere' material inferiority. Reading a book such as Field Marshal Erich von Manstein's *Lost Victories*, one looks in vain for acknowledgement that military virtuosity is the icing on the cake of overall national power – including alliances. Nazi Germany became wedded to the concept of *blitzkrieg* (lightning war) in part because of a desire to avoid a protracted war, and the country mobilized fully only once the tide of war had turned. *Blitzkrieg* was in some ways a giant bluff, likely to fail when it encountered adversaries who were not dazzled by its emphasis on psychological dislocation, or who, like the Russians, could trade space for time.

For all that, 'Wehrmacht envy' not only influenced Allied operations during the war but carried over into post-war doctrine. Field Marshal Sir Bernard Montgomery famously hung a portrait of Rommel in his personal caravan, and the Arnhem debacle owed something to his desire to show that he too was capable of imaginative and daring generalship. Patton was similarly fixated and found no less wanting when he came up against serious opposition. They simply could not overcome the yawning gap in culture between their own and their opponents' forces – and were invariably punished when they tried to do so.

Christopher Browning's chilling *Ordinary Men: Reserve Police Battalion 101 and the Final Solution* quotes a middle-aged German, not even a member of the Nazi party and one whose personality was formed before the rise of Hitler, saying that he and his fellows lived by the rule: 'Whatever serves the state is right, whatever harms the state is wrong.' We should not be surprised that the citizens of countries where the state, in principle, served the people tended to be at a disadvantage in a war with those who believed the opposite. While emphasizing that this refers to median performance across mass armies, it seems undeniable that men who wholeheartedly believe and loyally accept that they are no more than cogs in a vast and unquestionable machine will go further and stay longer than those who see themselves as individuals, with rights enforceable against the collectivity. Compounded by deficiencies in doctrine, training and equipment though they were, the relative military shortcomings of the British and American armies also faithfully reflected the better values of their societies, and we cannot wish for it to have been otherwise.

Nonetheless, the feeling of being a part of something greater than yourself is an integral part of even the most individualistic person's response to war. The decidedly 'bolshie' poet Keith Douglas, wounded in North Africa and killed in Normandy, wrote:

> We may talk in the evening, after fighting, about the great and rich men who cause and conduct wars... They are out for something they want, or their governments want, and they are using us to get it for them. Anyone can understand that: there is nothing unusual or humanly exciting at that end of the war... But it is amazing and exciting to see thousands of men... all enduring hardships, living in an unnatural, dangerous, but not wholly terrible world, having to kill or be killed, and yet at intervals moved by a feeling of comradeship with the men who kill them and whom they kill, because they are enduring and experiencing the same things... to read about it cannot convey the impression of having walked through the looking-glass which touches a man entering battle.

This not an uncommon sentiment, and it underlines how little the experience of war is touched upon by histories that dwell on the captains and the kings. As Douglas said, there is nothing *humanly* exciting about the sacred monsters of history, and our fascination with them is a function of the degree to which we cannot imagine being them. Yet we can have fellow feeling for the youngster trying to make the transition from adolescent to adulthood, even though we were not compelled to make it under circumstances where a step in the wrong direction could be our last; we can smile reminiscently at the fumbling of sexual discovery, even if our own early experiences were not given added urgency by the threat of extinction; and we can appreciate how love sprouted among the ruins, for have not most of us found it in unlikely places? What most of us cannot know, and may well envy, is the feeling of intense comradeship, which is all that makes war endurable. In *Rough Road to War*, Sir David Cole recalled returning to his unit at Anzio:

> The truth was that for an infantryman, his battalion, however harrowing its circumstances, was his home, indeed his world. There his friendships, his pride, his loyalty and his duty, his memories of war both happy and terrible and his own little place in history were all embodied. A rest and a fling out of the line and away from all responsibility and danger were good, indeed at times essential. But soon enough the magnetism of his battalion drew him back to be again where he belonged, whatever the price.

For the last twenty years, the historiographic pendulum has swung away from a top-down view of warfare, towards the worm's-eye view of the squaddy, the *poilu*, the dog-face, the *landser* – the man at the point of the battering ram. I am not so certain as I once was that the internalized imperative of small unit cohesion is the be-all and end-all of combat motivation, and I am now more inclined to believe that external forces are sometimes equally important. As the military historian Hew Strachan has pointed out in his chapter in the invaluable *Time to Kill*, some 15,000 formal and uncounted thousands more casual executions in the Wehrmacht during the war probably had as much to do with the cornered rat phenomenon as either ideology or the Allies' demand for unconditional surrender. We must also consider that for some, notably the SS and the Japanese, knowledge that their opponents were as disinclined to accept their surrender and treat them decently afterwards as they would be if the roles were reversed made the rhetoric of fighting to the death a self-fulfilling prophecy.

Another under-explored theme is that, for many, service overseas was a time of personal liberation. For so many British conscripts it came as a relief from the penny-pinching squalor in which they were warehoused at home, along with a recovery of a sense of purpose and worth after a long period of stagnation. They were freer than they ever had been or ever would be again, living in the here and now in a manner that civilian life does not permit, relieved of making most decisions, even basic ones such as what to wear or eat. Also, deep within our limbic systems there often lurks an urchin desire to blow things up, to the suppression of which much parental and societal effort is devoted. Cry havoc, and what was once frowned upon and punished is encouraged and rewarded. Nobody who wishes to understand either war or crime can be blind to the psychic and sensual rewards they offer. Young men are the common currency of both, and their behaviour in peacetime is not such as to encourage a belief that warfare is either an unnatural activity, or necessarily an unwelcome one to many of those caught up in it. The further away from the front line, the more unambiguous the rewards can be, with easy money to be made, easy sex to be had and the sheer irresponsible joy of not having to pay for what you break.

While the essence of war is destruction and homicide, and theft, rape and murder flourish in its long shadow, a vein of redemption is to be found in the fact that most soldiers are governed by the 'do as you would be done by' principle, especially in combat. This is not mere pragmatism, as shown by the amount of training necessary to overcome distaste for 'pouring it on' against a fleeing enemy, even though every soldier knows that those allowed to escape may well regroup and hit back. Not many Allied airmen obeyed orders to machine-gun Luftwaffe pilots dangling from their parachutes, yet they knew the men they spared could be back in the air the next day, trying to kill them. Some element of fair play appears to be hard-wired in the human psyche, along with grudging admiration for a tough opponent, and as we shall see this was particularly apparent at Cassino and Arnhem. The most sickening atrocities are generally committed by those dealing in death while being in no danger of it themselves; the principal difference between the oppressor and the oppressed is opportunity and those far from the front lines are often the most bloodthirsty, at least in utterance.

What I seek to illustrate in this book is what I have been exploring all my professional career – the meaning of war as a parallel universe in which human nature and social organization operate at a subtly different level. It is not merely in wartime that the powerful use us to get what they want, that ambitious individuals wrap their designs in the flag, that bureaucrats seek to extend their power and that personal vanity wrecks collective endeavour. What moves – or fails to move – societies no less than armies is that sometimes a bit more and sometimes a bit less than enough people are prepared to throw themselves into the traces and break the inertia. Combat leadership is usually decisive only when a relatively small impetus can tip the scales, and Lieutenant 'Birdie' Smith's vivid description of the moment before he earned his Distinguished Service Order at Tavoletto is representative:

> For a second no one moved, then 9 Platoon under Jemedar Jitbahadur went forward a few yards, very slowly. God, I thought, we really have had it, no food, no guts left and a suicidal attack. In desperation I shouted: 'What about your proverb – it's better to die than be a coward? Right, stay here; Rambahadur and I will go forward alone. Ramu, come on.' The effect was electrifying, as if I had touched open nerves to unleash all the pent up fear, frustration, anger, all compounded by hunger and lack of sleep. On our left Jemedar Jitbahadur shrieked 'Ayo Gurkhali', the cry was repeated on the right by 7 Platoon – then they were off. At last, they were moving, but not as I intended, not according to the orders that had been explained to them during the afternoon. A steady advance should have been maintained for the first two or three hundred yards, before we met the first German machine gun post. All my orders and instructions were forgotten; the leading platoon set off like a pack of hounds baying for blood, shouting and shrieking as if they were charging the final objective.

Immensely dramatic though such attacks are, unless they occur within the context of heavy pressure along the whole front, or can be properly exploited by astute local commanders, they will be often contained and driven back, thus demanding a consistency of high performance that needs to extend far beyond those directly involved in combat. However, some minor cause may indeed have a wildly disproportionate effect – someone who forgot to check the hydraulics on an anti-aircraft gun may have caused it to jam instead of shooting down a bomber that went on to cripple a warship, without whose gunfire a shaky company gave way, with knock-on effects at battalion, brigade, corps and army levels. Acute awareness of this is what lies behind military 'bull', which is in essence an effort to emphasize the overriding importance of things like routine and preventative maintenance, and to ingrain the right reactions to given stimuli no matter how frightened, tired, cold, hungry and confused the individual may be. In many ways this indoctrination is even more important for those not suffering from the exceptional hardships of the front line.

The enervation of routine can lead to fatal carelessness and a sleepy truck driver who goes over a cliff is just as dead as an alert one hit by a shell.

The human cost of war includes the lives ruined by post traumatic stress and families or whole communities blighted by enforced separations and the violent dislocation of expectations. The surge in juvenile delinquency that occurred in all the Allied nations, even the USA and Canada, was in part the product of homes broken by the conscription of parents into the services and other war-related work, while loneliness and increased temptation destroyed marriages that might otherwise have remained stable. Casualties include those whose predisposition to alcoholism might have remained no more than that within normal social and economic constraints, while the easy pickings of war made potential peacetime criminals of many who might otherwise have remained law-abiding. Worse, perhaps, was that those who loyally abstained from black marketeering, bought War Bonds and paid their taxes, saw that those who had not done so prospered unpunished. Not the least casualty of the war was the corrosion of the minimum social solidarity without which civilization is just a word.

The breakdown of social norms cannot be seen in isolation from the cutting edge, because they affected not merely its sharpness but also the strength behind it. No accurate accounting of the amount of Allied supplies lost through pilfering and other wastage has been made, but a conservative estimate is about a third, with some categories such as penicillin at times approaching 100 per cent. Logistical constraints slowed Allied breakthroughs in Africa, Italy and north-west Europe, thereby lengthening the war, but the degree to which this was due as much to parasitism as to the standard infrastructure explanations is one that deserves more consideration. It is a sobering thought that at times interdiction by air and sea may have choked off supplies to the better disciplined Axis armies little more effectively than wholesale plundering by their own rear echelons inflicted on the western Allies.

To mention these things is neither to devalue nor diminish the achievements of US and British arms – quite the contrary. A commander who has it within his power to execute deserters, looters, saboteurs and even the merely negligent would have to be either remarkably humane or seriously incompetent not to obtain a better flow of supplies and a greater concentration of fighting power than another who respects the fact that his men are citizens first and soldiers sometimes a long way second.

The Commonwealth War Graves Commission cemetery at Cassino, with the restored monastery in the background.

Precisely one GI in Europe, the unlucky Private Eddie Slovik, was executed for (repeated) desertion in the face of the enemy, and the career of Patton, regarded by the Germans as their most dangerous Anglo-American opponent, was nearly brought to an end by his crude attempt to shake a couple of soldiers out of combat-induced despair. Bill Mauldin, creator of the cartoon GIs Willie and Joe, commented that the aristocratic Patton believed soldiers were peasants to be led and not cattle to be driven, which made him an anachronism within the managerial US Army but a figure instantly recognized and appreciated by his British peers, something his rivalry with Montgomery has been permitted to obscure. Both were skilled motivators of not very warlike men and it is against the example they set, not against the culturally unattainable standards of their opponents, that the leadership qualities of other Allied commanders must be measured.

As to the far from ordinary people to whom this book is dedicated, the essays that follow touch upon their shared experiences, but the strongest bond may well be the one identified by Peter Roach: 'While they fought, struggled and died they had a dream of life as it should be and saw a side of the human soul which was finer than anything they had known. When they returned to drab and spiritless Britain they didn't abandon themselves to disillusion but locked away their dream so that none should laugh it to scorn. Sometimes behind those eyes it comes to light.' If, in the following pages, an elegiac tone creeps into my writing, it is because it is difficult to remain convinced that even this most just of wars was worth the massive snuffing out of the constellations of hope and promise buried under serried headstones or recorded on memorials. None, surely, is more throat-catching or challenging to modern complacency than that of the thrice-betrayed Poles on the aptly named Monte Calvario, behind the restored abbey of Monte Cassino:

FOR OUR FREEDOM AND YOURS
WE SOLDIERS OF POLAND
GAVE
OUR SOUL TO GOD
OUR LIFE TO THE SOIL OF ITALY
OUR HEARTS TO POLAND

ALAMEIN
THE EIGHTH ARMY'S DESERT VICTORY

Victory by the Eighth Army at the second battle of Alamein in October–November 1942 brought to a close a period during which flaws in British military leadership, doctrine, training and equipment were pitilessly exposed, giving the battle a resonance out of proportion to the numbers involved. Whether it was, as Churchill declared, 'the end of the beginning', remains a matter of debate. The revisionist view is that the Western Desert campaign was a strategic sideshow, of importance only to the Italians and the British. The older, and in my view better, argument is that there was nowhere else Commonwealth forces could have fought the Germans or the Italians on land after the fall of France in 1940, and that the humbling of Mussolini, the man whose rhetoric, title (*Duce/Führer*) and extended-arm salute Hitler had borrowed, was an important objective in its own right. The Germans, who might be said to have had the deciding vote in the matter, belatedly rushed reinforcements into the theatre and, when Axis resistance in North Africa finally ended in May 1943, two panzer armies had been destroyed and German losses in men and material were greater than those suffered at Stalingrad three months earlier.

And prior to that, Abyssinia had been liberated, the Italian alliance had been turned into a military liability for the Germans, several potential Axis allies in the theatre had been coerced or intimidated, and control over

---

OPPOSITE, TOP Cruising the sea of sand: a patrol of the Long Range Desert Group (LRDG).
OPPOSITE A New Zealand LRDG truck. It mounts a Lewis machine gun in front and a Boys anti-tank rifle in the rear.

the vital oilfields of the Middle East had been maintained. Before the oil in the region became a primary geopolitical concern, permanent British involvement in the area grew from a desire to control the short route to India through the Suez Canal. Cairo became the headquarters for essentially colonial wars against Turkey during the Great War and Italy during the sequel, and if the defeat of Germany's lesser allies did not greatly hasten the end of either war it undoubtedly served the interests of empire. It was not until shortly before second Alamein that troops from Britain outnumbered the Australians, Indians, New Zealanders and South Africans in Eighth Army, reminding us that although echoes of the imperial idea have now died away, half a century ago it was a cause to which English-speaking volunteers rallied from all over the world.

In August 1939 the separate army commands of Egypt, the Sudan and Palestine came under the new Commander in Chief Middle East, General Sir Archibald Wavell. His remit included support of direct British rule in Aden, British Somaliland, Palestine, Sudan and Cyprus, and the enforcement of defence treaties imposed on nominally independent Egypt, Transjordan and Iraq. The core of his command consisted of about 40,000 British garrison troops, plus the crack British-officered Arab Legion in Transjordan and the Sudan Defence Force. There were also some units equipped with light tanks and vintage Rolls Royce armoured cars, organized and trained as the Mobile Division (later 7th Armoured, the 'Desert Rats') by Major General Percy Hobart, a firm believer that armoured forces should operate independently of the other arms, whose legacy lingered after he was replaced in November 1939. The nucleus of the future Western Desert Air Force was equipped with three squadrons of Gloster Gladiator biplane fighters and four of twin-engined Blenheim bombers. There was one squadron of Lysanders, robust aircraft able to operate from unprepared ground, which was designated 'Army Co-Operation', but the airmen were even more convinced than Hobart that the technology they controlled had rendered the traditional combat arms obsolete.

Until Italy declared war in June 1940, Wavell's main concern was that German propaganda might put a spark to the tinderbox created by large-scale Zionist immigration following the Balfour Declaration of 1917 in favour of a Jewish homeland. A 1937 proposal to divide Palestine among British, Arabs and Jews provoked the two-year Arab Revolt led by the Mufti (religious leader) of Jerusalem. Fear of a repetition led, tragically for many would-be refugees, to severe curtailment of immigration and an

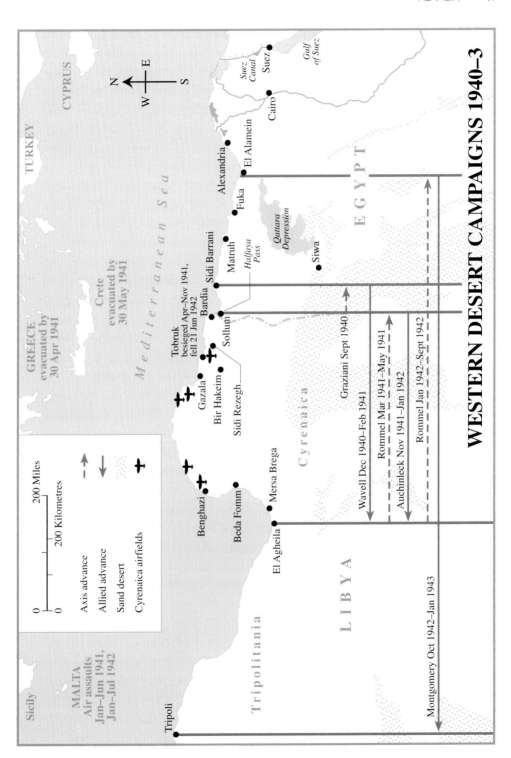

WESTERN DESERT CAMPAIGNS 1940–3

Suez Canal

Gulf of Suez

Suez

Cairo

El Alamein

Alexandria

Fuka

Matruh

Qattara Depression

Sidi Barrani

Halfaya Pass

Bardia

Siwa

Tobruk besieged Apr–Nov 1941, fell 21 Jun 1942

Sollum

Gazala

Bir Hakeim

Sidi Rezegh

Mersa Brega

Benghazi

Beda Fomm

El Agheila

Tripoli

CYPRUS

TURKEY

GREECE evacuated by 30 Apr 1941

Crete evacuated by 30 May 1941

Mediterranean Sea

Sicily

MALTA
Air assaults
Jan–Jun 1941,
Jan–Jul 1942

EGYPT

Cyrenaica

LIBYA

Tripolitania

Graziani Sept 1940

Wavell Dec 1940–Feb 1941

Rommel Mar 1941–May 1941

Auchinleck Nov 1941–Jan 1942

Rommel Jan 1942–Sept 1942

Montgomery Oct 1942–Jan 1943

N E
W S

0   200 Miles
0   200 Kilometres

Axis advance
Allied advance
Sand desert
Cyrenaica airfields

outbreak of Jewish terrorism, which hardened positions on both sides. Thus although at the outbreak of war one-third of the Palestinian Jews volunteered to serve with British forces and Churchill promised that a Jewish Legion would be formed, Wavell felt compelled to veto it. He thereby alienated the Jews without appeasing the Arabs, with dire consequences for British authority underlined as early as 1944 when Jewish terrorists assassinated Minister Resident Lord Moyne in Cairo.

Defeat in France and Italy's opportunistic declaration of war transformed the strategic equation in the whole theatre into one of imminent menace, just when almost every man and item of heavy equipment that Britain could produce was needed for home defence. The Italians had about 160,000 of their own men, and 350,000 African troops in Abyssinia and Libya divided roughly 3:2 in favour of the southern army, and although their aircraft and armoured vehicles were generally even more obsolete than the British, they had three times as many. Prewar contingency planning assumed the British and French would operate together against the two Italian armies, the French having the primary role in Libya and the British in Abyssinia, but, after failing to persuade the French to continue the war from overseas, Churchill ordered the Royal Navy to neutralize their powerful Mediterranean fleet. Although the flotilla at Alexandria agreed to disarm, the larger part of the fleet based at French African bases refused to do so and was attacked. In retaliation, the new Vichy regime in France broke off diplomatic relations, ordered an air strike on Gibraltar and granted the Germans military facilities in Tunisia, West Africa and Syria.

Whatever value we may ascribe to the action taken against the French fleet as a signal, not least to the USA, that Britain intended to continue in the war, the situation in which it thrust Middle East Command was unenviable. The Italo-Libyan army, now free to concentrate against Egypt, advanced ponderously across the border – and then dug in. The Italo-Abyssinian army was more aggressively led and made incursions into Sudan, Kenya and British Somaliland. Wavell judged the last untenable once support from French Somaliland was no longer forthcoming and evacuated it, incurring the ill-will Churchill reserved for those who drew attention to the costs of his policies. This had consequences elsewhere in the theatre because, having offended the Prime Minister once, neither Wavell nor Chief of the Imperial General Staff (CIGS) General Sir John Dill felt on sufficiently firm ground to argue with him over honouring an

Christmas Day 1940: British soldiers kneeling at mass just after a chilly desert sunrise.

undertaking to defend Greek sovereignty. This was at first limited to sending two bomber squadrons to assist them in repulsing an Italian invasion from Albania in late October 1940, but in November the Royal Navy won control of the eastern Mediterranean by attacking the main Italian naval base at Taranto with torpedo bombers, and those ships not sunk or damaged were withdrawn to the north-west of Italy.

Wavell's hand was strengthened by the arrival of the three infantry divisions of the First Australian Corps under Lieutenant General Thomas Blamey and the New Zealand Division under Major General Bernard Freyberg. Also available were the manpower resources of the mainly British-officered Indian Army and, in Kenya, two divisions recruited from West and East Africa, later joined by the 1st South African Division under Major General Dan Pienaar, while Rhodesian and South African squadrons came to form the backbone of the Western Desert Air Force.

The human quality of these volunteer troops was excellent, but they had no modern artillery or armoured vehicles and, with the exception of the Indian Army, they had done little more than basic training.

Although a breathing space had been bought, the closure of the Mediterranean to normal traffic meant that shipping had to travel an extra 10,000 miles to reach the Middle East via the Cape of Good Hope. Both the distances and the perils of that route could have been greatly increased at any time if Vichy France or Spain had opted to throw in their lot with Germany. Bombers could still fly from Gibraltar to Egypt via Malta, but shorter-range aircraft had to be shipped to the Gold Coast (Ghana), then flown to Sudan along a series of landing strips known as the Takoradi route, and then down the Nile to Cairo. This was able to operate because the Free French seized control of French Equatorial Africa, through which it passed, while in March 1941 Colonel Philippe Leclerc led a raid from northern Chad to neutralize the threat posed by an Italian base at Kufra in southern Libya. But the Italian presence on the Red Sea remained the most acute threat to British lines of communication, not least because for as long as it was a combat zone it was closed to US-flagged vessels, no small consideration when so much British registered shipping was being sunk.

Much that followed can only be understood bearing in mind that Abyssinia was necessarily Wavell's first priority, and that the attack made by the small Western Desert Force under Major General Richard O'Connor in December 1940 was designed to concentrate Italian minds and resources elsewhere. It succeeded beyond anyone's wildest hopes. The heavy infantry support Matildas of the Royal Tank Regiment proved virtually invulnerable to Italian anti-tank guns and helped the Indian infantry drive the Italians out of their defensive positions at the Egyptian frontier, then did the same with the Australians at Bardia and Tobruk as they advanced into Libya. Meanwhile 7th Armoured Division, led by 11th Hussars in their venerable Rolls Royces, cut across the bulge of Cyrenaica behind the retreating Italians and by early February about 120,000 men, 400 tanks, 900 guns and 1,000 aircraft had been destroyed or captured. In hindsight, Wavell should not have ordered O'Connor to halt at El Agheila, but the operation had already isolated the Italians in Abyssinia and, in terms of the eastern Mediterranean as a whole, the need to shore up Greek resistance to an imminent German invasion loomed larger than the arrival in Libya of a German 'light blocking force' under the command of one Lieutenant General Erwin Rommel.

Erwin Rommel in campaigning garb. The rank badges are those of a lieutenant general, dating this from the first half of 1941.

The serious fighting in Abyssinia lasted from 19 January to 16 May and involved invasions from the north by two Indian Divisions and the Sudan Defence Force, and from the south by the three African Divisions. In the midst of this Wavell had to cope with a pro-Axis *coup d'état* in Iraq on 3 April, followed by a siege of the British air base at Habbaniya and loss of control of the Mosul oil fields. Iraq was invaded by a battle group built around the Arab Legion from Transjordan, while 10th Indian

Division under Major General William Slim disembarked at Basra, and the revolt had collapsed by 30 May. The Vichyite authorities in the Middle East had lent their territory to German agents and aircraft in support of the rebels, so the two task forces then marched north to join an attack launched out of Palestine and spearheaded by Free French forces. From 8 June to 14 July Syria and Lebanon were conquered in a hard-fought campaign (in which the future commander of the Israeli Defence Force and Minister of Defence Moshe Dayan lost an eye) that culminated in a battle in Damascus between opposing elements of the Foreign Legion. Honour satisfied, many Vichy legionnaires now joined what became the 1st Free French Brigade under Brigadier General Marie Pierre Koenig. 'Gaullists, swashbucklers and criminals of twenty different nations,' sniffed Rommel's chief aide Alfred Berndt, but along with a strong contingent of Palestinian Jews they were to distinguish themselves at Bir Hakeim in May–June 1942, holding up Rommel's attempt to encircle Eighth Army at Gazala for sixteen days.

Meanwhile, the situation elsewhere for the Allies deteriorated disastrously. On 6 April the Germans marched through Yugoslavia virtually unopposed and crushed Greek resistance in three weeks. By 30 April some 60,000 British, Greek, Australian and New Zealand troops had been evacuated, 42,000 of them to Crete, abandoning all their heavy equipment. The New Zealanders' Freyberg was given the task of defending the island, but his scattered command was outfought by a German airborne force of about 23,000 men that began to land on 20 May and after bitter resistance a further evacuation was ordered. Amid appalling attrition of warships and transports by German dive-bombers, 6,000 navy and army personnel were killed or wounded and over 12,000 captured. It was scant consolation that in return they killed or wounded one-third of the German paratroopers and as a result Hitler declared they were never again to be used in the airborne assault role.

For the Australians and New Zealanders, Crete occupies a place in folk memory akin to Gallipoli in the Great War. They fought superbly – Kiwi Second Lieutenant Charles Upham, one of only three men ever to be

OPPOSITE, TOP Genuine combat shots are relatively rare, but this apparently unposed image shows German parachutists advancing under fire during the invasion of Crete, 1941.
OPPOSITE The Junkers Ju 52 was the workhorse of the German fleet: this one disgorges parachutists and equipment on Crete.

awarded a bar to the Victoria Cross, gained the first for sustained heroism between 25 and 30 May – but they were defeated and lost confidence in British political and military leadership. Less often remembered is the heroic resistance of the Greeks and Cretans. Colonel (later Major General Sir) Howard Kippenberger recalled an episode when the languid 'P. G. Wodehouse character' Captain Michael Forrester of The Queen's Regiment led a counter-attack, 'at the head of a crowd of disorderly Greeks, including women; one Greek had a shotgun with a serrated-edge bread knife tied on like a bayonet, others had ancient weapons – all sorts. Without hesitation this uncouth group, with Forrester right out in front, went over the parapet and headlong at the crest of the hill. The enemy fled.' Greeks manned three squadrons of the Western Desert Air Force, their Sacred Regiment (officers serving as troopers) became part of the SAS, and at Second Alamein a Greek brigade held the centre between 4th Indian and 50th British Infantry Divisions.

The loss of all British gains in Libya except Tobruk in March and April, and the capture of O'Connor and his successor Lieutenant General Philip Neame in a daring attack by Rommel's Italo-German force and its armoured component, the Deutsches Afrika Corps (DAK), was partly a perverse result of the breaking of the Enigma machine cipher used by the Axis. The product, known as Ultra, had been so invaluable to Wavell in planning the Abyssinian campaign that he fell into the trap of depending on it too much, and in this he was for once perfectly in step with Churchill, who was impatient to turn this secret advantage into a tangible military accomplishment. Hans-Otto Behrendt, who rose to be Rommel's chief of intelligence, commented: 'Even if the most efficient deciphering of the most important enemy messages provides a clear advance picture of the enemy's intentions, it is no substitute for either modern armaments like tanks, artillery and aircraft, or for operational skill and soldiers with battlefield experience.' Reassured by Ultra decrypts that revealed how small Rommel's force was and also that his instructions were to remain on the defensive, Wavell believed he could send his experienced infantry and armour to Greece and hold the Libyan front with a light screen. Unfortunately Rommel's own intelligence service revealed the opportunity this presented, so he disobeyed his orders and seized the ascendancy in morale he was to enjoy for the next eighteen months.

Thus fine Commonwealth units with reason to be proud of having driven the Italians out of Africa and which might, given time, have learned to work together and with their slowly arriving modern weapons, were defeated in detail, and mutual confidence among the nationalities in Eighth Army was eroded. The siege of Tobruk brought matters to a head. Two brigades of 9th Australian Division under Major General Leslie Morshead held the port from April to December 1941, fighting off repeated attempts to storm the defences and making a sortie that mauled two Italian infantry brigades. Churchill signalled, 'The whole Empire is watching your steadfast and spirited defence of this important outpost of Egypt with gratitude and admiration', but the Australian government demanded immediate action to relieve the garrison. Not chastened by experience, Churchill continued to use the insights he thought Ultra granted him to pressure Wavell into launching the tentative Brevity attack of 15 May and the major Battleaxe offensive of 15–18 June, in which 220 tanks were lost to the DAK's twenty-five. In October the Australian Labour Party under John Curtin, who owed his parliamentary seat to votes from troops in the Western Desert, won a general election and insisted that Morshead and his men should be withdrawn. After the Japanese entered the war in December, Curtin recalled two of the Australian divisions, although the 9th remained and played a crucial role at Second Alamein.

The new Tobruk garrison was composed of British troops and the Polish Carpathian Brigade, under the command of Major General Stanislaw Kopanski. The Carpathian Brigade was made up of soldiers who had escaped through the Balkans after the fall of Poland to join French forces in Syria, followed by a move to join the British in Palestine to escape coming under Vichy control after the fall of France. Among them were pilots who joined the RAF in the Middle East and here, as they did during the Battle of Britain, they distinguished themselves by reckless valour. Air Commodore Raymond Collishaw, the Canadian commander of the Western Desert Air Force and Great War ace, described them in terms that could be applied to all the Free Poles, on land, sea or air: 'They're terrific. The only thing they do all day is thinking up new ways of killing Germans. For the British it's a sport, but for them it is a religion. The Poles have two speeds: full out and stop.' Joined by comrades released from Soviet internment after Hitler invaded Russia in June 1941, they were another of the many nationalities that contributed to the unique character of Eighth Army.

On 1 July Wavell was ordered to exchange places with General Sir Claude Auchinleck, becoming C-in-C India where once again and at the hands of the Japanese he came up against hard realities for which neither he nor the empire he served so faithfully was prepared. The Eighth Army he left was a heterogeneous force in which the hard core of the original Western Desert Force was very much more at home in the desert than the later arriving reinforcements. It excelled in many peripheral areas such as the highly successful deception operations of Brigadier Dudley Clarke's 'A Force' and the intelligence gathering of the Long Range Desert Group (LRDG), but was seriously deficient in the core competencies. Auchinleck was determined not to be rushed into premature action and would not move until he had built up a numerical superiority of men and armour that prompted Churchill's remark: 'Generals only enjoy such comforts in Heaven. And those who demand them do not always get there.' But 'the Auk' was an Indian Army officer and not one to transform army attitudes from those formed in the imperial police role into those needed for the more demanding task of fighting a modern war.

Symbolic of the sea change among the rank and file was the manner in which slang based on Arab words crept into army vocabulary, alongside older terms drawn from India. Thus one looking for something might take an Arab *shufti* or a Hindi *dekko* to obtain Hindi *pukka* gen (reliable information) which was judged to be Arab *quois kateer* (very good) by his fellows or else, if they were in an *alakeefik* (I don't care) mood, they might let drop the quintessential Arabism *maleesh* (it doesn't matter). The Hindi *cha* (tea), *dhobi* (washing) and *wallah* (person) remained embedded, but local features acquired new names – a gully became a *wadi*, a ridge a *djebel* and a rarely seen woman a *bint*. In his *Recollections*, Rifleman Alex Bowlby described fellow Greenjackets who 'moved with the relaxed assurance of successful poachers. Their accent and wit alone marked them as Londoners. Although they hankered for the Smoke they missed the Desert. Cockney Arabs, with a touch of the sand.' Eighth Army even borrowed its anthem – from the Germans. In a poignant episode after the surrender in Tunisia, a column of British soldiers marched past a column of German prisoners, both singing 'Lili Marlene' in their respective languages.

The operational metamorphosis required is well illustrated by Keith Douglas in *Alamein to Zem Zem*. His regiment, the Nottinghamshire Sherwood Rangers Yeomanry, performed a cavalry charge with sabres drawn to scatter rioters in the streets of Jaffa shortly after landing in Palestine in January 1940. Three years later it was dodging German shells in Crusader tanks near Tripoli amid the following radio chatter:

'Uncle Tom, what's the going like over this next bit? Can we bring the, er, unshod horses [trucks] over it?' 'Uncle Tom, I'm just going over Beecher's myself, you want to hold 'em in a bit and go carefully, but after that it's good going for the whole field.' 'King Two Ack,' says someone who has broken a track. 'I shall need the farrier, I've cast a shoe.' Someone else is, 'having trouble with my horse's insides. Could I have the Vet?'

It has been argued that class, that all-purpose explanation for national shortcomings in peace and war, lay behind the army's slowness to adapt to changed conditions, and that if the infantry support model of the Royal Tank Regiment with its heavy tanks had been built upon instead of mechanizing the cavalry, much grief could have been avoided. Possibly, but surely the point is that cavaliers like the Sherwood Rangers were already there, as were the under-gunned, under-armoured but fast Crusader tanks, and use had to be made of both. The class argument overlooks the more obvious fact that a small peacetime army unable to pay competitive salaries and offering glacial promotion cannot be expected to produce generals or staff officers who know how to handle large armies, or indeed talent in depth. Both US Army Chief of Staff General George C. Marshall and CIGS General Sir Alan Brooke, who replaced Dill in December 1941, had to deal with the dilemma of knowing that many of their field commanders were unsatisfactory, but that possible replacements were from the same mould. There are no dragon's teeth – you fight a war with the army you bring to it.

On the vexed question of guns and armour, the German advantage lay as much in the manner in which they employed their weapons as in the superiority of their anti-tank guns, including the dreaded dual purpose 88mm gun, first devised as an anti-aircraft weapon but the outstanding anti-tank gun of the war. But the evolution of tactics is usually a function of the weapons available, so it is not surprising that the British were slow to copy the Germans' aggressive use of anti-tank guns when they continued to be issued the utterly useless Boys Rifle and the 2-pounder (40mm) long after they had been shown to be inadequate. The false dichotomy between light 'cruiser' and heavy 'infantry' tanks was likewise perpetuated by production decisions, and the evolutionary approach employed by the aircraft manufacturers – which would in due course have produced the right combination of gun, armour and engine – was eschewed in favour of

A German 88mm gun comes into action in the desert. It was the best anti-tank gun of the war, although its high silhouette, clearly visible here, made it very vulnerable.

introducing entirely new types, each requiring retooling and a period of debugging in the field. The low silhouette and sloped armour of the Crusader pointed in the right direction, but by the time it was belatedly up-gunned with the 6-pounder (57mm), the long 75mm was being installed in the German Panzer Mark IV.

In *Fire-Power* Shelford Bidwell and Dominick Graham suggest a parallel between the Duke of Wellington's 1806–13 campaign in Spain and the Desert War as theatres where British forces were 'able to engage more or less in isolation a fraction of the army of a great continental power [and] an army composed of valorous but dissociated regiments and corps was gradually welded together and learnt its business, as an *army*'. But in Spain it was the British and the Portuguese who were under the command of a bold general with an unequalled eye for terrain who enjoyed a broad measure of autonomy, whereas in North Africa it was the Germans and Italians. Bidwell and Graham also argue persuasively that the professional culpability of British senior commanders lay in their repudiation of the lessons of the Great War, in particular the combined operations of artillery, armour, infantry and air force in the grand offensive of 1918, but it would be at least as true to say that they never lost sight of the principal lesson – that modern warfare involved casualties on a scale they shrank from incurring. This in turn undermined morale, for soldiers quickly detect infirmity of purpose in their officers. Both desertion and willingness to surrender declined sharply among British – and Italian – troops once they felt they were being decisively employed, despite the higher losses this involved.

Mental unpreparedness was not confined to the army – witness the Royal Navy's lack of provision for the renewal of the U-boat offensive it had barely managed to contain during the Great War, and a shipyard capacity so inadequate that Churchill was reduced to begging Roosevelt for old destroyers decommissioned from the US Navy. But for sheer unbending intellectual rigidity, neither of the older services came close to the dogmatism of the newest and most technologically advanced service. Until ordered to do so by the C-in-C Middle East himself, the RAF refused to take Royal Artillery observers aloft or to lend aircraft to support the LRDG – and resented even having to service the civilian aircraft scrounged by that resourceful outfit. It was also culpably slow in developing the techniques of close air support (CAS) because these smacked of acting as 'airborne artillery' and of subservience to the army. The Luftwaffe, with its purpose-built Stuka dive bombers, had no such reservations and even the Italians were quicker to adapt their inadequate aircraft to the ground attack role.

As we shall examine further when we come to the bombing offensive, the RAF's inability to deliver on the promises its doctrine embodied came close to costing Air Chief Marshal Sir Charles Portal his job in 1941, not the least of his troubles being failure to achieve air superiority in the Middle East. In October 1940, on receipt of an order of battle indicating a front line strength of fewer than 200 aircraft, Churchill wired Air Marshal Arthur Longmore, Air Officer Commanding-in-Chief (AOC-in-C) Middle East: 'I was astonished to find that you have nearly 1,000 aircraft and 16,000 air personnel in the Middle East… Pray report through the Air Ministry any steps you may be able to take to obtain more fighting value from the immense amount of material and men under your command.' Longmore's honest answer was that many of the aircraft were obsolete, that the desert sand made maintenance a nightmare, that losses in combat were less than those in transit and training and that extra aircraft sent from Britain were barely keeping up with attrition.

The careers of most officers who erred on the side of candour in their dealings with Churchill did not prosper and Portal sacrificed Longmore on 1 June 1941. He was replaced by Air Marshal Arthur Tedder, who soon aroused the Prime Minister's anger over the same issue of front line strength and salvaged the situation only by the demeaning expedient, urged upon him by Portal, of revising down his estimate of enemy strength and falsifying the serviceability of his own aircraft. Thus was born the vicious circle of claiming more than had actually been achieved and asking more of men and machines than they could realistically be expected to deliver.

When, despite these adjustments to reality, the RAF still did not win air superiority over the battlefield, Churchill issued the following remarkable instruction: 'Upon the C-in-C in the Middle East announcing that a battle is in prospect, the AOC-in-C will give him all possible aid and irrespective of other targets, however attractive. The Army C-in-C will specify to the AOC-in-C the tasks he requires to be performed. It will be for the AOC-in-C to use his maximum force against these objectives in the manner most effective.'

Here we see, over a year after the fall of France had revealed the effectiveness of close tactical co-ordination between German air and ground forces, how little had been learned. The army and air force commanders were still treated like rival princelings and the C-in-C Middle East was authorized to demand inter-service collaboration only when a battle was imminent. It was not until 1942 that large marker arrows on the ground, first used to direct close support aircraft in 1916, were adopted in the Western Desert; and when 'tank busting' Hurricanes equipped with 40mm cannon were deployed, no communications procedures were in place for front line troops to identify targets to them. The two services had taken the first steps towards working together only by the time of Third Alamein; the situation was prevailing even during First Alamein, as memorably encapsulated by South African commander Pienaar's furious radio communication with his RAF liaison officer:

If you've got to bomb my trucks, you might at least hit them, but you missed every bloody one... My father fought the British in the Transvaal forty-two years ago, and all I want to know is, what side

I'm supposed to be on. Because if I'm on Rommel's, say so, and
I'll turn around and have him in Alexandria within twelve hours.
Just work it out, and let me know as soon as you've decided.

It was a grim fact that aircrew survival rates decreased dramatically the
lower they flew, the lowest in both senses being the torpedo bomber crews,
calculated in November 1942 to have a 17.5 per cent chance of surviving
a first tour of duty and a negligible 3 per cent chance of surviving a second.
Light flak was the big killer and, until their own fighter cover was defeated, the high level approach and low level delivery of the German Stukas
was not only markedly more effective but also incurred less severe losses.
Collishaw lacked the appropriate aircraft; but even after ground attack
fighters became available to Air Vice Marshal Arthur Coningham, the
New Zealander who replaced him in August 1941, it took the experience
of having his forward bases overrun to concentrate his mind on the virtues
of CAS. Even so, it was not until near total air superiority was won during the Italian campaign that procedures comparable to the German standard evolved, with aircraft overhead in radio communication with
Forward Air Controllers, and it remained the poor relation of the massive
US and British investment in high and medium level bombers.

The desert was not a neutral factor in this war: it was said that the
Arabs endured it, the Italians made it flower, the French civilized it, the
Jews made it produce, the Germans subdued it – but the British surrendered themselves to it. In fact the vast majority, of all nationalities, hated
it with an abiding passion, but there was truth in the generalization. Even
the matter-of-fact Peter Roach felt it: 'The land burned with a fierce heat
and solid waves hit me, but I didn't wither. I realized with joy and fierce
pride that I could stand upright, unbowed and resilient; I could enjoy the
endlessness, the simplicity and the hardness of this proud and distant
land.' The pride may well have been in the heart of the beholder, for it
really was a dreadful place where only the most undemanding of shrubs
managed to find some sustenance in the bleached soil, armoured insects
battled for camel droppings and were themselves the prey of scorpions
whose rapidly lethal poison testified to the need to expend as little energy
as possible in pursuit. Many a man brought away from the desert a fond-
ness for the locally manufactured rubber-soled suede desert boots – and
the habit of shaking them upside-down before putting them on in the
morning, for stories of the shrieking agony endured by those who failed

to do so were told as far away as training camps in Britain.

But above all there were flies, multiplying exponentially on the cornucopia of rubbish that is mankind's unfailing contribution to any landscape. They were everywhere, their spattered remains caking every windshield, blocking carburettors and getting into ears, noses and mouths, a torment for the wounded and a sickening shroud for the dead. They even settled on food as it moved from a frantically fanned plate to a mouth already puckering at the thought of the 'crunchy bits' it would contain. It was said that one should time one's visits to the latrine to coincide with mealtimes, because that was when they shifted their area of operations, a grimly humorous reminder of the pre-war public health ditty:

> *Straight from the rubbish heap I come, I never wipe my feet,*
> *And every single chance I get, I walk on what you eat.*

Mosquitoes abounded in the Nile delta but the desert was generally too inhospitable for them and for rodents, the other traditional disease carriers, to proliferate. As though to compensate, two lots of British soldiers took perverse pride in calling themselves rats. The first were the 'Desert Rats' of 7th Armoured Division whose divisional badge was the jerboa, a charming little creature about a foot long, half body and half tufted tail, that can leap up to ten feet at a bound. The others were the garrison of Tobruk during the siege of 1942, who took their name from a sneer broadcast about their largely subterranean existence by the Nazi broadcaster William Joyce (Lord Haw-Haw), just as their fathers proudly adopted the name of 'Old Contemptibles' after the Kaiser spoke of Britain's 'contemptible little army'.

One thinks of the desert as a place of blasting heat, yet the abiding memory most veterans have is of near freezing nights, the change in temperature so abrupt that rocks cracked audibly. It also precipitated such little humidity as the air contained, providing not only just enough moisture for the sparse vegetation but also creating a treacherous crust on top of soft sand that could seem like firm going and indeed would be for a vehicle with the special fat, soft desert tyres – for as long as it kept moving. For the vast majority of soldiers, the terrain they knew was the rocky coastal stretch that could bear the heaviest traffic, but where erosion from the passage of countless tracked and wheeled vehicles produced sand so fine that it seemed like a liquid and accumulated in surface irregularities.

A man could sink up to his waist in it and require help to get out, and it could wrench a steering wheel out of a driver's hands without warning. In the unmitigated sandy waste of the deep desert, men also learned to cope with the wind-driven, convex barchan dunes, and the awesome barriers of the *seifs*, semi-permanent dunes hundreds of feet high and tens of miles long, formed parallel to the prevailing wind or by crosswinds. Finally there were the towering sandstorms reaching thousands of feet into the sky, which could blot out the horizon and even the sun for days and sometimes required troops to don their detested gas masks.

The Sahara is incomparably the largest desert in the world and the Libyan Plateau, over which the Desert War was fought, runs along its northern edge, bounded by the Gulf of Sidra in the west and the Qattara Depression, a huge salt marsh at its deepest 440 feet (135 metres) below sea level, which runs south-west from Alamein near the Egyptian coast some 200 miles towards the Siwa oasis, south of which the aptly named Great Sand Sea stretches unbroken to the Sudan. There was only one, coastal, road; the lack of prominent and permanent features on the plateau, natural or manmade, led to a proliferation of signposts and to the army learning some of the navigational skills of its sister services.

The desert remains a place dotted with anomalies, where dependence on magnetic compasses could be fatal, so new techniques, pioneered by the LRDG, had to be learned. The simplest remained dead reckoning: a course would be calculated using a vehicle odometer and a sun compass, in which the shadow of a central needle falling on a small circular table graded through 360 degrees could be interpreted according to the time of day. For expert navigators who could get hold of them, theodolites were used to get an accurate astrofix at night. This was essential for the war fought in the deep desert, which was won by men who shared the feelings expressed by David Lloyd Owen of the LRDG:

> … those human beings who are with you are probably fairly well known to you, and are there for the same reason that you are – they know the dangers and delights of solitude just the same as you do, and they will react to the unblemished and staggering loveliness of a huge expanse of desert sky, deep blue by day and of a marvellous purple at night sprinkled haphazardly with hundreds of thousands of stars silently lighting that great canopy of night-time that drifts down with the close of day.

Even today this vast landscape remains profoundly disorientating to the uninitiated. While filming the Alamein episode of the series that this book accompanies, modern maps and a Global Positioning System did not solve all my problems. The ridges I had once written about with such confidence were barely perceptible: but once on top of them I could see that they offered a field of view worth fighting for. Distances were deceptive, the going changed radically and without warning from good to impassable, and the long, shimmering shots so eagerly sought by David Wilson, my director, were impeded by the fact that hidden wadis, into which I stumbled with oaths which amused the sound recordist, seemed to crease even the flattest piece of desert. I was regularly hammered against the anvil of the desert by a midday sun so directly overhead that my parked 4 x 4 threw no shade, and then, after the sun dropped quickly below the horizon like an orange ball, was so cold that I scarcely knew what to do with myself.

A classic image of the Desert War is the heavily bearded men of the LRDG returning from reconnaissance missions in their pairs of specially modified 15-cwt and 30-cwt Chevrolet trucks, wearing burnooses and lacking only a Jolly Roger on their radio antenna to complete their resemblance to the buccaneers of old. Four of the LRDG teams were from New Zealand and two from Rhodesia, but there were two patrols of Guardsmen and two from the Yeomanry, while the Indian Army contingent had four patrols of its own, further proof that 'bull' does not drive out spontaneity and that you cannot predict who will make an effective soldier on the basis of social class or national origin. The Germans were full of admiration but were unable to mount anything similar – an officer told his LRDG captors: 'We Germans could not do this sort of thing – out five hundred miles from our base for days or weeks on end. We like to go about in a crowd.' Yet they were perfectly capable of mounting damaging small unit operations behind enemy lines in other theatres, which suggests that in some way the desert itself repelled them.

The proliferation of irregular units on the British side owed much to Wavell, who issued such as Captain Ralph Bagnold, creator of the LRDG, with what he called 'talismans', notes instructing all heads of departments or branches to meet any requirement by the bearer 'immediately and without question'. Perhaps the strangest and most tragic of them was the

OPPOSITE An LRDG soldier mans a truck-mounted Lewis gun with the steep walls of the Qattara Depression as a backdrop.

non-Jewish Zionist Lieutenant Colonel Orde Wingate. Frustrated by Wavell's veto of a Jewish Legion, he turned an appointment as liaison officer with the followers of Emperor Haile Selassie into a fighting command he named the Gideon Force, which reached the Ethiopian capital of Addis Ababa ahead of the Commonwealth columns. His reward at the hands of the Auchinleck administration was dismissal for exceeding his orders, followed by attempted suicide. Reclaimed by Wavell for service in the Far East in mid-1942, he captured the imagination not only of Churchill but also the hard-headed US Chiefs of Staff, and pioneered the concept of deep penetration columns (Chindits) supplied by air. Although the technique proved to be a bad investment in the jungle, it might have had a better chance of success in the Western Desert, where the experience of the LRDG and the bases of the Takoradi route could have been built upon.

Auchinleck was not averse to the idea on a small scale and in October 1941 he authorized Lieutenant David Stirling to recruit the SAS to raid behind enemy lines. He also authorized the formation of the Middle East Commando which, under Lieutenant Colonel Geoffrey Keyes – posthumously awarded the Victoria Cross – attempted to kidnap or kill Rommel, who with his usual good luck was away at the time. The raid took place the day before Auchinleck launched his long prepared Crusader offensive on 18 November 1941, which ground forward to relieve Tobruk and drove Rommel's army out of Cyrenaica, at the cost of completing the disenchantment of the Dominion infantry contingents with both the British armoured brigades and the overall direction of the campaign. A key figure in this breakdown of trust was acting Major General Eric Dorman-Smith, Auchinleck's deputy chief of staff and operations officer, who failed to appreciate that German success was not based on the unilateral armoured manoeuvres in which he and his friend the military theorist Basil Liddell Hart believed so passionately. Nor did the German tanks withdraw after an engagement to form a self-defensive 'leaguer' (from the Afrikaans *laager*) during the night, leaving their infantry with the entirely correct impression that they had been abandoned.

The doctrine associated with Hobart, Liddell Hart and Dorman-Smith did produce results before the advent of the Germans, partly because fast moving independent columns played into the historical strengths of the British army. Wavell's handling of the theatre, including O'Connor's brilliant campaign through Cyrenaica, reflected the imperial style, with widely separated divisions and task forces outmarching and outfighting a poorly led and technologically inferior enemy. At a deeper level, as Artemis Cooper points out so wonderfully well in *Cairo in the War 1939–45*, the politico-military establishment in Cairo, like its counterpart in New Delhi, was created to serve purposes other than waging war. The key ingredient of the imperial mystique was to give the appearance of winning effortlessly, and the ineffable air of complacency among the denizens of the civil and military administrations reflected a commitment to an expansive imperial idea rather than to a besieged nation state, to the privations of which few had any desire to return. This was irksome not only to Dominion troops and Americans, but also to new arrivals from Britain.

For many the abundance and glitter were offensive and the 'social whirl' obscene, but to uniformed snobs and social climbers it was paradise because here, in sharp contrast to the easygoing army in the field, class and rank distinctions could be taken to extremes and there were always 'the natives' to look down on. Despite being run by and for foreigners, Egypt was a legally sovereign state, and Egyptians with an education, from the playboy King Farouk down to the humblest member of the *effendi* (clerical) class, wore the flowerpot-like tarboosh to mark them apart from the despised peasantry. But to British troops all Egyptians without distinction were 'wogs' (from 'working on government service,' a designation from the era of direct British rule), and the tarboosh was an irresistible target. As elsewhere, carelessness of local sensibilities fanned hatred in the class of indigenous collaborators essential to the maintenance of imperial authority.

Of course this is to use hindsight at several clicks of magnification. Those involved know little and care less about the great currents of history in which they are caught up, and sensibly devote themselves to extracting the maximum enjoyment from the passing moment. For all save the small number who sensed that things would never be the same again, there were no complaints about the decadence of Cairo and Alexandria – quite the contrary: it made them unbeatable places to unwind, and the authorities kept inflation, crime and venereal disease under markedly better control in Egypt than in any other theatre of the war. All of these indicators moved upward during 1942 as military discipline began to fray under the pressure of repeated humiliations in the field.

Until Alamein, the Desert War was a seesaw struggle across the

The blunt end of war: a sentry guards a Cairo bridge while the city goes about its business.

Cyrenaican bulge, with each side making use of vehicles captured from the other. In combination with the dust that covered everything, this sometimes led to enemy formations running alongside each other, until whichever side woke up first took the other prisoner. In Italy, one of Bowlby's companions recalled it fondly: 'It was a different kind of war. There were no civvies mixed up in it. It was clean. When we took prisoners we treated them fine and they treated us fine. The fighting was different, too. There wasn't any of this hanging around in the enemy's pockets. We had a go at them, or they had a go at us. Then one of us fucked off.' In so doing the British left behind the means for Rommel to sustain his advances far beyond the point where logistical analysis, by both sides, confidently predicted they must come to a halt. Had the Germans committed half the resources they were later to throw into North Africa they might have tipped the balance in 1941, but Hitler believed that peace could be dictated to the British after the greater latent menace in the east had been eliminated; on 22 June he launched Operation Barbarossa against the USSR, which was supposed to achieve a decisive result before winter set in. The ease with which Rommel had turned the land campaign around in Libya encouraged Hitler in his belief that the British threat was a fly to be swatted at leisure, and this was revealed as the mistake it was only once the greater gamble failed.

By the time Barbarossa was launched, Rommel's command was known as Panzer Group Africa, name changes matching further promotions later: general of Panzer Army Africa, field marshal of the German–Italian Panzer Army and finally of Army Group Africa. The hard core remained the DAK (15th and 21st Panzer Divisions), but the Italians and Libyan Askaris, including the Ariete and Littorio Armoured Divisions, at all times outnumbered the Germans under his command. Although they never had fully competitive armour or aircraft – they called their tanks 'herring cans' – under Rommel's leadership they were notably less effective than their German comrades only in attack, and were often their equals in defence. In *Alamein 1933–1962* Paolo Caccia Dominioni put the following words in the mouth of a veteran Italian general on the eve of First Alamein:

[Rommel's] instinct tells him immediately where a difficult situation is likely to develop, and off he goes with his *Kampstaffel*, which he treats like a sort of Praetorian Guard, and puts things right, charging around like a junior officer. No matter how large the enemy forces are, Rommel is always calmness itself; with bullets and shrapnel flying all over the place and mowing people down all around him, he never gets hit. He just puts things right.

Belief that the Italians were a weak link may have been fed by Ultra intercepts of communications in which Rommel made scapegoats of them when things went wrong, as during First Alamein when he blamed his mainly Italian logistics tail for not doing the impossible and where, although the Ariete stood while 21st Panzer retreated, in his account it was the other way around. Successful generals are as ruthless with the truth as they are with anything else that serves their purpose, and there were political reasons for his denigration of the Italians, as there were for his complaints about allegedly undisputed British air superiority, something RAF casualty figures did not support. Rommel's despatches sought to claim any success for himself and to undermine the authority of his titular superiors, the Italian High Command and Luftwaffe Field Marshal Albert Kesselring, over whose heads he regularly appealed directly to Hitler in Berlin. This led to further strategic errors.

Perhaps the most important of these was that the Axis never eliminated the threat from Malta, whose fate rested on a knife-edge throughout and influenced the Desert War to a degree it would be difficult to overstate. When the RAF could operate out of airfields in Cyrenaica, it could provide cover for convoys to the island from Alexandria and double the range of its bombers, which could fly one way between the mainland and Malta or vice-versa instead of having to return. But when the Axis held them, in combination with bombers based in Crete they could make the cost of fighting supplies through from the east as prohibitive as it already was through the narrows between Sicily and Tunisia in the west. In April–May 1941 the Luftwaffe achieved control of the skies over Malta, and an airborne invasion such as was launched against Crete would almost certainly have succeeded. But Rommel's recapture of Cyrenaica seemed to render an assault unnecessary, and some Luftwaffe units were redeployed for Barbarossa. The respite enabled the British to turn Malta into a formidable fortress.

In mid 1942 the Germans again slighted an opportunity to settle the theatre outright. From December 1941 to May 1942, heavier air attacks than London had experienced during the Blitz resumed; in conjunction with extensive mining, these neutralized Malta as a base for attacks on Axis shipping. And Rommel's second advance through Cyrenaica, this time including the capture of Tobruk – which Churchill called 'one of the heaviest blows I can recall during the war' – once again seemed to doom the island. But the Italian Folgore division and the division-sized German Ramcke brigade, previously earmarked for an airborne assault on the island, were instead flown to serve as reinforcements in Egypt, a misuse of a unique and expensive resource compounded by their lack of heavy equipment, without which even the best infantry were at a grave disadvantage in the desert.

To a certain extent Rommel was hoist by his own petard. He had used the chimera of a triumphal entry to Cairo to seduce Mussolini, who flew to Tripoli with his white horse and sent ceremonial uniforms forward to his incredulous troops, and to beguile Hitler, who made him Germany's youngest field marshal. This trumped his German and Italian superiors in the theatre, who wanted him to wait for the inevitable British counter-attack to dash itself against his anti-tank guns while they consolidated his logistics base. Instead, he exploited windfall captures of trucks (he said 85 per cent of his transport was captured), petrol, oil, lubricants (POL), food and ammunition to charge across the Egyptian border, and was funnelled into the Alamein bottleneck, where the Qattara Depression closes to within 30 miles of the coast. Here extensive British minefields covered by prepared defensive positions, as well as what Kenneth Macksey calls 'the logistics equalizer', brought him to a halt.

Failure to hold Tobruk – or at least to ensure the destruction of POL stocks – plus the 'flap' in Cairo, where the civil and military authorities burned their files on what became wryly known as Ash Wednesday (which spread panic as well as charred paper over the city), outweighs much of the credit due to Auchinleck and Dorman-Smith for First Alamein. According to the ever-quotable Pienaar: 'Everybody here knows perfectly well [Tobruk] was lost because certain people couldn't make up their minds whether it should be held or not. So Rommel made it up for them. You can't blame the men for doing nothing when they know they're being buggered about, can you?' The British commanders were mentally defeated, their army was demoralized and desertion soared, occasionally degenerating into banditry. No less important was that Auchinleck had lost the moral authority to stand up to Churchill, and CIGS Brooke set about recovering this prerequisite by installing a new team. When the Prime Minister insisted on flying to Cairo himself at the same time, Brooke put his job on the line to buy time for the army to regroup under new leadership. Even so, if Churchill's first choice, Lieutenant General 'Strafer' Gott, had not been killed on his way to assume command, Eighth Army might still have been committed to another premature offensive.

The breakdown in army morale also owed something to new drafts arriving without the necessary mental conditioning. After taking over in mid-August, Brooke's nominee Lieutenant General Bernard Montgomery made training, at every level, his first priority because he realized that his senior subordinates no less than the brigades under their command had ceased to pull together. For soldiers there was the ultimate sanction of the brutal glasshouse outside Alexandria featured in the film *The Hill*, but Caccia Dominioni recounts an episode on the eve of the battle when Montgomery formed up a group of senior officers and put them through close order drill, insultingly repeating every order, and rubbed it in with a closing homily about the need to set an example. Even if the anecdote is not true, it captures the spirit of the moment after Auchinleck and Dorman-Smith departed.

While Montgomery was getting Eighth Army back to basics, Cairo was being purged by General the Hon. Sir Harold Alexander, the new C-in-C Middle East, and well-connected staff officers found themselves obliged to justify their existence or return to their regiments. The need to reintegrate these men may have made Montgomery's job more difficult in the short term, but it was an indispensable measure if the army was to snap the link with the past. It was no less essential that a Guardsman and the younger son of a lord wielded the new broom, although perhaps you have to be British and over a certain age to understand why. And there were to be key changes in those personal relationships which make such a difference. Montgomery and Alexander became teamed respectively with Major General Francis de Guingand, previously Auchinleck's Director of Military Intelligence, and Major General A. F. 'John' Harding (his initials believed to stand for 'All Fucking Hurry'), who commanded 7th Armoured Division until severely wounded in January 1943 and then went on to be Alexander's Chief of Staff in Italy. Harding compensated for Alexander's lack of application and de Guingand for Montgomery's lack of modesty and tact, and the British army in the west fought the rest of the war under their leadership.

Montgomery, the recently arrived commander of the Eighth
Army, briefs senior officers on the ground. Lieutenant General
Brian Horrocks of XIII Corps is in profile behind him.

We shall be exploring Montgomery's dark side when we come to the
Arnhem debacle, so here let us dwell on why his inappropriately fuzzy
bronze effigy stands in front of the Ministry of Defence in London. He
was physically unimposing and had an unpleasant voice, his showmanship
was transparent and his manner awkward, he was not even liked by most
and certainly loved by few – yet many who served under him, as I know
to my cost, will react sharply to criticism of him, and he inspired respect
in the way that only great commanders do. This was in part because at this
stage of his career he listened to his subordinates and not only took the
trouble to explain the reasons for his decisions but also insisted that
similar briefings were given at every level. Bombardier Louis Challoner
of the Royal Horse Artillery commented: 'It should be obvious to the
meanest intelligence that when men are ordered to fire, to retreat, to
advance, to switch right and left without any explanation they soon lose

all interest and begin to think the war is a game the higher-ups play.' This nurtured the process akin to osmosis peculiar to armies, in which the men under Montgomery's command felt confident that he knew his business and would not spend their lives unnecessarily. They felt this at once, even before he led them to victory, and the remarkable thing was that he had this effect on all nationalities, including Dominion troops who had two generations' worth of reasons (and a good deal more mythology) to be highly sceptical of British generals. The only point on which all agree is that he believed in himself so completely and unquestioningly that it radiated from him.

The new army commander received an added bonus when a key component of Rommel's apparent magic was revealed. For the first six months of 1942 he was accurately informed not only about the British order of battle but also and crucially about their intentions, thanks to what was known as the 'good source', the US Military Attaché in Cairo who sent regular and comprehensive reports to Washington in a code German intelligence had broken. Behrendt quotes the following intercept for 1 June:

> Personnel losses of the British are fairly light but loss in material heavy. It is estimated that 70 per cent of British tanks engaged were put out of action and at least 50 per cent permanently destroyed. The air ground liaison was poor and the RAF repeatedly bombed own forces. The ground units of the armoured divisions were never present to occupy the ground captured by the tanks.

Ultra's greatest single contribution to the campaign may have been that it belatedly permitted this leak to be identified and plugged on 29 June, while on 10 July Rommel's other eye was put out with the loss of the excellent intelligence from 621 Radio Intercept Company, which ventured too close to the front line near Alamein and was captured in a daring raid by the Australians. The loss of this specialist company was by itself a body blow to the Germans, but in addition the documents that fell into British hands revealed how extremely damaging their own lack of radio security had been. Rommel never fully recovered from this setback, but conversely the discovery was so shattering to the British that fear of eavesdropping may have hampered the development of tactical co-ordination in the field.

The dates for First Alamein are usually given as 1–4 July 1942, but the fighting was only a little less intense during the weeks that followed and Charles Upham, now a captain, was wounded and captured while winning the bar to his Victoria Cross in savage fighting on the Ruweisat Ridge at the heart of Eighth Army's position on 14–15 July. Although Mussolini and his horse returned to Rome, Rommel still thought he could break through. Despite the fact that it was not until mid-August that Brooke was able to get his team installed in Egypt, the defeat of Rommel's next attempt to outflank the British position with the DAK in the battle of Alam Halfa between 30 August and 7 September owed relatively little to Auchinleck's prior dispositions for defence in depth all the way back to the Canal. On the contrary, Montgomery shared the army's hatred of Dorman-Smith's isolated infantry brigade 'boxes' with dispersed artillery around which the armoured battle was supposed to flow, so he brought forward reserves to solidify the front and forbade tactical withdrawal. A shortage of effective anti-tank guns meant he still had to counter enemy armour with tanks, and disproportionate losses among these dissuaded him from trying to cut off the DAK. A further complication was that the Italian units holding the hinge of the DAK advance were equipped with captured armoured vehicles, multiplying the incidence of 'friendly fire' amid the enveloping dust.

Although better handled than in the recent past, it was still the old army that fought First Alamein and Alam Halfa. The delay that Brooke, Alexander and Montgomery now insisted upon was no less essential for training and reorganization than for the build-up of a two-to-one superiority in men and tanks shipped in fast convoys from Britain. Montgomery inherited not one but several blunt instruments and could not hope to weld them together in the time available, but he could and did ensure that decisive mass was never again committed piecemeal. Undeniably the delay also permitted Rommel to improve his tenuous logistics and to bring up his air support, and gave him time to build on the extensive British minefields already in existence, covering them with machine-gun, mortar and artillery emplacements often blasted out of the bedrock. But his own appreciation of the situation was an accurate reading of the writing on the wall: 'The line could not be turned, so the war assumed a form very familiar to both sides, each having so much experience and theoretical knowledge that it could not surprise the other with any new development. In static war, the side that fires the most wins.' After Alam Halfa he knew he was doomed to a battle of attrition that he could not win, so long as the British were prepared to accept significantly higher losses than they had previously.

Among Montgomery's preparations was an elaborate deception operation designed to convince Rommel (or rather his deputy, General P. Stumme, as Rommel himself went on sick leave between 23 September and 25 October) that the attack would come from Lieutenant General Brian Horrocks's XIII Corps in the south. The effort was largely wasted because Rommel had created a formidable barrier designed to absorb the standard British artillery preparation and infantry attack, with lightly held forward posts covering extensive and heavily booby-trapped anti-personnel and anti-tank minefields, backed by strong anti-tank gun positions. The front was manned by his infantry divisions, 164th Light and Trento in the north, Bologna, Ramcke (Airborne) and Brescia in the centre, Pavia and Folgore (Airborne) in the south. Behind these he placed his armoured divisions divided into six groups, three formed by 15th Panzer and Littorio in the north, three by 21st Panzer and Ariete in the south and at the far right of his line the German Kiel Group, equipped with captured Stuart light tanks. His reserves, the motorized 90th Light and Trieste, remained in the north. Like Rommel's own advance over the same ground during Alam Halfa, an attack in the south would have pushed on a swinging door with an armoured hinge.

It requires an acute eye for topography to detect the ridges and hills marked on maps. Save to one under fire, for whom the slightest unevenness can spell the difference between life and death, the Alamein battlefield seems a featureless plain made to measure for the flat trajectory of the high velocity German anti-tank shells, which skimmed so low over the ground that their flight could be tracked by the swirl of sand in their wake. Sand-filled undulations in the rocky surface made it a lottery for the infantry whether a mortar bomb sank into the latter or hit the former to fill the air with lethal fragments. It was a nasty, naked experience to advance over this terrain on foot and even worse inside a tank, knowing that the tracks were kicking up a tell-tale cloud of dust and listening dry-mouthed for the characteristic crack of the dreaded 88s. Eighth Army now had a superiority in men of about 195,000 to 105,000 and in battle tanks of 1,000 to 500 but, if allowance is made for the greater effectiveness of their anti-tank guns, the Germans still had near parity in artillery. The British armoured brigades had lost all enthusiasm for massed charges but the army was still a long way from developing the necessary combined arms expertise, so the battle went forward much as Rommel predicted.

Royal Engineers training with a mine detector. The sapper on the right is alerted to a mine by a sound in his earphones.

The first stage of Montgomery's assault, code-named Lightfoot, called for a lightning artillery bombardment to be followed immediately by a night assault out of the coastal salient towards Miteiriya Ridge by the four infantry divisions of XXX Corps under Lieutenant General Oliver Leese. The scheme was for the veteran divisions, 9th Australian in the north of the salient, and 2nd New Zealand and 1st South African at the southern end, to attack on slightly divergent axes, with the recently arrived 51st (Highland) advancing into the expanding gap between them. 1st and

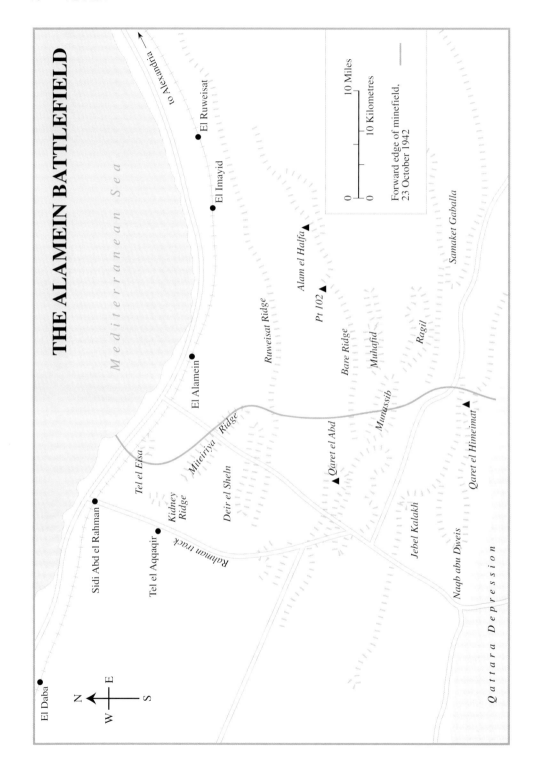

THE ALAMEIN BATTLEFIELD

Mediterranean Sea

to Alexandria

El Ruweisat

El Imayid

Alam el Halfa

Pt 102

Ruweisat Ridge

Bare Ridge

Muhafid

Ragil

Samaket Gaballa

El Alamein

Miteiriya Ridge

Qaret el Abd

Munassib

Tel el Eisa

Deir el Shein

Kidney Ridge

Qaret el Himeimat

Sidi Abd el Rahman

Tel el Aqqaqir

Rahman track

Jebel Kalakh

Naqb abu Dweis

El Daba

Qattara Depression

N
E
S
W

0 | | | | | 10 Miles
0 | | | | | 10 Kilometres

——— Forward edge of minefield,
23 October 1942

A British 25-pdr field gun makes its contribution to the preliminary bombardment at Alamein, 23–4 October 1942.

10th Armoured Divisions of X Corps under Lieutenant General H. Lumsden were then to attack on either side of the 51st to establish blocking screens – the problem of having to use tanks instead of anti-tank guns once again asserting itself – while the infantry turned north and south to cover the Royal Engineers, who had to open passages in the minefields at the rate of about 200 yards an hour, and to widen the breach in the German front in a process Montgomery called 'crumbling'.

Challoner described the preliminary bombardment during the night of 23/24 October in words evocative of the Western Front during the Great War. 'The roar from the massed guns defied any description. No fury of sound had ever assailed our ears like that before, it cuffed, shattered and distorted the senses, and loosened the bowels alarmingly.' The effect on the Axis front line positions can readily be imagined. Simultaneously, parties of infantry that had infiltrated around the enemy outposts during the preceding night moved swiftly to occupy them, and Captain Grant

Murray of 5th Seaforth Highlanders looked back from a trench as the artillery thundered overhead: 'Then we saw a sight that will live for ever in our memories – line upon line of steel helmeted figures with rifles at the high port, bayonets catching in the moonlight, and over all the wailing of the pipes.'

As an aside to those unfamiliar with British army nomenclature, several of the infantry battalions in 'Indian' divisions were mainland British, and there were a large number of Lowland Scots and Englishmen in the 'Highland' Division, itself a wartime-raised replacement for the original 51st Division, captured under tragic circumstances at St Valéry in 1940. These may not have fully shared Murray's enthusiasm for the bagpipes and they were all newcomers to the desert, but the 51st shook out smartly to occupy a line along Miteiriya Ridge that was almost double the width of its start line.

But the crucial development was that the Australians were able to achieve a deep penetration between 164th Light and Trento and then wheeled to pin the former against the coast, drawing the reserve 90th Light and Trieste. It helped that on the 24th Stumme died of a heart attack while under fire in this sector, and Rommel did not return until the next day, but this was balanced by the fact that in the south the Pavia and Folgore Divisions held against XIII Corps's 44th Infantry and Harding's 7th Armoured Divisions, while the Kiel Group ambushed a Free French advance near the Qattara Depression. The failure of this attack, downplayed to the point of misrepresentation by Montgomery but convincingly if vituperatively described by Caccia Dominioni, freed 21st Panzer and part of Ariete to shift north.

Tanks did not survive long on Miteiriya Ridge; David Beretta, crewman in an Italian 75mm self-propelled gun, described the carnage he witnessed before a shell fragment ripped off his face.

> We barely managed to halt their advance, failed to force them to withdraw, but it was a miracle that we stopped them. In the evening we counted 20 Shermans and Grants and some Valentines and Cruisers [Crusaders], but the price we paid for that uneven battle was too high. We had no choice, we were so used to Lady Death's presence that we did not fear her any more. We understood that the most difficult courage was not to die but to continue to live and fight in that hell.

The US-supplied Sherman tank became the workhorse of British armoured divisions, and played an important part at Alamein.

In an effort to advance along rather than over the ridge, infantry and armour got badly out of step with each other in the battles for Snipe and Woodcock, strongholds on either side of the topographical continuation of Miteiriya called Kidney Ridge. 2nd Rifle Brigade fought a classic infantry versus armour action on Snipe, knocking out at least thirty-seven armoured vehicles. Its commanding officer, Lieutenant Colonel Vic Turner, brother of a VC holder from the Great War, earned a VC of his own. Yet somehow Keith Douglas's experience captured the rudimentary level of co-operation between British infantry and armour:

Presently an infantry patrol, moving like guilty characters in a melodrama, came slinking and crouching up to my tank. A corporal... leant against the tank, saying: 'You see them Jerry derelicts over there, them two?' He indicated the two burnt-out tanks to our right front and added: 'They've got a machine gun in that right-hand one. We can't get up to them. They open up on us and pin us down, see?' 'Well, what would you like us to do?' 'I should have thought you could run over the buggers with this,' he said, patting the tank. 'Well, we'll see. I'll have to ask my squadron leader.' I indicated his tank. 'Will you go over and tell him all about it?' 'Very good, sir,' said the corporal, suddenly deciding I was an officer.

His description of the local attack that followed, which in fact silenced several machine guns and netted forty German prisoners, deserves inclusion in any anthology of men at war. The sense of isolation even at the heart of a great battle, the bizarre casualness of some in contrast to the intensity of others, and the way the Germans seemed to pop up at his feet are all vividly conveyed. What neither he nor anyone else on the spot appreciated was that chaotic though their own situation seemed to be, somehow they had stopped Rommel's main armoured counter-punch and he lacked the fuel to throw another without sacrificing the means to salvage his remaining tanks. Thanks to Ultra, the British High Command was aware of this but despite yelps of outrage from Churchill, Montgomery desisted from the grinding attack on Kidney Ridge and regrouped for the final stage. He claimed this was part of the original plan, but in fact it emerged from negotiations with his divisional commanders.

Supercharge was launched the night of 1/2 November, with the New Zealanders opening the way for 1st Armoured Division through the last of Rommel's defensive belt, north of Kidney Ridge and close to where the remains of his own armour were concentrated, as much with a view to escaping along the coast road as to containing the ever-aggressive Australians. As late as 3 November, 9th Armoured Brigade was virtually annihilated here, with 102 out of 128 tanks knocked out and 240 men killed, 10 per cent of the fatalities suffered by Eighth Army during the whole battle. Its commander wrote: 'There was no mercy shown to crews – tank crews or gun crews. We shot them up as they ran – they did the same when we baled out. It wasn't such a gentleman's war as a lot of people like to make out it was.' Meanwhile in the south, perhaps aware that they were about to be abandoned, the Axis infantry became porous. Two squadrons of the Royals in armoured cars ran through the lines that had previously stopped the whole of 7th Armoured Division and spread havoc. 'The enemy was too astounded to do anything as we came through, or else the Italian section thought we were Germans and the German section thought we were Italians. They waved swastika flags at us with vigour and we replied with "Achtung!" and anything else we could think of which, with an answering wave, would get us through their lines.'

Although it was, in the circumstances, a masterpiece of double-speak, Rommel's dispatch of 4 November begging Hitler to authorize the head-long retreat he had already embarked upon also conceded that he was facing a single-mindedness as great as his own:

> I am fully aware of the necessity of holding the line to the utmost and not to yield one inch. But I believe the tactics employed by the British in destroying one formation after another by rigorous fire concentration and constant air attack is turning the tide against us and increasingly exhausting our troops. Therefore, as I see it at present the only possibility of doing further damage to the enemy and preventing the loss of North Africa lies in mobile warfare, and contending with the enemy for every foot of ground. I ask for approval for this.

In later years Montgomery alleged that when interviewing a prospective staff officer he would ask him two questions: was he truthful and was he lucky? Rommel was truthful only on occasions, but he was astoundingly lucky for most of his career and never more so than when heavy and sustained rain turned the desert terrain into a quagmire and grounded the Desert Air Force during the crucial first days of his disengagement from Alamein. The Italian armoured divisions were mostly shattered and the infantry left behind, although Ramcke's tough paratroopers marched north out of the bypassed centre of the line at Alamein, captured a convoy on the coast road and caught up with their rapidly retreating mechanized brethren. Ramcke could barely contain his anger when he met Rommel, but it must have been tempered by seeing how little of the army had got away. The DAK stood to the bitter end and its commander was captured. It was to re-form in Tunisia and strike one last blow, against US II Corps in the Kasserine Pass in February 1943, but by then there was little left of the old guard and, having 'fought itself to the condition where it can fight no more', it surrendered on 12 May with one last *Heya Safari!*, the war cry of German African troops in both world wars.

Montgomery built on Eighth Army's known strengths in artillery and infantry and a crushing logistical advantage to batter a path for his armoured divisions, and kept doing it until the enemy cracked. The longer the process continued, the more certain it was that this time the pursuit would continue beyond Cyrenaica. He certainly entertained hopes of cutting off the retreating Germans but soon learned that a determined enemy can always get away in the desert, and that if his army was at last off the starting blocks, it was not yet ready to go to the finish. He had been able to restore self-confidence and to make his great numerical superiority in men and material prevail, but there was still a gulf between the most inspired performance of even his best armoured units and the bedrock norm on the Axis side. Michael Carver, a dedicated professional serving in 7th Armoured, the most experienced British formation, summarized his experience as follows:

> Nobody knew where anybody or anything was, where minefields started or ended. There was always somebody firing at something and usually somebody being fired at, but who and what it was and why was generally a mystery. To try and find out led from one false clue to another. The information one gleaned would probably be wrong anyway. In the end one gave up trying to tie everything up and went one's own sweet way, hardening one's heart to the inconvenience, annoyance and anger it might cause to somebody else. The longer the battle went on, the less patient one became, the less inclined to obey orders and generally take trouble.

Only towards the end of the war, when training had become abbreviated and the loss of leadership cadres unsustainable, could this have been written by anyone who served under German command. Generations of taking war seriously gave them a superiority in standard operating procedures, command and control, staff work and an instinct for battle so great that the only way they could be defeated was by ruthless attrition. Montgomery knew this, and if later he claimed more credit for his generalship than the facts support, it was in part because the truth was so unpalatable not only to him but to the nation and the cause he served.

Four days after Rommel conceded defeat, Operation Torch landed 65,000 mainly US troops under the command of Lieutenant General Dwight Eisenhower in French North Africa, and set in motion a sequence of events that ended with the Germans occupying Vichy France, and overseas France at last declaring for the Allied cause, although not before the Vichy authorities in Tunisia had permitted Axis reinforcements to flood in from Sicily unopposed. The 'what ifs' begin to acquire critical mass at this point, for in fact this made the magnitude of the eventual Axis defeat much greater, while if the occupation of North Africa by the Americans had been akin to an easy ride they would not have taken their first useful but bloody lessons in the school of hard knocks, headmaster Erwin Rommel.

The Americans were no more blessed with talented generals than the British, but they had the enormous advantage of coming in on a flood tide. By contrast, the officers and men of Eighth Army stood alone for two years in the path of a current flowing the other way, and if they too had to learn the hard way how to deal with the previously omnipotent Wehrmacht, they learned nonetheless and in the process dispelled the myth of German invincibility.

THE BATTLE-FIELD TODAY Although I had written about Alamein in the past, I had not visited the battlefield before working on this project, and am reminded, yet again, of the unwisdom of imagining that one can really understand a battle without seeing the ground. Getting to El Alamein itself is relatively easy. There is a good road along the coast from Alexandria, whose proximity shows just why that particular piece of desert was so important. Cairo is about three hours away by a new road, which curls across the desert to join the coast road just east of El Alamein. The coast is now heavily built up, with village upon village of new condominiums north of the road, and quarries from which their stone has been extracted to the south. El Alamein, easy to miss in the sprawl along the littoral, contains a good-ish Second World War museum. If one might wish that the exhibits were better explained – or those outside better maintained – there are some unmissable items, like a Chevrolet truck recently discovered in a sand-dune in a southern oasis which worked perfectly when recovered, and an 88mm gun whose new paint job only thinly conceals the original white 'victory bands' – each denoting a tank knocked out – round its barrel.

Nearby is the Commonwealth War Graves Commission's El Alamein War Cemetery, with 7,943 graves, and a cloister memorial, which commemorates soldiers, sailors and airmen killed in a wide area of Africa and the Middle East, bearing another 11,868 names. The cemetery, beautifully maintained – as is almost always the case with those in the Commission's care – contains headstones with personal inscriptions which bring one up sharply. A Yeoman's wife tells us that:

> *To the world he was a soldier*
> *But to me he was the world.*

Two brothers, captains in the 3rd Hussars, who died within days of one another, lie side by side. Their headstones bear the biblical inscription:

> *They were lovely and pleasant in their lives*
> *and in their death they were not divided.*

There is a Greek cemetery close by, another timely reminder of the war's polygonal character. A forbidding, fortress-like German war cemetery stands on the coast to the north-west, with an Italian cemetery on the coast road.

Visiting the battlefield itself is difficult unless one is travelling as part of an organized group. South of El Alamein station, where the old ticket office stands empty beside a smart new building, a metalled road runs due south into the desert, just on the British side of the line at the beginning of the battle. There are still abundant signs of defensive positions, like occasional bulldozered scrapes for tanks, some concrete emplacements just south of the railway and, deeper into the desert, stone sangars (circular infantry breastworks). Trench systems have often been filled in by sand, but this has retained the moisture better than the surrounding desert, and so their lines are often marked by patches of green or brown against the ochre. If navigation in what is still an unforgiving environment remains one problem (hence the advisability of travelling in groups), mines are another. There is an Egyptian army camp south of Alamein, with Russian-supplied mine-rolling tanks parked just outside it, and lines of stone cairns alongside roads and tracks mark cleared areas. But most of the desert is not cleared, and large circular anti-tank mines, British and German, still speckle its floor. While we were there an Egyptian army truck was blown up by a mine, and a Bedouin boy was killed by one. Whenever we travelled off a metalled road we were accompanied by a Bedouin guide, Hagi Domo, who led us among the minefields with a gentle confidence that I did not always share.

There are security concerns about travel on the southern edge of the battlefield, probably connected with the growing number of oil wells in the area, but we were able to gain permission to travel, with a pistol-packing escort, to the edge of the Qattara Depression. This is far more dramatic than I had imagined, with the desert dropping suddenly and dramatically down cliffs strewn with petrified trees into a deep and uneven moonscape stretching away beyond the horizon. The Himeimat feature, towards the southern end of the German–Italian position, is one of the few ridges that looks worthy of the name, and dominates a wide sector around it. Ruweisat Ridge, away to its north, is, like most desert ridges, far more gentle, but the track that runs squarely along it gives a surprisingly good view.

All around lies the jetsam of war. Rusty ammunition boxes and jerry cans – the latter a 5-gallon British copy of the German petrol can that was markedly more efficient than the aptly nicknamed British 'flimsy' – are common. We saw live small-arms ammunition and empty brass cases, shell fragments, barbed wire and its retaining pickets, empty bottles – one of which had contained Black and White whisky – and, especially in Italian positions, sardine cans. The watchful Hagi Domo even discovered pieces of 1942 German newspaper, its uniform size leading one to suspect that it had been torn up for what the seventeenth-century antiquary John Aubrey would have called 'a domestic purpose'.

When we were following the route of 51st Highland Division's advance, near the northern edge of the battlefield, we were reminded that the coast road and the railway which parallels it follow an ancient trade route. One of our guides pounced on something glinting in the sand – with my mind on the script I was a second or two too late – and picked up a coin with a Hellenistic head on one side and the attributes of Egyptian kingship on the other. It was a gold stater of one of the Ptolemies, a dynasty that ruled Egypt after the death of Alexander the Great. It had lain there for perhaps two thousand years, and its discovery helped put the strivings of twentieth-century warriors into some sort of context.

ALAMEIN: CHRONOLOGY

1940

10 Jun	Italy declares war on France and Britain.
3 Jul	Royal Navy bombards French fleet at Oran, Mers el Kébir and Dakar.
4 Aug	Italians invade British Somaliland from Abyssinia.
12 Sep	Italians invade Egypt from Cyrenaica (Libya).
28 Oct	Italians invade Greece.
11 Nov	Royal Navy attack on Italian fleet at Taranto.
9 Dec	Start of British offensive against Italians in Cyrenaica.

1941

Jan–June	First siege of Malta.
19 Jan	Start of British offensive against Italians in Abyssinia.
Mid Feb	German 'light blocking force' under Rommel arrives in Libya.
24 Mar	Start of German–Italian counter-attack in Cyrenaica.
28 Mar	Royal Navy victory at Cape Matapan.
3 Apr–30 May	Pro-Axis revolt in Iraq.
6–24 Apr	Fall of Yugoslavia and Greece.
7 Apr	Start of siege of Tobruk.
15–17 May	British offensive (Brevity) in Cyrenaica.
16 May	Surrender of Italian forces in Abyssinia.
20 May–1 Jun	Battle of Crete.
8 Jun–14 Jul	Campaign in Syria and Lebanon
15–18 Jun	British offensive (Battleaxe) in Cyrenaica.
22 Jun	German invasion (Barbarossa) of the USSR.
1 July	Auchinleck replaces Wavell as C-in-C, Middle East.
18 Nov	Start of British offensive (Crusader) in Cyrenaica.
10 Dec	Relief of Tobruk.

1942

Jan–Jul	Second siege of Malta (awarded George Cross on 16 April).
21 Jan	Start of Rommel's second offensive in Cyrenaica.
26 May–17 Jun	Battles of Bir Hakeim and Gazala.
21 Jun	Fall of Tobruk.
1–4 Jul	First Alamein.
11 Aug	Relief convoy (Pedestal) fought through to Malta.
30 Aug–7 Sep	Alam Halfa.

24 Oct	Second Alamein, first phase (Lightfoot).
2 Nov	Second Alamein, second phase (Supercharge).
4 Nov	Rommel breaks away.
8 Nov	Allied landings (Torch) in French North Africa.

1943

23 Jan	Fall of Tripoli, capital of Libya.
19–22 Feb	Battle of Kasserine Pass.
13 May	Surrender of Axis forces in North Africa.
10 Jul	Allied landings (Husky) in Sicily.

CASSINO
ATTRITION IN ITALY

While Axis forces were surrendering in North Africa, Churchill and Roosevelt and their retinue of advisers met for the Trident Conference in Washington to decide the development of Allied strategy. Once it had been agreed to postpone the invasion of France until the following year, it was logical to employ Allied forces in the Mediterranean theatre to eliminate Italy from the war, but theatre commanders Generals Dwight Eisenhower and Sir Henry Maitland Wilson, despite their pleas, were not granted the right to offer the Italians anything other than the 'unconditional surrender' formula announced by Roosevelt at Casablanca in January. In the absence of a diplomatic solution, the Allied armed forces proceeded to the frankly shambolic invasion of Sicily where they continued the process of learning to work together, always competitively and sometimes acrimoniously. Meanwhile, despite near absolute Allied air and sea superiority, the bulk of active Axis forces were able to escape across the Straits of Messina to the mainland.

The Americans were never convinced that there was much to be gained by invading the Italian peninsula, and the campaign that followed was originally intended to exploit an unexpected chance for a rapid advance to the very borders of the German Reich. That Churchill persisted in pursuing it long after the window of opportunity slammed shut is

OPPOSITE, TOP The restored monastery of Monte Cassino.
OPPOSITE The monastery in ruins after its capture by the Allies, May 1944.

another matter, but at the start Eisenhower reacted with commendable speed and daring to secret overtures made by the new Italian government, following the deposition of Mussolini in late July 1943. It took considerable moral and physical courage on the part of King Victor Emmanuel and the Fascist Grand Council to act when they did, and several of them paid with their lives for doing so, but changing sides in mid-war requires finesse and decisiveness, qualities in short supply after twenty years of submission to dictatorship. The king and his prime minister, Marshal Pietro Badoglio, were not the men for such a moment.

Before Richard Lamb's *War in Italy 1943–1945*, the specifically Italian military dimension had received little attention in English. It is a story of such intricacy that I can only touch on it here, but the turning point seems to have been not so much defeat in North Africa and Sicily as a prior countrywide revulsion against the German alliance, sparked by Italian survivors of the battle of Stalingrad returning home to tell of being sacrificed and abandoned. The same had happened at Alamein, but the feeling of betrayal was more intense in the face of a merciless enemy. As a result there was a moment when, properly led, important parts of the Italian army might have turned on the Germans, offering the Allies a possibility of opening an immediate 'second front' not merely in Italy but also in Greece, Albania and Yugoslavia. But the Germans, as always, reacted faster. Their massacre of Italian soldiers who fought against them and then surrendered, notably of the Acqui division on Cephalonia – the background to Louis de Bernières' wonderful novel *Captain Corelli's Mandolin* – had the desired effect of discouraging resistance elsewhere.

While the window was still open Brigadier General Maxwell Taylor, second in command of the US 82nd Airborne Division, put himself in the hands of Italian military authorities – with whom he was still technically at war – in order to co-ordinate a projected landing at airfields around Rome, to coincide with the announcement of an armistice. Boarding an Italian naval vessel at sea he landed at Gaeta, unaware that it would be nine months before another American set foot in it, and from there he was driven to Rome, noting that German troops were thin on the ground, but only to find that Italian preparations were rudimentary. Fresh from having his men scattered over Sicily like grass seed, when not being shot down by the nervous anti-aircraft gunners of the Allied invasion fleet, he had no hesitation in aborting the whole risky scheme and with it the only reason for the invasion of mainland Italy found convincing by the Americans.

But by this time the Churchill-generated momentum to attack 'the soft underbelly of Europe' was unstoppable, although a glance at a topographical map shows how unpromising this approach was. Even if the Allies and the Italians had managed to retain control of central Italy in September 1943, there were still the Alps to contend with. During the Great War the Italian army nearly bled to death trying to penetrate them and the Germans could have held the Alpine passes indefinitely against any assault it was logistically conceivable for the Allies to mount. Had the issue been properly thought through, once Mussolini was gone there was no reason to proceed with the invasion of the mainland, and the late-arriving rationale that it would draw in troops that might otherwise have been used against the Normandy landing was thin. Almost as many German troops could have been tied down had the Allies made Corsica and Sardinia into credible invasion staging posts, forcing the Germans to commit massively to the defence of southern France as well as northern Italy. It was precisely on this fear that the elaborate deception operations preceding the invasion of Sicily had played, helped by the fact that, to the Germans, what the Allies chose to do instead made little strategic sense.

There followed a bitter campaign in which Allied soldiers eventually prevailed against the best that the Wehrmacht could field, battling their way up a peninsula seemingly designed by nature to negate aerial and numerical superiority – and to break an attacker's heart. Command of the sea should have provided the trump card, but the amphibious resources that might have been used to bypass German defensive lines were required for the invasion of Normandy, and after the initial landings in the south of Italy in September 1943 these were available for only one more large operation, at Anzio on 22 January 1944. This in turn forced Allied commanders to rush their first attempt at Cassino, and everything else followed from the very human tendency to insist that, because a large investment has been made in a failed project, more must be spent to redeem it.

No engagement fought in western Europe between 1939 and 1945 evoked the experience of the Great War quite as much as the linked operations at Cassino and Anzio. In his biography *Neither Fear Nor Hope*, Lieutenant General Fridolin von Senger und Etterlin, in charge of the defence at Cassino, judged it to be the battle that reflected most highly on the fighting quality of the German soldier – in either war. In March 1944, after two of his own best infantry divisions had been checked by the German Parachute Division despite a devastating preliminary

General Sir Harold Alexander (right), Commander-in-Chief of 15th Army Group, 1944.

bombardment, Allied Army Group commander General Sir Harold Alexander wrote: 'Unfortunately we are fighting the best soldiers in the world – what men! I do not think any other troops could have stood up to it perhaps except these para boys.' A month earlier he had been more forthright in a letter to his subordinate army commanders, Lieutenant Generals Mark Clark of the US Fifth and Oliver Leese of the British Eighth: '[The Germans are] quicker at regrouping forces, quicker at thinning out on a defensive front to provide troops to close gaps at decisive points, quicker in effecting reliefs, quicker at mounting attacks and counter-attacks, and above all quicker at reaching decisions on the battlefield. By comparison our methods are often slow and cumbersome.'

We do not know what Leese's reaction was to this statement of the painfully obvious, but Clark took it personally. Vaulted to army command without intermediate experience, he was over-conscious of being the standard-bearer of US arms in Europe and fiercely resented any suggestion that he had anything to learn from the British. He also found Alexander's patrician manner unsettling, and here he was not alone. The Army Group commander did not get a grip on the campaign for far too long, giving rise to doubts about his dedication as well as suspicions about his motives. His army commanders seemed likewise incapable of inspiring their subordinates, and a striking feature of the Italian campaign was the widespread lack of confidence in military direction at all levels.

Another peculiarity was that, despite a belief that much of their own suffering was unnecessary, Allied soldiers recognized that the worst effects of the campaign were felt by the civilian population, in particular the southern Italians who were already among the most wretchedly poor in all of Europe. The barren landscape was the result of this, denuded by centuries of culling for firewood, and it is difficult to match today's mountainsides cloaked in vegetation with the moonscape photographs taken during the war. Still less can one imagine the ruins that once stood where prosperous communities bustle today, or look at the elderly and imagine what it was like for them when every combination of directed and careless cruelty was being visited upon them. Yet although they were cast adrift by their leaders, divided among themselves and despised by both sides, they found not only the strength to survive but the generosity to feed, shelter and guide some 10,000 Allied prisoners of war back to their own lines. German reprisals for this and for partisan activity, encouraged and then thoughtlessly betrayed by the Allies, took at least as many Italian lives, to which must be added those killed, wounded and bombed out in the battle zones, the physical abuse, looting and wanton destruction that usually followed, and the debauchery of society at large by uncontrolled inflation and organized crime.

It may seem prim to talk about a 'proper' way of waging war, but there are sound military as well as moral reasons for maintaining order behind the lines. Therefore, however shocking it may be to democratic sensibilities, it is not surprising to find that standards of civil order, public health, basic services and even food supplies were markedly higher until the very end in the German occupation zone. In *Naples '44*, former Field Security Officer Norman Lewis recorded the following exchange with a sardonic *carabiniere* (Italian rural policeman) on the subject of the wholesale hacking up of landlines for their copper content that frequently interrupted Allied telegraphic and telephone communications: 'I reminded him that the Germans shot wire-cutters on the spot. "Of course they did," he agreed. "Thank God, you're a civilized and humanitarian people, and you liberated us from those barbarians. You've taught us what democratic justice is all about and we can't thank you enough." Not a muscle moved in his face to show that he was laughing at me.'

Italy was no stranger to invading armies and conquering cultures, but in this war her own tradition of rural social banditry was returned to her, professionalized by passage through the big cities of the USA, to become an incubus that has yet to be fully excised. One cannot argue with Lewis's indictment of an Allied Military Government linked at the highest level with gangsters such as Vito Genovese and 'Lucky' Luciano:

> A year ago we liberated them from the Fascist monster, and they still sit doing their best to smile politely at us, as hungry as ever, more disease-ridden than ever before, in the ruins of their beautiful city where law and order have ceased to exist. And what is the prize that is to be eventually won? The rebirth of democracy. The glorious prospect of being able to choose their rulers from a list of powerful men, most of whose corruptions are generally known and accepted with weary resignation. The days of Benito Mussolini must seem like a lost paradise compared with this.

The feeling of shame that pervades Lewis's account also colours Joseph Heller's great novel *Catch-22*, based on his experiences while flying medium bombers over Italy. A decade before opposition to the war in Vietnam made it fashionable, Heller mocked the American way of war in what, beneath the light-hearted surface, is a very savage book indeed. He was Jewish, with no doubts about the seriousness of purpose which is all that can possibly justify war, and this may have given an added edge to the fury inspired in him by the personal triviality he perceived in many of those in authority. He was not alone in this. 'I thought the caste system was restricted to India,' wrote one aggrieved GI. 'These officers think they are tin gods or the next thing to it.' Nor was Heller alone in excoriating the waste and corruption he observed, although it is hard to decide whether this was because it was more flagrant than usual in Italy or because of the frustration bred by military stalemate.

Feelings of futility and resentment were not confined to US servicemen. The mutiny at Salerno was a case of miserable man-management, in which soldiers proud of belonging to Eighth Army and the Highland Division 'downed tools' on being assigned, at short notice, as replacement drafts to the British contingent in Clark's Fifth Army. An army psychiatrist's

Once the allies were ashore at Anzio, the fighting there took on some of the grim attrition of the First World War.

conclusion at the time was that the ringleaders were those 'with the highest divisional morale and a combative family spirit', who felt that an essential social compact had been broken. The justice of the case was not entirely clear-cut, for at least some of those fighting for their lives beneath the torrent of the German counter-attack were to observe that they wanted help, not a lesson in the divisional cohesion, and argued that the mutineers 'deserved everything that came to them'. However, the episode was handled neither humanely nor intelligently. Almost 200 were court-martialled and punishments ranging from demotion through terms of imprisonment to death sentences – thankfully commuted – were passed upon them.

No such example was made of the marauding packs of heavily armed multinational deserters allied with local *banditti*, which on occasion had to be engaged in combat by specially formed units of military police. A patrol of Popski's Private Army (the official designation for a long-range raiding group led by Vladimir Peniakoff, a Belgian of Russian parents), as usual informally dressed, was captured by the Free Poles and nearly shot out of hand on suspicion of being one such gang. Most personal accounts record frequent cases of temporary or permanent desertion, which accounted at times for as much as 10 per cent of the troops in the line, but they are understandably more reticent about the incidence of venereal disease, which caused more (albeit generally short-term) manpower loss to the Allied armies than all the efforts of their enemies. The contrast was so great that an intelligence unit identified by Lewis as part of the 'A Force' contemplated infiltrating infected prostitutes from Naples into the German occupation zone, where sensible procedures kept the problem under control.

A related and by no means insignificant drain on Allied fighting power was that the pandemic of crime reduced the number of military police available for battlefield duties, making it necessary to draw troops out of the already thinly stretched line to help maintain order. How much a shortage of Redcaps contributed to the traffic jam that slowed pursuit to a crawl after the breakthrough at Cassino in May 1944 is hard to say, but on a subsequent occasion 'Birdie' Smith remembered that orders from the top, 'reiterated over and again... that once the pursuit had begun, the road discipline, convoy control and traffic arrangements had to be first class.' In no other theatre was the provost service so severely tested, and on the western side of the Italian peninsula it was literally overwhelmed.

There, the manpower loss directly or indirectly attributable to criminality paled next to a logistical haemorrhaging that would have disabled any army in the world except the American. It was estimated that two-thirds of the economy of Naples was devoted to the recycling of stolen military supplies, and Lewis wryly noted in his diary that on 5 February 1944, 'thieves scaled the walls of Castellamare castle, which houses the Field Security Headquarters for Italy, removed the wheels from all the vehicles, and escaped back with them over the walls, which are 30 feet in height. This will provide splendid material for the ballad-singers of the area, whose audiences revel in colourful villainy.' Nor was the looting of the Fifth Army cornucopia limited to individual initiatives. Finding their own vehicles seriously inadequate for the conditions in the Apennines, British units borrowed US four-wheel-drive trucks on a massive scale and generally forgot to return them, while on one occasion an American officer offered a ride by a French colleague was indignant to discover the jeep was one that had vanished from outside his command post some weeks earlier.

A British Bren-gun carrier comes ashore during the early stages of the Anzio landing.

All of this before even considering the losses caused by appalling weather and nightmarish terrain, compounded by the most comprehensive demolition and sabotage that history records. In Naples the Germans not only wrecked and booby-trapped port facilities and public utilities, they also concealed a number of very large bombs on long delay fuses under buildings likely to be employed by Allied forces. Not to be outdone, the unreconciled commandos of Prince Junio Borghese's Italian 10th Flotilla MAS, whose debonair insignia was a skull with a rose in its teeth, infiltrated sometimes very young saboteurs as well as torpedoing or planting limpet mines on Allied shipping. Every road and rail bridge, tunnel, causeway, culvert and cutting was destroyed and sown with an assortment of mines, sometimes laid on top of each other to kill the sappers who had to remove them.

Cassino became a battlefield because it lies at the mouth of one of the few valleys running along instead of across the Italian peninsula. It is formed by the Liri, which runs between the Abruzzi and the Aurunci mountains to join the Gari near the village of Sant'Ambrogio to form the Garigliano, which in turn runs into the sea near Minturno. During the four months the Allied armies took to reach this, the narrowest point of the

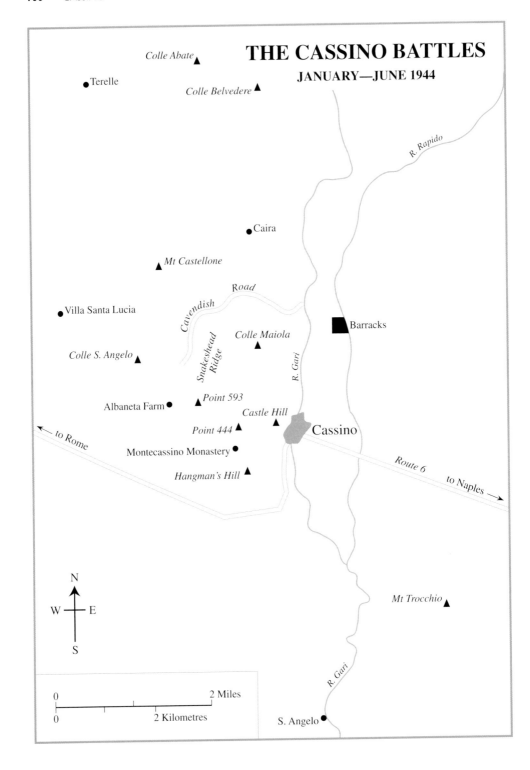

THE CASSINO BATTLES
JANUARY—JUNE 1944

Italian peninsula, the Germans had plenty of time to construct the infamous Gustav Line by flooding the valleys and riddling the reverse slopes of the mountains beyond with deep gun emplacements and mortar pits, while the forward slopes were dotted with camouflaged concrete pill boxes and even some dismounted tank turrets.

Before confronting this, the Allies had to overcome the forward defences of the Bernhard Line, unfortunately identified as 'the Winter Line' by war correspondents who thereby raised false expectations, for the worst of the winter and the best prepared German defences lay beyond it. The moment of truth for David Cole of the Inniskillings came when he first saw the Gustav Line and realized that it could be breached only by the massing of troops on a scale not yet admitted by the Allied commanders: 'Now death had to be faced with cold calculation. And the arithmetic was not encouraging. Of the thirty-six or so fellow officers who had landed with me in Sicily, fourteen had been killed and sixteen wounded, some of them twice and some so badly as never to return.'

German engineers built the Gustav Line, and Allied engineers such as Sapper Richard Eke of 754 Army Field Company, Royal Engineers, had to crack it. Eke did not think of himself as heroic and after getting involved in a firefight vowed: 'Never again would I be infected with this front line madness.' Yet he and his fellows had to demolish the obstacles, clear the mines, bridge the rivers and build causeways across the swamps because only then could the Allied armoured formations perform the task for which the fast but desperately vulnerable Sherman tank was suited. But the river crossings and their approaches were well covered by German artillery, so before anything else could happen the infantry had to put out its eyes.

One really has to see it to appreciate how Monte Cassino dominates the battlefield. 'You felt as if the monastery was watching you,' one veteran recalled. 'It was an eerie feeling. You had to keep looking up to check if you could see it. If you could, then it could see you.' A German–Italian staff appreciation concluded the position was impregnable and it eventually fell only after it was outflanked, despite being bombed and shelled as few other topographical features have ever been. The fact that it was crowned by the father abbey of the Benedictine monastic order really should have been irrelevant. On 29 December 1943, the day before he relinquished command in Italy, Eisenhower issued the following guidance:

> If we have to choose between destroying a famous building and sacrificing our own men, then our men's lives count infinitely more and the buildings must go. But the choice is not always so clear-cut as that... Nothing can stand against the argument of military necessity... [but] the phrase... is sometimes used where it would be more truthful to speak of military... or even personal convenience. I do not want it to cloak slackness or indifference.

That, one would have thought, was that. The monastery deserved consideration as a fine artillery observation post and, although the Germans were not using the building as such, they ensured its destruction by installing guns in the many caves in the slopes below it, and by blasting further fighting positions from the rock within the shadow of the monastery walls. When New Zealand Corps commander Lieutenant General Bernard Freyberg insisted on the saturation bombing of the crest, it was not only in the hope that the position would be neutralized thereby, but also to take the handcuffs off the Allied artillery, previously severely limited in the support it could give to operations around the monastery.

Written soon after the battle, Fred Majdalany's intense *The Monastery* records no slackness or indifference, only the delight felt by his fellow Lancashire Fusiliers over the systematic 'working over' of the monastery ruins by an 8-inch howitzer known as 'Horace' to the British and 'Belching Bitch' to its American crew. Those within sight of it came to hate the building with a passion seldom evoked by an inanimate object and, regardless of what their generals said, the survivors of the US 34th and 36th Divisions, which had suffered severe losses in assaults on either side of it, were very bitter that it was not bombed earlier.

It is less easy to justify repeated assaults on what was by far the strongest point of the Gustav Line. The battle did not have to be fought that way, and Clark's first offensive in January unwittingly came close to success without doing so. Bearing in mind that the timing was dictated by the availability of landing craft for the Anzio operation, and that Fifth Army had only just fought its way up to the Gustav Line, his plan was for the French Expeditionary Corps (CEF) to press its advance well north of Cassino into the Abruzzi, while British X Corps was to attack to the south, along the coast and into the Aurunci. He hoped these flank attacks would cause the Germans to weaken their centre in the Liri valley and permit the two infantry divisions of US II Corps to secure the far banks of the Gari river (usually identified as the Rapido in accounts of this battle) preparatory to a charge by 1st US Armoured Division. When the German reserves had all been drawn into battle, the two US and two British infantry divisions of US VI Corps, plus Rangers, Commandos and other Special Forces, were to land behind them at Anzio.

Taking the Bernhard Line had already weakened Allied units and there was no respite between it and the Gustav Line. Peter Roach of 7th Armoured Division captured the moment in a laconic diary entry: 'One more minor advance. Bert found a bridge undamaged over the Garigliano and no one would believe him so he came back and brewed tea until he was wounded by a mortar bomb.' But it was reasonable to suppose that the retreating Germans had suffered more, and on the basis of a flood of Ultra decrypts as well as reports from agents behind German lines, Fifth Army's pre battle intelligence summary confidently declared: '… it would appear doubtful if the enemy can hold the organized defensive line through Cassino against a co-ordinated army attack. Since this is to be launched before Shingle [the Anzio landing] it is considered likely that this additional threat will cause him to withdraw from his defensive position once he has appreciated the magnitude of that operation.'

Against the enemy thus described, Clark's plan, even though rushed into execution, would have succeeded. As it was, according to Senger either of the flank attacks could have unhinged the Gustav Line – if followed through. He was already very nervous about his own Mountain Division's ability to hold the CEF in the days leading up to the first battle, and the assault by X Corps across the Garigliano, including an amphibious hook to Minturno, took him by surprise. Historically minded, Senger knew that the Spanish had destroyed a French army by crossing the river precisely where the British attacked towards Castelforte 440 years later. For a tantalizing moment the assault gained a vantage point over the German artillery positions in the Ausente valley, before a counter attack by reserves rushed from around Rome recovered the heights. Although the third part of the assault, towards Sant'Ambrogio, was not performed with vigour, Senger thought: 'It was the attack of the British X Corps that made it possible to land at Anzio… [it] had drawn our reserves from their dispositions in depth towards itself, so that when the landing occurred we lacked the forces that should have attacked in the first phase and might even have annihilated the landing force.'

For three months the main action moved elsewhere, but the

An American .30 Browning machine-gun crew in action at Cassino.

unceasingly savage battle to hold the Garigliano bridgehead and the mountains beyond showed the importance the Germans attached to the salient, while the French erected a monument near Rocca d'Evandro to honour their British comrades for winning the position from which they were to launch their breakthrough in May. Lieutenant Philip Brutton's spare description of the death toll for 11 February alone makes chilling reading:

> The first German attack against the Welsh Guards' lines came in at dawn and was repulsed by a bayonet charge led by the company commander, David Elliot, who was killed. His place was taken by Robin Barbour who faced, once more, an enemy

onslaught, and once again led a bayonet charge. He, too, was killed. Only thirty-eight men were now left in No 2 company; in the few hours' fighting, twenty-two had been killed and forty-nine wounded. Night patrols into no-man's land were constant. In one Anthony Schuster was killed, and a member of his platoon, Guardsman Walter Jones, took over. He himself was later killed. Christopher Williams-Ellis then took out a patrol. He, too, was killed.

To the north of Cassino, the advance by two divisions of the CEF into the Abruzzi also came close to dominating a valley of crucial importance to the Germans by seizing the heights beyond the village of Caira, from which the defences behind Cassino were laid bare. These constituted what John Ellis was right to call a 'vile tactical puzzle'. There are three major ridges. The first, ending at Monte Cassino, is in fact dominated by the second, which includes Snakeshead Ridge and its highest point, the ominously named Monte Calvario, which the Allies prudently chose to refer to as Point 593, and most accounts of the battles of Cassino dwell on the fighting along and on either side of these ridges. But beyond the third ridge, which includes Monte Castellone and the so-called Phantom Ridge, there is a broader valley running from a small plateau midway between Caira and Terelle to Villa Santa Lucia on the flank of the Liri Valley, which was as vital for the Germans at Cassino as the Ausente was for those holding the Garigliano front. CEF commander General Alphonse Juin realized how important this feature was, but unfortunately he was still in the early stages of winning Clark's confidence and his men had to press forward unsupported. A French commander of an Algerian *tirailleur* (rifleman) company recalled the savage struggle for Colle Belvedere:

> Visibility less than two yards. Pause every 150 feet of the climb. Arduous ascent. Muscles and nerves at the breaking point… explosions sixty feet above us. Men slip, fall six or seven feet, risk breaking their backs… Such human suffering! I joke with the riflemen. Night black, visibility zero, we trample over corpses; they're ours, one with no head, his guts spilling out.

Clark proceeded with the attack by US II Corps into the Liri Valley despite full knowledge that the CEF and X Corps flank attacks had not drawn German strength away, as his plan required. The assault shattered two regiments of the 36th (Texas) Division. The Texans never forgave Clark, demanding a Congressional enquiry after the war into why, just to reach the river, they had to carry their boats and bridging equipment over two swampy, mine-infested miles under fire from German artillery which had the ranges perfectly calculated, into interlocking fire from the machine guns and mortars of well-dug-in Panzer Grenadiers. In his first-rate study, *Cassino: The Hollow Victory*, John Ellis points out that Major General Fred Walker, commanding the 36th, went ahead with the attack without protest, despite confiding to his diary: 'I do not know of a single case in military history where an attempt to cross a river that is incorporated into the main line of resistance has succeeded. So I am prepared for defeat. The mission should never have been assigned to any troops with flanks exposed.' The explanation would seem to lie in the frame of mind revealed by Clark in his memoirs: 'I can only say that in the same circumstances I would have to do it over again – and if I am to be accused of something, thank God I am to be accused of attacking instead of retreating.'

Although the assault on the Gustav Line failed to achieve a break-through, it had indeed helped denude the Anzio area of German troops and Shingle, the landings at Anzio and Nettuno, achieved the absolute surprise predicted by Ultra. Unfortunately VI Corps commander Major General John Lucas obeyed his own cautious instincts and Clark's warn-ing not 'to stick his neck out', giving rise to Churchill's comment: 'Instead of hurling a wildcat on to the shore all we got was a stranded whale.' He was right – Shingle made operational sense only if it was to make an immediate and decisive contribution to breaching the Gustav Line.

The issue is often seen in black and white, as though Lucas had a choice only between charging towards Rome and certain destruction, or consolidating a shallow perimeter against the wrath to come, as he did. But there was an intermediate alternative – the terrain around Anzio was suited for swift movement inland, less so for defence; and while Lucas's large Special Forces contingent may have lacked heavy weapons, it was trained to raid German enemy communications. Instead it was to be sacrificed as line infantry, while the tanks that might have spearheaded an advance from the beachhead were retained for the chimerical charge up the Liri Valley that was supposed to crown the whole affair.

In *Cassino*, his history of the battle written many years after *The Monastery*, Fred Majdalany judged the effort made by Major General

Charles Ryder's US 34th Infantry Division north of Cassino, following the debacle on the Gari, to be beyond praise, ranking it among the finest feats of arms by any Allied troops throughout the war. Ryder and his corps commander, Major General Geoffrey Keyes, overflew the battle daily in their fragile Piper Cubs and, unlike their army commander and their successors on this front, seem to have been fully aware that the third valley, not Monte Cassino, was the key. It took the men of the 34th a week just to get across the Rapido valley, here deliberately flooded by the Germans, and then they had to claw their way up bare, steep slopes with every track mined, every crest swept by machine guns and every hollow visited by mortar fire. Although the ground was so broken that the effects of shrapnel were limited, this was scant consolation for men obliged by the thinness of the topsoil to crawl into crevices and construct the rock shelters familiar to British troops as 'sangars'. A single sniper could pin down a company by day, while at night any attempt to light a fire or even a cigarette courted death.

All along the Gustav Line, a platoon might believe it had cleared an objective and advance towards the next, only to find itself brought under fire from the rear and compelled to surrender by an enemy position that had held its fire while being overrun. Men might watch with satisfaction while artillery apparently demolished a machine gun nest in a house or barn, to learn expensively that the fire was coming from an intact steel or concrete pillbox constructed behind or beneath it. Morale was not improved when well-stocked dugouts with bunks and heaters were captured, connected by tunnels to firing positions and observation posts also equipped with braziers. By contrast, German flooding and artillery denied the Rapido valley to Allied vehicles, such that supplies came forward by pack animals and, up slopes where even mules refused to go, on the backs of men.

Belatedly, the remaining regiments of the 36th were sent to fill the gap between the right flank of 34th and the CEF, still fighting for the heights beyond Caira, and by 9 February the offensive had come, in Senger's words, 'within a bare 100 metres of success'. But the CEF and the 36th could not advance beyond Monte Abate towards the village of Terelle, and the 34th could not hold the vital crests of either Monte Castellone or Point 593. In the nights between 12 and 15 February the CEF had to over extend its front as far as Monte Castellone, while 4th Indian Division, brought over from the Adriatic, took over the rest of the ground won by the two US divisions. M. B. White, whose harrowing *Purple Heart Valley* was, remarkably, published in 1944, told of many unwounded survivors having to be brought down in stretchers, and of those able to walk out he wrote: 'It was more than the stubble of beard that told the story; it was the blank, staring eyes. The men were so tired that it was a living death. They had come from such a depth of weariness that I wondered if they would ever be able quite to make the return to the lives and thoughts they had known.'

One of the many paradoxes of war is that men who a few minutes earlier have been trying to kill each other may extend a lull in the fighting into a local armistice while the wounded are cleared away, and this is not always just a *quid pro quo*. Around Cassino, on numerous occasions, German troops who were capable of shooting unarmed old men, women and children in reprisals for partisan activity took pity on the Allied soldiers sent against them and granted unilateral respites for them to recover their casualties and even to withdraw from hopeless positions. In *Return to Cassino*, Harold Bond recalled the mercy they showed survivors of the 36th on the Gari, but he also remembered the other side of the coin, after an engagement for which he was later awarded the Silver Star, when his mortar platoon broke up a German counter-attack above Caira. He protested after his platoon sergeant continued firing until the screams of the wounded were silenced, to receive the quiet reply: 'They'll kill you if you don't kill them... I've been with this a long time, Lieutenant.'

The plain fact is that in no one place was Fifth Army strong enough to overcome the opposition it encountered, and Clark's or Lucas's shortcomings are less significant than the very serious intelligence failure that lay behind the whole scheme. Alexander was also lulled into a false sense of security and failed to co-ordinate even a diversion by Eighth Army on the Adriatic front, thereby freeing up the German units that soon put the Anzio beachhead under siege. This in turn lit the fire of suspicion in Clark's mind that 'the British' sought to fight the campaign with American lives, which would have come as a surprise to the Sherwood Foresters, quoted by Carlo D'Este, on the Anzio perimeter:

> It was every night, every night everybody was hunting Germans, everybody was out to kill anybody... we was insane... we did become like animals in the end... yes, just like rats... it was far worse than the desert. You were stuck in the same place. You had nowhere to go. You didn't get no rest, like in the desert... you

never expected to see the end of it. You just forgot why you were there.

Eighth Army had made a longer advance from the toe of Italy to Naples and then across the Apennines, and from the heel along the eastern seaboard. There had been little opposition before the final stretch, but it had to fight, on a more constricted front, about the same distance along the Adriatic as Fifth Army did along the Tyrrhenian coast. The British landings were virtually unopposed and, unlike thoroughly sabotaged Naples, the ports of Taranto, Brindisi and Bari were all captured in working order. The advance to the Foggia plain, roughly parallel to Salerno and considered a strategic objective of greater importance than Naples, was rapid and it was only afterwards that really determined resistance was encountered. At Termoli, 50 miles beyond Foggia, Commandos landed during the night of 2–3 October 1943 and held it for four days against fierce attacks until 78th Infantry Division came up, after which enthusiasm for amphibious hooks around German positions seems to have waned. This was regrettable because, as one British officer put it, 'in this country every five miles provides a fresh defensive position for a division, every five hundred yards for a company'. Then came the contested Sangro crossing, then Ortona where the Canadians became the Allied experts on street fighting, and then one of the worst winters ever recorded took hold, freezing men and machinery when not enveloping them in mud.

It was unfortunate that Montgomery departed at this crucial moment to become Eisenhower's land forces co-ordinator for Operation Overlord. Leese, his replacement, was no Montgomery and 'Birdie' Smith's description of a visit to his battalion by the army commander concludes: 'Wisely he did not attempt to ape his illustrious predecessor; indeed it was to his credit that he behaved like a cheerful Guards officer – which he was.' Montgomery and his staff took with them something of the spirit of the army as well as their mastery of the set-piece battles required to winkle the Germans out of prepared positions. Dominick Graham recalled a comment made to him by a German POW in November 1943: 'We thought we were bettering ourselves by leaving Russia for sunny Italy. Little did we know how much more devastating was British than Russian fire.'

But Montgomery cannot escape responsibility if Leese was not properly groomed to take over, and he deserves condemnation for poisoning the well by privately advising Clark to ignore Alexander as much as possible. It is hard to escape the suspicion that he was never very interested in the Italian campaign, but whether he was or not the effect of his departure on Eighth Army was profound. A growing 'what's the point?' attitude can be gleaned from war correspondent Christopher Buckley's *Road to Rome*, which reflected the thinking of John Harding, now Alexander's Chief of Staff:

> A *line* suggests something that can be pierced and, by implication, offers opportunities of exploitation when it is pierced. But the winter line was in reality a succession of river and mountain positions defended in depth. Our men battled across the Sangro, but behind the Sangro was the Moro, and behind the Moro was the Foro, and behind the Foro was Pescara. And when you had got to Pescara, where were you?

To answer this rhetorical question, at Pescara you were at the entrance to one of the two viable routes for an army through the south-central Apennines, leading directly to Rome. But Eighth Army was not in a position to explore the opportunity because by capturing the Foggia plain it had created a logistical bottomless pit behind it. There had been little thought given to what Eighth Army was to do beyond Foggia, reflected in a plan dominated by the shipping and onward land transport required to build or refurbish sixteen airfields and to bring in 35,000 air force personnel to serve the heavy bombers of the Mediterranean Allied Strategic Air Force (MASAF). But MASAF's primary mission was to attack southern Germany and the Balkans, not to assist the Allied armies in Italy, and, as Senger commented: 'It was a grave decision to build up this organization at the expense of the land front, the neglect of which allowed the Germans to strengthen their defences.'

We shall explore the evolution of bomber doctrine in greater detail later, but some mention of it must be made in the context of the Italian campaign, for it was here that the limits of even massive air power to influence ground operations was first demonstrated, although unfortunately not fully appreciated by Allied planners and commanders in Normandy. As early as the 1940 Norway campaign, the British had learned that their movements in mountainous terrain were not greatly inconvenienced by German air superiority, yet the Mediterranean Allied

Tactical Air Force (MATAF) was confident that with the far greater resources at its disposal it would be able to isolate the Gustav Line with the optimistically named Operation Strangle. The results were disappointing, not least because weather conditions precluded operations half the time, but also because much of the bomb damage was ephemeral. Bridges might be downed by day but night interdiction was neglected, with the result that the Germans kept a flow of essential supplies moving forward over ferries, pontoon bridges and structures they would dismantle and hide before dawn.

In June 1944, too late to influence planning for Overlord, Air Marshal Sir John Slessor, Deputy Commander of the Mediterranean Allied Air Forces, submitted a model of special pleading to US Chief of Staff Marshall and USAAF Commanding General 'Hap' Arnold, declaring that air power could not *by itself* defeat a well-organized army, but that it could weaken resistance to a *determined* land offensive and turn an orderly retreat into a rout. I have added italics to draw attention to the implied rebuke of the land forces that became the preferred air force excuse for failure to live up to its own promises. Strangle failed to force withdrawal by attrition of supplies, or prevent movement of strategic reserves to the front, or of tactical reserves from one part of the front to another, or of forward troops to new positions in the rear – simply put, it failed to achieve a single one of its objectives and Slessor's reduced claims were still overstated. Neither in Italy nor in northern Europe did air power ever succeed in turning a German retreat into a rout – even by day their route discipline, anti-aircraft and camouflage skills were too good.

MATAF was loath to adopt even the CAS procedures learned in combat by one of its components, the Desert Air Force, and the whole process of trial and error was gone through once more. Eventually the 'cab rank' system evolved, in which orbiting rocket- and cannon-equipped fighters could be summoned at short notice by Forward Air Controllers to assist ground operations. Montgomery had begun to integrate the air element within his elaborate artillery plans by the careful cultivation of inter-service harmony, with air force and army headquarters co-located down to divisional level, but although MATAF command was co-located with Fifth Army headquarters, this was in the 1200 rooms of the King of Naples' huge palace at Caserta, said to be haunted by lost souls doomed to seek orders along its corridors for all eternity. It was finally not Clark but rather Lieutenant General Ira Eaker, overall Commander of the

Mediterranean Allied Air Forces, who ordered an 'exchange of personnel' between MATAF and the army, too late to develop close co-operation in time to affect the outcome at Cassino. These problems were neither unique to Italy nor even to the Second World War, for the conceptual gulf between US air power advocates and what they call 'ground pounders' persists to this day.

Before returning to said ground pounders around Cassino, mention should be made of perhaps the most significant single contribution by air power to the Italian campaign: the Luftwaffe's severe curtailment of Allied naval support achieved by a handful of Dornier 217s equipped with 3,000lb Fritz X radio-directed bombs. These sank the 35,000-ton Italian flagship *Roma* on her way to surrender in Malta on 9 September, crippled her sister ship *Italia*, disabled the cruisers USS *Philadelphia* and *Savannah* off Salerno and left HMS *Warspite* dead in the water on the 16th. Heavy units and aircraft carriers were promptly withdrawn to Malta and a crucial Allied advantage negated. In Normandy, the Germans judged naval bombardment to be much the most devastating, combining as it did accuracy with weight of explosives and the excavating effect of semi armour-piercing shells, and although the army at Anzio had some heavy ordnance, the largest being two 240mm (10.9-inch) howitzers, the range and power of, for example, *Warspite*'s eight 15-inch guns might have kept the Germans at a more prudent distance.

To the Germans the assault at Cassino on 15–18 February by the New Zealand Corps, newly formed by 2nd New Zealand and 4th Indian Divisions with 78th British in reserve and Freyberg in command, was simply the final phase of the first battle. Allied accounts consider Second Cassino to be a battle in its own right, beginning with the symbolic destruction of the monastery, and therein lies a tale of objectives becoming blurred under the pressure of events. US 34th Division had pushed generally westwards across the ridgelines behind Cassino and had attacked to the south, along the line of the ridges and towards the town of Cassino, mainly to protect its flank. This was now changed to a southward drive by 4th Indian Division towards Point 593 and the monastery, with the original axis of advance becoming a holding action on the new flank. Responsibility for this lies with Clark, who virtually refused to accept authority over the unwanted addition to his army, but Alexander was also at fault for promoting the gallant Freyberg above his level of competence. Ryder and his officers also bridled at the newcomers' poorly concealed belief that 4th Indian would necessarily succeed where 34th had failed, and there was inadequate sharing of tactical information.

As a general rule, if a division finds itself attacking on a one- or two-company front this is nature's way of telling its commander that he has chosen – or been allocated – a poor line of advance. Major General 'Gertie' Tuker, commanding 4th Indian, wanted to hook around Monte Castellone on his right in combination with the 36th and the CEF, but Freyberg decided that with only 800 mules at his disposal he would not be able to sustain a further assault on the third ridge and chose instead to send Tuker's men across the front of the German base line. British commanders had more experience than their US peers of the Germans' habit of cutting off wide hooks at the elbow, but this was still a fateful departure. Given more time to prepare, things might have been different, but the reason for continuing the attack was the warning given by Ultra that Anzio was soon to face a major counter-attack.

Tuker drove to Naples to find a book on the construction of the monastery and was thus able to inform his superiors that it had walls 10 feet (3 metres) thick extending to a 25-foot (7.5-metre) talus at the base, pierced only by two tunnel-like entrances. In one of several strongly worded assessments, independently echoed by Brigadier Howard Kippenberger, commanding 2nd New Zealand Division, he argued that regardless of whether the monastery was currently occupied by the Germans or not, it would obviously be their fallback position. He told Freyberg that nothing would induce him to attack Monte Cassino unless 'the garrison was reduced to helpless lunacy by sheer unending pounding for days and nights by air and artillery'. Furthermore, he added, the usual 500lb and 1,000lb bombs would not do the job, and demanded that 'blockbusters' be employed.

Tuker was obliged by recurring illness to hand over command of the division to Brigadier H. K. Dimoline on 6 February, but he continued to bombard Freyberg with memoranda on the subject. Unfortunately, in the face of the US generals' unanimous opposition, his requirement that the massif as a whole should be pounded by the heaviest ordnance was lost sight of, and the argument narrowed to whether or not the prerequisite 'desecration' of the monastery should take place at all.

Perhaps inevitably, the bombing that followed combined the maximum political damage with the minimum military utility. On 15 February MASAF's heavies dropped 309 tons of 500lb bombs and 100lb incendi-

German parachutists defending the ruins of the monastery at Monte Cassino.

aries on Monte Cassino, followed by MATAF's mediums that demolished the upper works of the monastery with 126 tons of 1,000lb bombs. The massive foundations still reared up, uncracked, and since the weather rather than operational imperatives had dictated the timing, the bombing went forward thirty-six hours before 4th Indian was in a position to follow it up in strength. A number of refugees within the monastery were killed and wounded, but because the bombing was unusually accurate the Germans on the dominant Point 593, above and behind the monastery, escaped unscathed.

Nazi Propaganda Minister Josef Goebbels was quick to exploit the opportunity to denounce the 'Jews and Communists' unjustly waging war on Germany: 'The monastery has been destroyed several times, but then it was by barbarians... Today these barbarians are called British and Americans, whose wish is to exterminate these phenomena of a superior European civilization. Everything that has made our old continent beautiful, great and strong is to be systematically destroyed.'

During the nights of 15 and 16 February, the gallant 1st Royal Sussex lost twelve of its fifteen officers and 162 out of 313 men while trying to take Point 593 on its own, and it was not until the night of 17 February that something like a concerted attack was mounted. 4/6 Rajputana Rifles attacked along Snakeshead Ridge, 1/9 Gurkhas towards the intermediate Point 444 and 1/2 Gurkhas towards the monastery itself. Meanwhile, in the valley below, two companies of the New Zealanders' Maori Battalion advanced to the railway station south of the town of Cassino, supposedly to win a perimeter that would permit the engineers to build a causeway for armour across the rivers Rapido and Gari and the flooded areas between them. All were beaten back with heavy loss and, far from advancing the line they had taken over, 4th Indian held on only with difficulty in the face of fierce counter-attacks. John Ellis judges it to be one of the low points of Allied generalship during the war: 'a wilful failure at the highest level to take due account of the terrible problems involved in mounting a concerted attack across such appalling terrain [which] were still being grossly underestimated a full month later'.

The plan Freyberg put forward on 18 February was for more of the same, and it was duly approved by Clark and Alexander. Three weeks of unbroken rain might have been expected to provide time to reconsider the advisability of trying to squeeze more men into such narrow fronts, but instead the delay was used to plan a massive aerial and artillery programme, to be embarked upon once the weather cleared and the ground had dried out enough to support tanks. This was cognitive dissonance at work with a vengeance, for it was acknowledged that the bombardment would render the ground once more impassable to armour, especially within the town of Cassino. As astonishing was the misuse of one of the more remarkable combat engineering feats of the war, the Indian and NZ sappers' creation of a camouflaged track, the so-called Cavendish Road, from Caira along the valley between Snakeshead and Phantom Ridges. This was to be used to send tanks – without infantry support – around Point 593 towards the monastery, emerging one by one from a defile near Albaneta Farm, actually a medieval stronghold with a hospital above ground and the local German para regimental headquarters in the cellars.

Alexander and Clark cannot escape the overall responsibility, but there was something almost obsessive about Freyberg's behaviour from the moment he came before Cassino. The New Zealanders were not men to tolerate an unimaginative pounder and until this moment their informality and collegiate decision-making had been much commented upon. Yet before the second battle Freyberg brusquely refused to meet Dimoline and Kippenberger together, saying he did not want a 'soviet' of divisional commanders to gang up on him, and he insisted on a frontal assault without also insisting that diversionary attacks be made elsewhere. Kippenberger trod on a mine well behind the front on 2 March and lost both feet, and with Tuker gone as well there was no officer left in Freyberg's command with the seniority and experience to challenge him. I do not think it a coincidence that from the first he was like a moth to the flame of the positions held by the German paras, the very men who had bundled him humiliatingly out of Crete in May 1941.

Third Cassino opened with a full force effort by MASAF and MATAF in the morning of 15 March. Only half the 992 tons of 1,000lb bombs dropped were within a mile of the aiming point and only 8 per cent within 1,000 yards. This was followed by nearly 200,000 shells from 890 guns, the combined bombardment killing 160 of the 300 paras in the town. 'We now realized that they wanted to wipe us out, but we could not grasp that this terrible episode would go on for so long,' a survivor recalled. 'Scattered survivors, half crazy from the explosions, reeled about in a daze, avoiding all cover until they were hit by an explosion or disappeared.' But those remaining were sufficient to prevent 5th NZ Infantry Brigade from clearing the vital crossroads covered by the redoubt built into the cellars and cliffs around the ruined Continental (actually Excelsior) Hotel. Without this, it was to no avail that together with 5th Indian Brigade they seized Castle Hill (Rocca Janula) above the town and that a party of Gurkhas even took Hangman's Hill, across a steep ravine but almost level with the monastery. Around Albaneta Farm, an armoured NZ, Indian and US task force achieved complete surprise but in the absence of infantry support was halted by a handful of paras wielding Teller mines like hand grenades. The offensive was called off on 23 March and, amid a blizzard, the exhausted men of the Indian Division were relieved after six horrendous weeks in the line.

'Birdie' Smith recalled the exhaustion among his Gurkhas on the march from the hills behind the monastery back across the Rapido valley:

OPPOSITE, TOP Corporal Bartlett, a New Zealand sniper, at work in the ruins of Cassino.
OPPOSITE Indian troops entering Cassino.

'Officers, British and Gurkha, shouted at, scolded, cajoled and assisted men as they collapsed. At times we had no alternative but to strike soldiers who just gave up; all interest lost in everything, including any desire to live. By a dint of all the measures we could think of most of the battalion reached their transport.'

But, to remind us that war is the province of young men and that they are resilient, the entry in his diary for the very next day read: 'Everyone in high spirits.' There was nothing to choose between the determination, bravery and often the chivalry of the two sides. At Castle Hill the men of 1/4 Essex held against vicious counter-attacks, culminating in hand-to-hand fighting in the courtyard after the paras blew down a section of wall, burying twenty of the defenders. A captured para sergeant-major walked about almost like an umpire at an exercise and, when the attack was over, he bowed to the officer commanding, congratulated him on a fine defence and presented him with his own fur-lined gloves. Armistices to permit the recovery of the wounded followed most attacks, with stretchers lent and punctiliously returned. In what must have been a gesture of respect for the outstanding performance of the isolated Gurkhas on Hangman's Hill, they were allowed to withdraw quietly down paths dominated by German mortars and machine guns, and to return later for their wounded.

The crucial difference lay in higher leadership. During the hellish preliminary bombardment, corps commander Senger drove to within range of the Allied guns and then walked forward to join divisional commander Lieutenant General Richard Heidrich at the front line headquarters of the colonel of the 3rd Parachute Regiment. Senger was not alone in contrasting this and the 'follow me' leadership of the German battalion commanders with Allied practice, noting that battalion command elements of 5th NZ did not even enter Cassino for two days. But this raises a broader question – the Parachute Divisions were Nazi *corps d'élite*, so the number of aristocratic officers in them challenges some cherished postwar social and political assumptions. Likewise, even as the battles for Cassino raged, Senger and his army commander General Heinrich von Vietinghoff would on occasion gather with their respective chiefs of staff and talk sedition. They despised Hitler as a guttersnipe, felt humiliated by what Germany now stood for in the eyes of the world, knew that by delaying the Allies they were ensuring greater Soviet inroads to their beloved country – and yet they did their duty by their men to the bitter end. 'What will be the judgement of history on those of us who had the perspicacity and integrity to recognize that defeat was inescapable, yet continued to fight and shed blood?' Senger asked. A simple answer remains elusive.

On Monte Castellone the Irish Brigade took over from Juin's Algerians, who had been in the mountains since early January without suffering the kind of deprivation that disabled other Allied formations in far less time. Royal Irish Fusilier John Horsfall does not seem to have appreciated the significance of the resource entrusted to him: 'The following day I spent exclusively in the company of mules and Paddy Bowen-Colthurst, who seemed at home with the damnable creatures in spite of being a Scots Guardsman.' Some accounts speak of a world-wide shortage of mules, but the more serious lack was of men who knew how to handle them, and Horsfall noted that on his first effort to take supplies forward: 'We dropped several mules over cliffs and a good many others shed their loads.'

To the left of the Irish Brigade, in the stark, corpse-strewn hills behind the monastery overlooked from three sides by German snipers and artillery observers, Majdalany's Lancashire Fusiliers took over from the Gurkhas and discovered that the 'no-movement-by-day' order had to be taken very literally: 'As soon as it was dusk, the soldiers would crawl from their shelters, and you would see small groups of bare hindquarters showing white in the semi-darkness, like grotesque friezes: their owners fervently praying that they might complete the proceeding before a shell struck the area. For shelling – frightening at any time – is worst of all when it catches you with your trousers down.'

The hapless Lucas spoke for many Americans when he confessed to his diary that he did not understand the studied understatement of the British and thought their officers suffered more losses than they should. As though to illustrate the point, on one occasion when Alexander insisted on visiting the front line at Anzio, a request was radioed back that 'the guy in the red hat' should prove his courage elsewhere, as he was attracting artillery fire. Anglo-US misunderstanding, however, paled beside the distrust of both by other components of the armies in Italy. All were fighting for their own particular reasons, which for many did not include belief in the stated war aims or even the basic decency of the US or British governments. Talk of liberating Europe rang hollow to coloured troops, be they Americans or British and French colonial, while highly motivated men from German-occupied countries found both British and Americans insufficiently serious, maddeningly patronizing and, alas, occasionally treacherous.

These were not easy armies to run, and the difficulties involved in keeping everyone pulling in the same direction should not be underestimated. Like Eisenhower, Alexander should perhaps be judged more as a politician than a general, one furthermore tasked with overseeing a British-inspired campaign employing preponderantly US means. Second and Third Cassino are impossible to defend as military operations, but they make a great deal more sense when seen as symbolic efforts, to show willing while waiting for the worst of the winter to pass and for the Air Forces' logistical requirements for the Foggia airfield complex to moderate, thereby restoring operational mobility to Eighth Army.

When it came, the breakthrough was as usual the result of concentrating forces and co-ordinating operations. But bridging the gulf between knowing what you should do and actually doing it is what generalship is all about, and with Alexander and Clark marching to different drummers it seems likely that the credit belongs to Harding and Major General Alfred Gruenther, their respective chiefs of staff. After their experience with the New Zealand Corps they made no further attempt to send British reinforcements to 'Lieutenant General Mark W. Clark's Fifth Army', as he insisted correspondents should refer to it, so in order to achieve concentration it was necessary to redraw the army boundaries, with Eighth Army's front now extended from the Adriatic across the mouth of the Liri valley. Despite the addition of Lieutenant General Wladislaw Anders's newly formed Polish Corps of about 50,000 men and a smaller Italian Mountain Group, Eighth Army was not up to strength and never would be. So when 4th Indian joined 10th Indian on the 'quiet' Adriatic front, they were obliged to conduct many more fighting patrols than usual in order to conceal the departure of the rest of the army, while in the mountains 24th Guards Brigade and the Italians were likewise tasked with creating the illusion of far greater forces by generating disproportionate radio traffic and the nerve-racking ordeal of deliberately 'noisy' night probes of the German positions.

Both the deception and the redeployment, across frighteningly steep and narrow mountain roads at night and in complete radio silence, were performed impeccably and the Germans were to be taken so completely by surprise that Senger, Vietinghoff, Kesselring and their chiefs of staff were all on leave when the offensive, code named Diadem, was launched. Unfortunately the advantage was largely wasted because XIII Corps was committed to yet another attack into the Liri Valley, accompanied by an

The badges on his beret mark the officer giving this briefing before the fourth battle of Cassino as one of the gallant Poles.

assault against Monte Cassino by the whole Polish Corps. It was probably politically impossible to bypass the ruins of the monastery by now, but that does not excuse ignoring the more promising lines towards Terelle or along the Secco valley towards Atina, which were allotted to a single division, 2nd New Zealand, as a secondary operation to protect the Poles' flanks. When the time came, the gains made by what were only intended to be diversionary attacks by the Kiwis, the Guards and the Italians under-lined what might have been achieved. Frontal assault was once more preferred and 4th and 78th British, 8th Indian and 1st Canadian Infantry Divisions attacked across the Gari, while 6th British and 5th Canadian Armoured Divisions waited to charge, their momentum supposed to carry them through successive German lines of prepared defences further up the Liri valley.

Meanwhile Fifth Army shifted its weight to Anzio bringing VI Corps, commanded since February by the aggressive Major General Lucian Truscott, to a total of four US and two British infantry and one US armoured divisions, and the extremely aggressive Special Service Force. Along the Garigliano, the newly arrived 85th and 88th US Infantry

Divisions were squeezed into the Minturno salient while the CEF, now four and half divisions and about 130,000 strong, took over the Aurunci front. The half division was made up of Moroccan *Goumiers*, over 7,000 dark-robed mountain tribesmen led by 600 French officers and NCOs, organized into three groups of three *Tabors*, each consisting of three *Goums*. It is impossible to establish how many of them were mounted in traditional style, but each *Tabor* had an allotment of 785 mules, giving them a unique ability to sustain mobile operations in the mountains. They were also notoriously sexually predatory, and such was the terror they inspired that over on the Adriatic front, a Basuto cook with the British forces who politely knocked on the door of a farm house, hoping to buy eggs, was killed when without a word the lady of the house, mistaking him for a *Goumier* bent on rape, sank an axe into his head.

Like Eighth Army's redeployment under the noses of German observers on Monte Cáiro, Fifth Army's reinforcement of Anzio had to be done in full view of the Alban Hills (Colli Laziale), and by sea to boot. With a limited number of LSTs (Landing Ships Tank) but an abundance of vehicles, the Americans invented the roll-on roll-off technique and transformed amphibious logistics at a stroke, although too late to influence planning for Overlord. Meanwhile deception operations sought to convince the Germans that the US troops withdrawn from Cassino were massing in Naples for another landing north of Rome, but overall the preparations for the offensive were so well concealed that they did not draw in significantly more German troops than were there already. If the strategic objective was indeed to divert German troops from France, it would have been more appropriate to emulate the Indians on the Adriatic and Guards and Italians in the central Apennines by attracting as much attention as possible.

Then again, if Alexander's plan had been guided only by military considerations and fixated neither on Monte Cassino nor Rome, he might have gone around the lower Liri valley. For a double envelopment to succeed, the centre must hold the enemy's attention while flank attacks surround him. Allied intelligence on the German order of battle was better than ever and revealed a three to one numerical inferiority not only on the Cassino front but at Anzio as well. It also confirmed that absolute operational surprise had once more been achieved, and this time it was even right about the morale and determination of German troops around the beachhead. Once the German reserves were drawn into the Liri, the breakout from Anzio was as certain to succeed as any operation in war can be, which makes the rejection of an outflanking manoeuvre through the Abruzzi, in favour of thundering up the middle with more forces than Route 6 could handle, all the more unimaginative.

On 11 May Operation Diadem was launched with an artillery bombardment by more than 1,500 guns, which opened fire just as the Germans were conducting their surprisingly predictable nightly reliefs at the front. But still the defenders held, beating back the Poles' first assault on Point 593. 'Monte Cassino was like something out of another world,' a Polish cadet said. 'We lived in a shifting murk of drifting smoke, heavy with the pestilential reek of death. The very ground we clung to was trembling under the artillery barrage.' Despite the bombardment, the Germans also inflicted the same sort of damage on 8th Indian and 4th British Infantry Divisions along the Gari as they had on the US 36th months earlier, but a corps cannot be denied in the same way as a single division, and after three days the crossings were consolidated. While the Poles regrouped, German observers on Monte Cassino were deluged with smoke shells, but the main obstacle to progress now became one of the more intractable traffic jams of the war, with armour and vehicles so concentrated that the German artillery, even firing blind, could not miss. It was grim pounding, but on the 16th the German high command ordered a general withdrawal. Thus when the Poles finally planted their flag amid the monastery ruins on the 17th it was, save for their own justifiable pride and their place in the history books, a hollow achievement. The Germans withdrew from the Cassino front in good order and were pushed up the Liri valley.

A genuine breakthrough took place in the Aurunci where the CEF punched through a German line not held in sufficient depth and reached the Ausente valley while XIII Corps was still struggling to establish itself across the Gari. The Franco-Africans outflanked the next German defence lines (Dora in the Aurunci and Hitler, rapidly renamed Senger, across the Liri), designed to contain an attack up the valley, not through the mountains. The assault up the Liri drew the German army group reserves from around Rome to the Senger line, from which they were pushed by the Canadians in a set-piece battle between 22 and 25 May, although it would probably have been preferable to keep them as deeply as possible within the bag they were about to be put in by the breakout from Anzio. Alas, the element of national rivalry now destroyed the operational coherence of Diadem, as Juin discovered when Alexander refused to redraw army

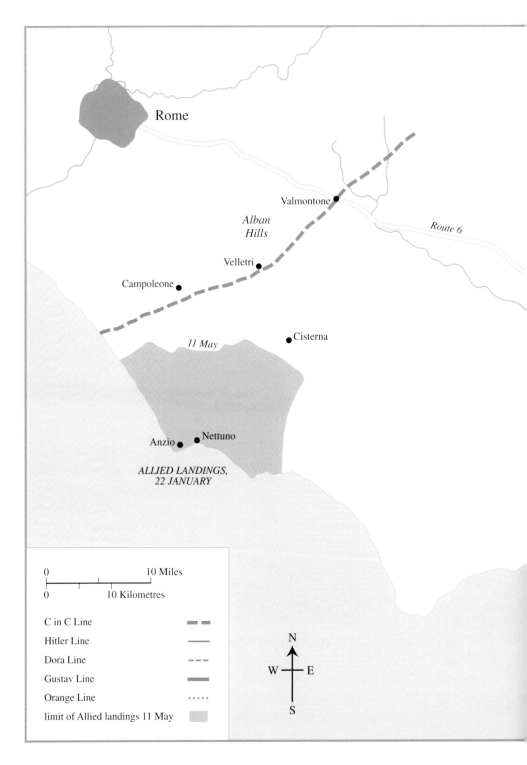

Rome

Valmontone

Alban
Hills

Route 6

Velletri

Campoleone

Cisterna

11 May

Anzio Nettuno

*ALLIED LANDINGS,
22 JANUARY*

0		10 Miles
0	10 Kilometres	

C in C Line

Hitler Line

Dora Line

Gustav Line

Orange Line

limit of Allied landings 11 May

N
W ——— E
S

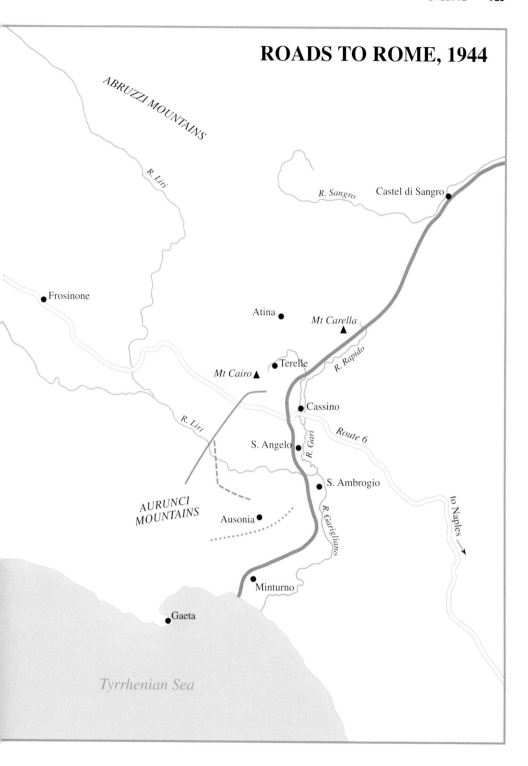

ROADS TO ROME, 1944

ABRUZZI MOUNTAINS

R. Liri

R. Sangro

Castel di Sangro

Frosinone

Atina

Mt Carella ▲

R. Rapido

Mt Cairo ▲ Terelle

Cassino

R. Liri

R. Gari

Route 6

S. Angelo

S. Ambrogio

AURUNCI MOUNTAINS

Ausonia

R. Garigliano

to Naples →

Minturno

Gaeta

Tyrrhenian Sea

boundaries so that the CEF could sever Route 6 behind the Senger line, 20 kilometres (12 miles) ahead of Eighth Army's ponderous advance. 'Once again we have run into one of the stumbling blocks of coalition warfare,' Juin wrote. 'The Allies cannot come to an agreement and co-ordinate their efforts. At the present juncture, questions of prestige are shaping events, each one wanting to make the entry into Rome. History will not fail to pass severe sentence.'

The CEF had also opened the door for the advance along the coast of US 85th and 88th Infantry Divisions, which had found it heavy going for the first week. Gaeta fell on the 19th and contact was made with the Anzio garrison on the 25th, a happy occasion demeaned when Clark insisted that it be restaged for the cameras, with him playing the lead. Meanwhile Alexander ordered Truscott to launch his long-prepared armoured assault through Cisterna towards Valmontone to cut off German Tenth Army, in obedience to the Diadem schedule. In his diary Clark bristled at what he chose to see as Alexander's 'interference' and he seems to have lapsed into what can fairly be described as paranoia about a British plot to reach Rome before him, an impossibility given that at Valmontone Truscott would have been standing across not only the Germans' line of retreat, but also Eighth Army's road to Rome.

What Clark was really concerned about was to get to Rome before Overlord relegated the Italian theatre to the inner pages and to ensure that only he and the US component of his army should get the credit. The CEF was sent east of the city while the British divisions at Anzio were sent towards Ostia in the west. Rome itself was undefended and US Special Forces, French and British reconnaissance patrols all subversively entered it ahead of the photographic corps led by Clark. His behaviour was so out-rageous that he forfeited the respect of Truscott and earned the outright contempt of Brigadier General Robert Frederick, commander of the Special Forces, who was compelled to lose men so that Clark could enter Rome while there was sufficient light for the cameras. In order to muddy the waters he invented a 'race to Rome' for the benefit of the official US Army historians after the war, but in the words of the eminent US military historian Carlo D'Este:

> Clark's decision on May 25 was a calculated act that was to prove as militarily stupid as it was insubordinate. The evidence, most of it supplied by Clark himself, is overwhelming that...

Lieutenant General Mark Clark, with Major General Lucian
Truscott on his far left, arrives to take over the city of Rome.

he deliberately committed what must rank as one of the most mis-
guided blunders made by any Allied commander during World
War II. About to win a stunning victory that would not only have
gained him the glittering prize of Rome virtually without a fight
but have earned him immortality as a great battlefield commander,
Mark Clark suddenly [switched the axis of attack] and in the
process sparked a controversy that continues to this day.

Some judged it a reasonable choice of parallel pursuit over uncertain
encirclement, and there it might have rested had Clark destroyed his
papers before he died. But these confirmed that he lied to both Alexander
and Truscott at the time and released a carefully edited, flag-waving version of his diary to the official historians later. One can only speculate
why he preserved the real one. Possibly he felt posterity would balance his
earlier lapses with his later performance as Army Group Commander in

Italy and as commander of UN forces while winding down the war in Korea – and perhaps it should. Like surgeons, generals usually bury their mistakes, and Clark deserves some credit for leaving us a true record of his thoughts while being taught his lonely trade by an unforgiving enemy.

THE BATTLE-
FIELD TODAY

Few battlefields reward careful study as much as that of Cassino. Driving down the Autostrada del Sole from Rome the mass of Monte Cáiro towers over the Abruzzi on the left, while on the right the Aurunci make their presence felt less dramatically. The monastery, lovingly recreated, and reconsecrated by Pope Paul VI in 1964, can be seen long before the motorway exit. The railway and Route 6 follow the same line as before, but Cassino itself was rebuilt to the south-east of its old location around Rocca Janula, now also being restored. The cableway from the railway station was never rebuilt and the gallows-like support structure that gave Hangman's Hill its name is long gone. As you drive past it on the serpentine road up to the monastery, there is a sign saying it is not safe, which will bring a wry smile to the lips of returning veterans.

Near the top, beside the Polish cemetery, there is a road (its entrance secured by a gate whose unlocking requires a local contact) that leads to the 3rd Carpathian Division memorial on the crest of Point 593, with the sad inscription I quote in the Introduction. You can see how it commands Monte Cassino, and how the cemetery in the saddle between the two hills seems to reach out to the monastery. During preparations for the fiftieth anniversary ceremonies, workmen found two skeletons near the memorial, Germans still holding their rifles. Even today, brush fires are punctuated by explosions as the flames find more of the munitions that killed and wounded so many souvenir hunters after the war.

The path continues along Snakeshead Ridge, to the 'Doctor's House' that was used by both the Royal Sussex and the Poles as their headquarters. Returning, another path winds beneath the western edge of Point 593 past the ruins of Albaneta Farm. It passes under the cliffs, pitted with caves where the German paras sheltered from bombardment (I found one surrounded by the tail fins of British 3-inch mortar bombs), and over which a section of Gurkhas, charging in the darkness, fell to their deaths. Follow the road from Albaneta Farm eastwards and you come to a shattered Sherman tank, with a cross made of welded tracks emerging from its empty turret ring, which marks where the 4th Polish Armoured Regiment emerged from the Cavendish Road. Some tracks are welded on the front and some pitiful extra patches of armour plate on the side – no use against the mine that destroyed it. You can follow the route of the Cavendish Road to Cáira, if you can stand the loss of blood to the thorn bushes and implacable mosquitoes.

It is safer to drive back down to Cassino and follow the signs to *Cimitero tedesco* ('German cemetery'), a reminder why British in Italy called the Germans 'Teds'. Here, 20,000 are buried, another 27,500 from the Anzio front at Pomezia – the cemeteries like bastions brooding over the land they once controlled. The French cemetery is over the hills at the railhead of Venafro where the CEF began its drive through the Bernhard line. South of there, at Mignano, the Italians who died fighting alongside the Allies are buried where the first of them fell, trying to storm Monte Lungo without artillery support. Back at Cassino, the Commonwealth cemetery, with British, Canadian, Gurkha, New Zealand, Indian and South African graves around ten columns with the names of the missing, marks XIII Corps's bridgehead over the Gari. There are no Americans here – all the Fifth Army dead are buried together at Anzio.

In Cassino the site of the Continental Hotel is occupied by undistinguished blocks of flats, but between them you can still see the deep caves in the cliffs, while the line of fire down the Corso della Repubblica, once the western limit of the town, explains better than words how a handful of paras in this location held up an army. In the Piazza De Gasperi a symbolically broken pillar is flanked by a rusting Sherman and a PAK 40. Behind them is the bookshop of Federico Lamberti, publisher of many books in several languages about the ordeal of Cassino. He was there as a boy – and subsequently served in the Royal Pioneer Corps! He deserves my thanks for many insights into the battle, and I cannot think of a better starting-point for a visit.

CASSINO: CHRONOLOGY

1943

14–24 Jan	Allied Summit Conference (Symbol) in Casablanca.
11–25 May	Allied Summit Conference (Trident) in Washington.
10 Jul	Allied landings (Husky) in Sicily.
25 Jul	Mussolini resigns, arrested.
17 Aug	Axis forces complete their evacuation of Sicily.
3 Sep	British Eighth Army crosses Straits of Messina (Baytown).
7 Sep	US Fifth Army landings at Salerno (Avalanche).
8 Sep	Italian surrender announced.
9 Sep	British 1st Airborne Division landed by sea at Taranto.
10 Sep	Germans occupy north and central Italy in force.
11 Sep	Eighth Army captures Brindisi.
27 Sep	Eighth Army takes Foggia; popular uprising in Naples.
1 Oct	Fifth Army enters Naples.
22 Oct	British 78th Division lands at Bari.
27 Oct	British Commandos land, battle for Termoli.
6–27 Dec	Canadian 1st Division battles for Ortona.

1944

11 Jan–12 Feb	First Cassino, assault by Fifth Army.
11–24 Jan	French Expeditionary Corps (CEF) drives to the Gustav Line.
17 Jan–9 Feb	British X Corps attacks on the Garigliano.
20–22 Jan	US II Corps attacks on the Gari.
22 Jan	US VI Corps landings at Anzio (Shingle).
25 Jan–3 Feb	CEF assault on Colli Belvedere and Abate.
24 Jan–12 Feb	US II Corps assault on the hills beyond Cassino.
15–18 Feb	Second Cassino, first assault by New Zealand Corps.
15 Feb	Bombing of the monastery.
15–16 Feb	Royal Sussex assault on Point 593.
17–18 Feb	4th Indian Division assault on the Cassino massif; Maori Battalion attacks towards Cassino railway station.
15–24 Mar	Third Cassino, second assault by New Zealand Corps.
15 Mar	Bombing of Cassino.
16 Mar	Indian and NZ units capture Castle Hill.
16–24 Mar	Gurkhas hold Hangman's Hill; NZ Division assaults into Cassino.
19 Mar	NZ/Indian/US armoured group assault from Cavendish Road.

11–18 May	Fourth Cassino, start of general offensive (Diadem).
12–17 May	British XII Corps assault across the Gari.
13–14 May	CEF breaks through in the Aurunci mountains.
15 May	US 85th and 88th Divisions break through along the coast.
17–18 May	Poles capture Point 593, Monte Cassino.
23 May	Canadian Corps assault on the Senger Line; US VI Corps begins breakout from Anzio beachhead towards Valmontone.
25 May	Clark orders change in axis of attack towards Rome.
4 Jun	US elements of Fifth Army enter Rome.
6 Jun	Allied landings in France (Overlord).

MARKET GARDEN

A DARING THRUST ACROSS AN AIRBORNE CARPET

After the Overlord landings in Normandy on 6 June 1944, the western Allies were locked in a battle of attrition with German Army Group B that was in many respects comparable to the grinding offensives of the Western Front in the Great War. A crucial difference was that in the later war the Eastern Front continued to absorb the bulk of German forces and on 23 June the Russians launched Operation Bagration across a 1,100-kilometre (680-mile) front in the area today known as Belarus. By the end of August this titanic offensive, the largest of the war, had smashed through German Army Group Centre and advanced over 500 kilometres (310 miles) into East Prussia and Poland.

On 20 July an assassination attempt against Hitler raised false hopes that the German domestic front would collapse as it had in 1918. Finally on 25 July the US and British armies at last broke out of Normandy (a process effectively initiated with American Operation Cobra, although the way had been prepared by dogged Anglo-Canadian efforts in eastern Normandy). By 25 August they had reached the Seine, while the US and French armies landed in the Riviera on 15 August (Operation Dragoon) were chivvying German Army Group G up the Rhône valley. By mid September the British had advanced to Antwerp and the Americans to Luxembourg and Nancy, meeting little serious resistance, while the rain of

OPPOSITE Dakotas drop men of the British 1st Airborne Division to join troops and gliders already on the ground, 17 September 1944.

German V-1 missiles on southern England that had begun on 13 June was curtailed as First Canadian Army overran their launch sites along the French coast. With the Kriegsmarine and the Luftwaffe reduced to shadows of their former strength, it was easy to believe that because victory was now certain it was also imminent.

Market Garden, the largest airborne operation ever undertaken, fell into a gap that now opened between hope and experience in the conduct of the campaign in north-west Europe. It marks the moment when Allied impetus was lost to the elastic band effect of supply lines that stretched back to Normandy, past the Channel ports held by the Germans until late September, exacerbated by the clamorous demands of liberated France and theft on a gargantuan scale. A further fly in the ointment was that the German garrisons in the major western French ports, through which supplies and reinforcements were intended to flow directly from the USA, held out still. At the same time, German forces fleeing the occupied territories began to recover coherence and strength as they fell back towards their own frontier, the compressed spring effect making itself felt as their lines of communications shortened and the fronts they had to defend narrowed. Leading Allied formations soon found they were paying a rising price for each day's progress and that the heady days of pursuit were over, but it took longer for this to curb galloping euphoria among those insulated by distance.

In mid September Allied political and military leaders met in Quebec and agreed to divert reinforcements intended for Europe to the Far East, the first dilution of the 'Germany first' strategy agreed in early 1942, according to which the Allies would pit their main strength against Germany rather than Japan. In France, Supreme Commander General Dwight Eisenhower (universally known as 'Ike') assumed overall operational command on 1 September and decreed a 'broad front' strategy, with British and US forces advancing side by side instead of massing for a single thrust into Germany. This was a politically necessary but militarily baneful departure from the principle of concentration, compounded by the fact that Eisenhower could not devote himself to the land campaign with the necessary single-mindedness. Churchill and Roosevelt were well past their best by this time, and few would argue that team spirit was much in evidence at Supreme Headquarters Allied Expeditionary Force (SHAEF), so the burden of keeping rivalry between the Allies and among their squabbling armed services under control fell to Eisenhower himself.

Generals Eisenhower (left) and Montgomery early in 1944.

Although SHAEF did become akin to the imperial court of Byzantium, this was in large measure because the ceremonial, civil and military functions Eisenhower was required to perform were those of an emperor.

However militarily sub-optimal the broad front advance may have been, it was politically impossible for Eisenhower to accept the (patently rhetorical) offer made by newly promoted Field Marshal Sir Bernard Montgomery (equally universally known as 'Monty'), commander of the Anglo-Canadian 21st Army Group, to serve under Lieutenant General Omar Bradley, commander of the US 12th Army Group, in a combined single northern thrust through the Ruhr. This was as likely as reining in Third US Army under the charismatic Lieutenant General George Patton, closing fast on the Saar in the south. Montgomery later blamed the failure of Market Garden in part on Eisenhower's alleged insensitivity to Britain's desperate need to end the war as soon as possible, but the evidence points to his being acutely aware of British exhaustion. He strained the limits of the politically possible by giving Montgomery US troops to command during the operation and later, a mark of professional trust and personal respect that his demanding subordinate was too graceless to reciprocate.

Montgomery also blamed Bradley and Patton for getting around Eisenhower's order to give Market Garden logistical priority, but British supply problems were as much a product of chronic flaws in a large number of their own trucks and of his own admitted failure to appreciate that a major operation was necessary to clear the Scheldt estuary in order to activate Antwerp. The port was miraculously captured intact on 4 September, thanks to the Dutch resistance. Resources were diverted to the airborne operation instead, permitting a German coastal army of 65–75,000 men not merely to escape encirclement but also to counter-attack the operation, while delaying the opening of the port for two vital months. Deepening the tragedy, the Dutch responded heroically to the call for a general strike made by their government-in-exile in the expectation of prompt liberation, and persisted in it amid German reprisals through the following winter, during which thousands starved and froze to death.

With Bradley's connivance, Patton did indeed finesse Eisenhower's instructions by advancing to an exposed position so that he would have to be supported, but that was precisely Montgomery's own intention, the main difference being that he was overt about it. When he met Eisenhower in Brussels airport on 10 September, Montgomery began by criticizing the broad front concept in terms that bordered on insubordination, leading Eisenhower to interject: 'Steady, Montgomery. You can't speak to me like that. I'm your boss.' Montgomery apologized, but when he went on to pro-pose Market Garden, essentially a scaled-down version of the single thrust, there cannot have been much doubt in Eisenhower's mind that it was intended to subvert the broad front strategy. Nonetheless he accepted the proposal, even though it meant putting the predominantly American troops and transport facilities of the Allied Airborne Army (AAA) under Montgomery's command. Ralph Bennett's *Ultra in the West* revealed that both generals were fully informed of, but chose to ignore, the absolute strategic priority attached to Antwerp by the German high command, and Eisenhower suppressed a section in the official US history that was high-ly critical of Montgomery for failing to clear the Scheldt opportunely. This suggests that the Supreme Commander shared his subordinate's hope that the operation would solve the logistical problem.

Like his army commanders, historians have been slow to appreciate the subtlety of Eisenhower's man-management skills and the strength of character that lay behind them. A lesser man would have balked at Market Garden, which clearly owed much to Montgomery's desire to reassert the role of land force co-ordinator he had exercised during the battle of Normandy. By contrast, Montgomery's patronizing attitude towards Eisenhower was in some ways the visible tip of the iceberg of British

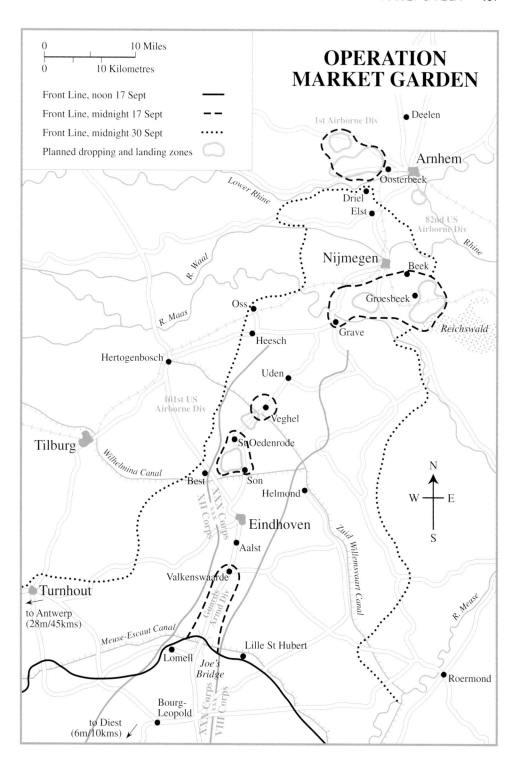

OPERATION MARKET GARDEN

0   10 Miles
0   10 Kilometres

Front Line, noon 17 Sept
Front Line, midnight 17 Sept
Front Line, midnight 30 Sept
Planned dropping and landing zones

1st Airborne Div

Deelen

Arnhem

Oosterbeek

Lower Rhine

Driel

Elst

82nd US
Airborne Div

Rhine

Nijmegen

Beek

R. Waal

Groesbeek

R. Maas

Oss

Grave

Reichswald

Heesch

Hertogenbosch

Uden

101st US
Airborne Div

Veghel

Tilburg

St Oedenrode

N

Wilhelmina Canal

Best

Son

W — E

Helmond

S

XXX Corps
XII Corps

Eindhoven

Zuid Willemsvaart Canal

Aalst

Valkenswaarde

Guards
Armd Div

R. Meuse

Turnhout

to Antwerp
(28m/45kms)

Meuse-Escaut Canal

Lille St Hubert

Lomell

Joe's
Bridge

Roermond

Bourg-
Leopold

to Diest
(6m/10kms)

XXX Corps
VIII Corps

resentment at growing US preponderance within the alliance, which was to have repercussions that extended beyond the war and helped to sour Anglo-US relations during the 1950s, when Eisenhower was President. At the purely human level, Montgomery should have been a great deal more appreciative of the fact that Eisenhower had backed him through difficult times in Normandy, particularly against the British contingent at SHAEF led by the Deputy Supreme Commander, Air Chief Marshal Sir Arthur Tedder, who on more than one occasion recommended Montgomery's dismissal from command even of 21st Army Group.

Tedder's attitude again illustrates that inter-service rivalries were often more intense than those between the nationalities. The British and US air force commanders had an essentially shared agenda and made common cause, and at sea even the abrasive Admiral King came to respect the professional expertise of his British counterparts. In Italy, although Alexander had to swallow hard on a number of occasions, overall a commonsense recognition that he who pays the piper calls the tune prevailed. Anglo-US friction threatened to get out of hand only in France and Germany, and some responsibility for this goes beyond Montgomery to Field Marshal Sir Alan Brooke, Chief of the Imperial General Staff, and his proxy struggle with General George Marshall, US Chief of Staff, over the direction of the campaign. Both had been bitterly disappointed not to be given overall operational command, and if Montgomery was Brooke's surrogate (the Americans would have preferred Alexander), the promotion of Eisenhower over the heads of 366 more senior US officers marked him as unquestionably Marshall's.

This rivalry shaped the awkward command structure of the AAA when it was brought into being in August 1944. The obvious candidate for overall command was the combat-tested US Lieutenant General Matthew Ridgway, but Brooke in effect blocked his appointment by lobbying strenuously for his own protégé, Lieutenant General Frederick 'Boy' Browning. This was despite the fact that Browning had not made a success of a previous appointment as Airborne Adviser to Eisenhower in the Mediterranean, where he had given offence by his patronizing tone ('My dear Ridgway, what you Americans fail to understand is...') and by his open contempt for the USAAF Troop Carrier Command. The compromise candidate imposed by Marshall was Lieutenant General Lewis Brereton, who had worked well with the British in India, in the Mediterranean and as commander of Ninth USAAF, a heavy bomber force. Browning was appointed his deputy as well as commander of the British Airborne Corps, consisting of 1st and 6th Airborne Divisions with two parachute and one airlanding (glider-borne) brigades each, the Polish Parachute Brigade Group and the air transportable 52nd (Lowland) Division, originally trained for mountain warfare. Ridgway had command of XVIII US Airborne Corps, consisting of the newly arrived 17th and the veteran 82nd and 101st Airborne Divisions, each of three paratroop and one airlanding regiments.

Although two of Ridgway's divisions were committed to the operation – and on 15 September Lieutenant General Bedell Smith, Eisenhower's Chief of Staff, offered Montgomery the use of the third – he was to be pointedly excluded from playing any part in Market Garden. Montgomery airily dismissed Smith's offer as superfluous to requirements, and while it was by that time certainly too late to contemplate any major change to the plan, the slighting of Ridgway's combat command experience in the preparation of the most ambitious airborne operation of the war was unconscionable. To compound the imbalance, the two air transport commanders, Major General Paul Williams of IX Troop Carrier Command, USAAF, and Air Vice Marshal Leslie Hollinghurst of 38 Group, RAF, were also more familiar with airborne operations than either Brereton or Browning. Brigadier 'Shan' Hackett, commander of 4th Parachute Brigade during the battle, wryly commented on the result of this air force preponderance at the top: 'They used to make a beautiful airborne plan and then add the fighting-the-Germans bit afterwards.'

Some under the fastidious Browning's command did not share Brooke's high opinion of him. Glider pilot Louis Hagen recalled in *Arnhem Lift* how angry he felt, as he and a lieutenant struggled to use the unfamiliar Piat (Projector Infantry Anti-Tank), at the emphasis on spit and polish during training: 'Why couldn't they have taught us about house-to-house fighting and the Piat gun?' Why indeed? Canadian veterans of Ortona had toured army camps to lecture on street fighting and the Piat had been in service since 1942. Nor is there any record of Browning using his influence to obtain improved radio equipment, despite crippling breakdowns reported by 6th Airborne after operations in Sicily and Normandy. In *Echoes from Arnhem*, Lewis Golden of the divisional signals detachment dropped at Arnhem argues convincingly that, considering how seriously deficient the planners knew it to be, the radio equipment in fact worked better than could have been expected. Browning must also bear some responsibility for British Airborne forces being far behind the Americans and the rest of the British army in the development of CAS procedures, so much so that the only Forward Air Controllers to accompany 1st Airborne Division during this operation were two teams of signallers borrowed at the last moment from a US fighter control unit. Given these known deficiencies, it is difficult to excuse Browning's decision to use precious gliders to fly in with his operationally useless headquarters on the crucial first day.

In *The Devil's Birthday* Geoffrey Powell, a company commander in the battle, gives the following explanation: 'Browning, like many another, had long waited for the day when he would lead into battle the troops he had raised and trained. And this battle was likely to end the war in the West and bring renown to both his airborne troops and himself. In such circumstances, few men given the opportunity would have acted otherwise.'

One who would have was Major Brian Urquhart, chief intelligence officer of the British Airborne Corps, whose attempts to dampen Browning's enthusiasm were dismissed as the product of 'nervous exhaustion' and got him sent him on compulsory sick leave. Another was the commander of the Polish Parachute Brigade Group, Major General Stanislaw Sosabowski. 'But the Germans, General, the Germans,' he exclaimed when Major General Roy Urquhart (no relation), commander of 1st Airborne Division to which the Poles were attached, outlined a rash operation planned for 10 September (Comet) upon which the unstable edifice of Market Garden was to be built. In early September Browning had threatened to resign over a dispute with Brereton concerning a proposed operation for which Browning felt there had been inadequate reconnaissance, and in which he judged excessive dependence was placed on enemy disorganization. Yet Comet, and Market Garden even more so, depended totally for success on German unpreparedness and he dismissed Brian Urquhart's photo reconnaissance evidence that there was German armour where the plan required it not to be. This may have been based on Ultra intercepts of reports from local German commanders, falsely claiming that their precious tanks were not battleworthy in order to evade orders to send them elsewhere, but a more experienced commander would at least have marked the map 'here be dragons'.

Until the publication in 1990 of the ground-breaking *It Never Snows in September* by Robert Kershaw, a professional parachute officer and fluent German speaker, historians also paid insufficient attention to

'You sure, Lieutenant?' An American airborne officer plans his route, 17 September. The censor has painted out his divisional shoulder patch in this photograph.

Sosabowski's comment, yet the defining characteristic of the campaign in north-west Europe was the phoenix-like ability of the Wehrmacht to recover from crushing defeat, despite being directed by a man no longer in touch with reality who at the end wished only for as many as possible to die with him. Having wrecked the first line German army formations on both fronts, the Allies now encountered a peculiarly lethal combination: previously unblooded troops of variable quality and enthusiasm, led by officer and NCO cadres whittled down to a hard core of the most highly skilled, motivated – and lucky – individuals of the most efficient fighting machine since the Roman legions, whose attitude was summed up by 'Enjoy the war while you can, because the peace will be terrible.' Additionally, every platoon seemed to have its 'crazy Helmut', a man who had lost everything to Allied bombing and lived only for revenge.

The Allied ground forces were at different points along the bell curve of combat effectiveness, with the Americans in the ascendant as increased experience and confidence matched their rising numbers. British enthusiasm as well as relative strength had been on a downward slope even before Normandy, where bitter fighting had cut deep into reserves of both. The spirit of the army resided in the veterans of the North African and Italian campaigns, many of whom felt they had done enough and all of whom judged that the powers that be should have learned more, much more, from earlier setbacks. Peter Roach's thoughts upon returning to England to prepare for D-Day were probably representative:

> Now we had to learn how to be soldiers, how to drill and march and shout orders, how to put on equipment and clean boots so that we could join the army at home which had been suffering these horrors unendingly... We knew the capabilities of the German army and had the very greatest regard for it, but what was this? We knew that the German army would never reduce us to tears, and we knew that the British army had done so many times.

Performance was further degraded by the manpower shortage that forced Second British Army to cannibalize infantry and armoured regiments at the expense of unit cohesion, while keeping some formations in action for too long. It still proved impossible to keep the front line battalions up to strength and, despite a long advance through towns full of cheering civilians, the prevailing mood was one of wary cynicism. The men were not tired or demoralized – with the end of the war in sight they were simply not prepared to take unnecessary risks. There was still a willingness to 'do their bit', but the dreadful attrition of junior officers and NCOs in Normandy testified to an increasing need to pull men into battle by personal example. The typical British attack had become the short rush forward, dig in and await the inevitable German counter-attack. These were soldiers who could grind the enemy down, or hold a defensive position to the death, but they had acquired neither the battlefield habits nor the confidence in their leaders necessary for a blitzkrieg-style operation such as Market Garden.

Napoleon said that one has a limited time for war, and by late 1944 most senior British commanders had probably exceeded it, the dreadful execution of the Great War making itself felt in the age gap between them and the next generation of leaders. Montgomery was already wrestling with the delusions of grandeur that were in time to produce among the most self-serving memoirs ever written, while the spare style of

Lieutenant General Miles Dempsey, the opaque commander of Second Army, is captured by an order he issued in early September: 'Dear Horrocks – You will capture (a) Antwerp (b) Brussels.' Of his corps commanders, Lieutenant General Richard O'Connor (XII Corps), hero of the early days of the Desert War, was a ghost of his former self after more than two years as a prisoner of war, while Lieutenant General Neil Ritchie (XII Corps) was a plodder, and even the dynamic Lieutenant General Brian Horrocks (XXX Corps) suffered from attacks of debilitating fever as the result of a near fatal wounding in North Africa. The latter once said: 'The main – perhaps the sole – function of a corps commander in battle is ruthlessly to ensure that the aim of the operation is maintained,' but he was unable to do this during Market Garden, and the fairest verdict is that it asked too much of the officers and men involved.

In most campaigns, barring those that end in mutual exhaustion, there comes a moment when a commander judges his enemy to be off balance or sufficiently weakened by attrition to permit the killing stroke. With Eisenhower's qualified support, this was what Montgomery sought to administer, in an operation so out of character that Omar Bradley, who came to resent deeply Montgomery's patronizing attitude, recalled it with bemused admiration: 'Had the pious, teetotalling Montgomery wobbled into SHAEF with a hangover, I could not have been more astonished than I was by the daring adventure he proposed... [Although] I never reconciled myself to the venture, I nevertheless concede that Montgomery's plan for Arnhem was one of the most imaginative of the war.'

The aim was to go around the Siegfried Line or 'West Wall', which ran from Switzerland to Cleves parallel to the French Maginot Line, likewise bypassed by the Germans through Holland in 1940. Market, the airborne plan, involved the simultaneous delivery of three airborne divisions: US 101st to capture bridges over the Wilhelmina canal at Son, the River Dommel at St Oedenrode and two bridges each over the River Aa and the Willems canal on either side of Veghel; US 82nd to seize a large bridge over the River Maas (Meuse) near Grave, two even larger ones over the Waal at Nijmegen and four smaller bridges across the Maas-Waal canal in between; and British 1st to capture at least one of the three bridges over the Lower Rhine at Arnhem. Garden, the ground plan, required Second Army to advance from the Meuse-Escaut canal into Holland, and XXX Corps to charge along the 100-kilometre (60-mile) corridor opened by Market while VIII and XII Corps protected its flanks.

XXX Corps was to reach the 101st on the first day, 82nd the next, the spearhead at Arnhem on the third and then advance beyond it to cut off German forces in western Holland, secure airfields for the arrival of the air-transportable 52nd (Lowland) Division and position the army to advance on the Ruhr from the north.

In common with many other commentators, Bradley wrote of Arnhem, where British 1st Airborne Division was destroyed, rather than of Market Garden as a whole, in which the two US airborne divisions, the greater part of the army dropped behind German lines, no less heroically fulfilled their missions. But the Rhine crossing was the whole point of the operation and, like every man in the Allied armies, Bradley had his eyes fixed on its spearhead. For many the aching feeling that it should have been reached in time persists, and criticism by the US Airborne of the slow advance by the British Guards Armoured Division through the corridor they held open was echoed by Lieutenant Colonel John Frost, who held the northern end of the road bridge at Arnhem with part of a single battalion for longer than the operational plan required of the whole division. He had these thoughts after Patton's Third Army liberated him from captivity in 1945: 'All ranks of this army, when they saw our red berets, would say: "Arnhem. Aye. We'd have gotten through. Yes, sir. We'd have gotten through." I could not help believing that they would have. There was nothing slow or ponderous about them and they didn't stop for tea or the night for that matter.'

This and the sharp paragraphs that follow about Browning must have been painful for a career British officer to write. Frost published his memoirs in 1980 after a successful career in the army, and this was the mature and informed judgement of one who had every patriotic and professional reason to mute his criticism. Peter Harclerode presents a good case for the defence of XXX Corps in *Arnhem – A Tragedy of Errors*, arguing that it was at the end of its tether after battling through the Low Countries against hardening German defence, but as Hackett commented in the Foreword: 'How long, some of the defenders at the bridge or those around me in Oosterbeek might have asked, is a tether, and how much more had ours still to run out?' Part of the answer is that the outstanding combat performance of the airborne element in Market Garden was bought at the expense of the land forces, not only by drawing off the most highly motivated officers, NCOs and men but also the air transport that might have been used instead to sustain a more methodical advance. Against which, the Allies had made a major investment in the AAA; it was by this time their sole strategic reserve and with seventeen operations planned and then cancelled since Normandy it was collectively champing at the bit. It is doubtful that Browning ever uttered the caveat about 'a bridge too far' attributed to him by Cornelius Ryan in his book of that title, as he seems to have been no less convinced than any man in the AAA that they could storm the gates of hell if given the chance.

Allied airborne forces came into being in response to the extremely effective interventions by German paratroopers early in the war, in particular – and fatefully for their British and US emulators – in May 1940 by detachments that seized Belgian river crossings and neutralized the fortress of Eben Emael and by two full divisions dropped into 'Fortress Holland' around Rotterdam, which were severely handled but managed to hold key bridges across the Waal and Maas rivers until ground forces raced to relieve them. Like the Stuka dive bombers that so ably supported them, the German paras enjoyed the psychological impact of tactical innovation on an unprepared enemy, false reports of their further use generating growing demoralization among British and French troops in the campaign that followed. But when the Allies tried to repeat the Germans' exploit over much the same ground in 1944, they were dropped among troops deployed and trained to counter a fully expected airborne assault, and the German ground commander of the area due to be bisected by Market Garden was none other than Luftwaffe General Kurt Student, father of the German Airborne Corps and architect of the 1940 operations.

As we have seen, Student's men had discovered the cost of an airborne assault on troops who did not panic during the invasion of Crete, where they lost a third of their number. Less than half as many of Browning's men were dropped at Arnhem and they did not receive the CAS that tipped the scales in Crete, and of 10,000 landed north of the Rhine, about 1,400 were killed, 6,300 (mostly wounded) were captured and only 2,300 were evacuated across the river. We have seen how the Germans chose to use their airborne troops in the later years of the war and what they could achieve given armour and heavy artillery support. The fate of the no less tenacious 1st British Airborne Division, lacking these elements, seems to confirm that the success of the airborne assault concept in 1940 was unique and perhaps unrepeatable.

Market Garden's chances of success were paradoxically improved by the fact that German Army Group B was now under the command of Field

Marshal Walther Model, known as the 'Führer's Fireman' from his exploits on the Eastern Front, who had moved to Oosterbeek, near Arnhem, two days previously. War has its moments of hilarity, and one came when Model's Chief of Staff interrupted his lunch on 17 September with the words: 'What an absolute swine! There are two parachute divisions on top of us!' Later in the day Urquhart's men ambushed and killed the garrison commander, Major General Friedrich Kussin, but they came close to bagging a far greater prize. Allied accounts dwell on what went wrong, but much went better than could have been expected, in particular the fact that the Germans, with plenty of time to do so, failed to blow the bridges over the Waal. They were captured intact not because the fleeing Germans abandoned them but because the aggressive Model hoped to counter-attack over them. Had he been killed or captured they would have been opportunely demolished, dooming the spearhead even more certainly.

As we observed at Cassino, intelligence officers are often under pressure to go with their commanders' flow, but here it seems that Montgomery as well as Browning chose to ignore explicit warnings that the two divisions of II SS Panzer Corps under General Willi Bittrich, 9th 'Hohenstaufen' under Colonel Walter Harzer and 10th 'Frundsberg' under Colonel Heinz Harmel, were regrouping to the north and east of Arnhem. Both divisions were reduced to a fraction of their full strength (from 18,000 each to about 2,500 and 3,000 men respectively, with only a handful of armoured vehicles), but they were powerful battle groups nonetheless. The intelligence (under) estimate for Comet had still warned of one Panzer division 'much the worse for wear' with about fifty tanks in the immediate area, but only a few days later Browning assured Roy Urquhart that he would encounter only 'low category troops in brigade strength with a few tanks' around Arnhem. Everything that followed stemmed from this failure to evaluate existing intelligence correctly, because in fact Urquhart's division landed among 'alarm groups', smaller units deployed to attack them immediately, backed by some of the most highly motivated, disciplined and experienced armoured units under Model's command.

One of the reasons for this failure is that warnings about II SS Panzer Corps from the Dutch Resistance were disregarded because German counter intelligence had run a successful 'radio game' against the British secret services between March 1942 and April 1944, using captured Dutch radio operators to send back false intelligence and to encourage the

A German infantryman, summer 1944. He carries the fast-firing MG42 and hand-grenades for good measure: news that his cause is doomed seems not to have reached him.

The Guards Armoured Division, which spearheaded XXX Corps, was often confined to single narrow roads, ideal for German ambushes. Here an ammunition truck blazes.

dropping of further agents and supplies into German hands. Rather than admit their own negligence, the London controllers chose to blame the field operatives, with the result that the word was out among the British that the Dutch were not to be trusted. Not only did this infect intelligence assessment and planning, it also led XXX Corps planners to ignore the expertise of their Dutch liaison officers, and inhibited Roy Urquhart and his subordinate commanders from availing themselves of the help offered to them by members of the Dutch Resistance in Arnhem. By contrast the Americans made full use of their own liaison officers and of local volunteers in their areas of operations, to great advantage.

Unlike the planners of Market, those responsible for Garden had plenty of experience of ground warfare and it is a measure of their discipline and loyalty that none of them, at the time or later, pointed the finger at the absurdity of the following directive from Montgomery: 'The thrust northwards to secure the river crossings will be rapid and violent and without regard to what is happening on the flanks.' No less than the airborne plan, this could work only if the Germans played the helpless role assigned to them. Since they did not, the artillery and armour of XXX Corps was not only required to help the lightly armed airborne troops take some of the key objectives, but also had to be dispersed along the salient to hold off converging attacks from the flanks it was supposed to disregard. There is more than a hint here of Montgomery's desire to emulate his old opponent Rommel or his current rival Patton, but it was a deeply unrealistic directive to issue at the end of an already long advance, to an army now compelled to concentrate available logistics behind a one-corps advance along one road that on occasion narrowed to a one-tank front.

Nor should it be forgotten that just to reach Arnhem was not enough – the whole operation was designed to achieve exploitation beyond the final bridgehead. Even if the Guards Armoured Division had reached Arnhem on schedule, it would then have had to fight house to house against SS troopers liberally equipped with anti-tank weapons, backed by tanks and tracked assault guns – with some of these, only the one Sherman per troop equipped with the long 17-pounder (76mm) gun could compete. A Cassino-like flattening of the town would have followed, but after it was all over the Allies would have won only a slightly longer salient, still going nowhere. When, eight days after the first landings, Horrocks cancelled a planned assault across the Lower Rhine and ordered the evacuation of what was left of the British Airborne Division, it was in recognition that the delays inflicted by the Germans had long since defeated the purpose of Market Garden.

But once all the background politicking and pettiness is discounted and the strategic and operational illusions are revealed for what they were, there remains an epic of arms such as would have inspired fireside ballads among our warrior ancestors. There have been many much longer and bloodier battles, but it is unlikely that there was ever one where a comparable concentration of extremely original and articulate men came together in conditions of such acute hardship and savage peril. As Martin Middlebrook noted after interviewing hundreds of survivors, those who flew the transports no less than the men who fought on the ground share an intense pride in having taken part. Why some battles achieve this apotheosis and not others is hard to say, but the annual pilgrimage of pensive veterans and the veneration they are shown by the Dutch confirms that something rare happened here. It was captured by the words of a cross-eyed (whether by birth or from exhaustion we cannot know)

German NCO to Lieutenant Tom Ainslie after the fight at Arnhem bridge: 'Good evening. That was a lovely battle, a really lovely battle. Have a cigar, we are human too.'

Hackett was right, the air part of Market was beautifully planned and executed. During the night and into the morning of Sunday 17 September, the heavies of Bomber Command and Eighth USAAF hammered German airfields and flak positions along the approach routes, followed by a comprehensive ground attack effort by Ninth USAAF and British Second Tactical Air Force. When over 1,500 troop carriers and nearly 500 glider–tug combinations took off from twenty-four airfields throughout south-eastern England, they were escorted by over 1,000 USAAF and RAF fighters, which pounced on the few German aircraft that rose to challenge them and on any flak batteries brave enough to fire at the stupendous air-borne armada. The southern approach by 101st Airborne over Eindhoven ran into the most serious flak, but only three of the thirty-five transports lost went down before dropping their troops. The men in the gliders were less fortunate: thirteen of the US and twenty-three of the British failed to arrive. Although most were the victims of broken tow ropes and landed elsewhere, one glider in each force broke up horrifyingly in mid air. Amazingly, no British tugs or transports were lost, against a worst-case predicted attrition of 40 per cent for the whole force, with the spearhead expected to suffer the worst. Six British and eighteen US battalions, their morale sky high, landed with minimal dispersion.

The contrast with the 'fighting-the-Germans bit' on the ground could not have been more stark, the first and nastiest shock being administered to the Irish Guards as they charged from their bridgehead over the Meuse-Escaut canal. The Royal Artillery had delivered the sort of preliminary bombardment for which it was by now justly famous, followed by well co-ordinated CAS, but the Guards ran into a paratroop training unit. Although the unit's anti-tank gun company had been destroyed by the bombardment, it coolly let the leading squadron through before springing an ambush with hand-held *Panzerfausts*. Nine tanks were knocked out in two minutes and, in what was to become the signature of XXX Corps's painful advance, everything stopped until infantry came forward to clear the way.

'We watched as nine of our mates brewed up,' said a tank crewman. 'There was hardly anything we could do as we were lined up one behind the other on the road – and we couldn't get off it to go round.' The first

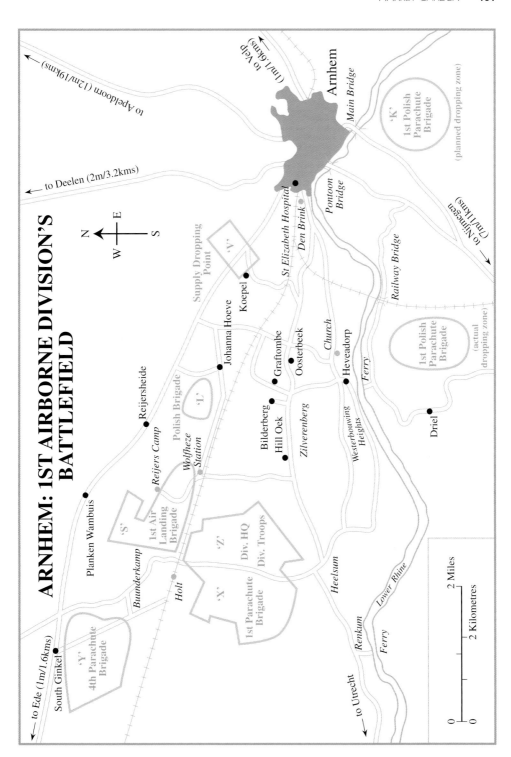

ARNHEM: 1ST AIRBORNE DIVISION'S BATTLEFIELD

Arnhem

Main Bridge

to Velp (1m/1.6kms)

'K' 1st Polish Parachute Brigade

(planned dropping zone)

to Apeldoorn (12m/19kms)

to Deelen (2m/3.2kms)

Pontoon Bridge

Den Brink

St Elizabeth Hospital

Railway Bridge

to Nijmegen (7m/11kms)

Supply Dropping Point

'V'

Koepel

Johanna Hoeve

Church

Oosterbeek

Heveadorp

Ferry

1st Polish Parachute Brigade

(actual dropping zone)

Graftombe

Reijersheide

Polish Brigade

'L'

Bilderberg

Hill Oek

Zilverenberg

Westerbouwing Heights

Driel

Planken Wambuis

Reijers Camp

Wolfheze Station

'S'

1st Air Landing Brigade

Buunderkamp

Holt

'X'

'Z'

Div. HQ

Div. Troops

1st Parachute Brigade

Heelsum

to Ede (1m/1.6kms)

South Ginkel

'Y' 4th Parachute Brigade

to Utrecht

Renkum

Ferry

Lower Rhine

Ferry

N
W — E
S

2 Miles

2 Kilometres

0   2
0   2

engagement often sets the tone for the whole battle, and for a serious check to have come so soon into a 'set-piece' attack was a brutal blow. The Guards Armoured Division employed the same brave but blunt tactics in Normandy during Operation Goodwood, its first battle, and two months later it was little nearer to becoming the equivalent of a Panzergrenadier division, with all arms working together like the fingers of one hand.

For the airborne 'carpet' over which XXX Corps was supposed to roll, the drop zones (DZ) and glider landing zones (LZ) were chosen strictly with an eye to keeping the vulnerable transport aircraft away from flak concentrations – Deelen airfield was wrongly believed to be especially well defended, and its proximity to Arnhem itself induced planners to keep aircraft well away. But the planners also believed that open fields and distance from known German positions would facilitate unharried assembly. All previous airborne insertions had been crippled by dispersion and suffered heavy losses because the Germans won the race to regroup, and Kershaw argues that in an operation involving such large numbers the sacrifice of the surprise factor in favour of prompt concentration was the correct solution to the Germans' deployment in 'alarm groups'. But all experience indicated that at the same time small storming parties should have been dropped as close as possible and on both sides of all the target bridges, because a surrounded demolitions party will often think twice before enraging the men to whom it will shortly wish to surrender. The British and the 82nd were dropped 9–12 wooded and built-up kilometres (5–7 miles) away from the key bridges over the Waal and the Lower Rhine, and the fact that any of these were intact when they reached them was because of German errors of judgement that could not possibly have been predicted.

To deal with each sector sequentially, the main DZs and the LZ for 101st Airborne (the 'Screaming Eagles') were inside a triangle formed by the first bridges XXX Corps would need to cross, at Son and the alternative at Best across the Wilhelmina canal and at St Oedenrode over the River Dommel. But the 501st Regiment was dropped separately outside Veghel and by a happy mischance one battalion landed on the other side of the Aa river and the Willems canal. Major General Maxwell Taylor, he of the ill-fated mission to Rome in September 1943, had the largest area to seize and the least time to do it, so his first lift consisted largely of infantry and jeeps, leaving the support elements to follow in the second and third lifts. His calculation proved correct at lightly defended Veghel and St Oedenrode, but neither of the Wilhelmina canal bridges was reached in time to prevent their destruction. The Screaming Eagles found themselves severely outgunned in an encounter battle with German infantry that came up to support some fifteen 88mm guns at Best.

Horrocks had prudently assembled 9,000 Royal Engineers with 2,300 vehicles of bridging material, while 43rd Wessex Division had been specifically trained for contested river crossings, but instead of pressing on during the night when news of the loss of the Son bridge reached them, the Guards Armoured stopped well south of Eindhoven and the bridging operation did not take place until the night of 18/19 September. The most likely explanation for this delay is that they expected the city to be more strongly defended than it was, but the failure even to probe forward with infantry was still a puzzling decision. Night fighting was an area where the British enjoyed a rare tactical advantage over the Germans and which 'Monty's moonshine', the illumination of clouds with powerful search-lights, had been devised to exploit. The reason why Market did not start with a dawn drop and only one lift was scheduled for each day was because IX Troop Carrier Command's Williams, commander of by far the larger transport fleet, judged that the moonless conditions and the lack of experience of his air crew, many of them recent arrivals, made pre-dawn and dusk operations impossibly hazardous. It was unfortunate that a factor which worked against the success of one part of the operation could not have been turned to compensating advantage in the other.

The high drama of events further north and their own headline defence of Bastogne during the Battle of the Bulge three months later have overshadowed the crucial role played by 101st Airborne in keeping open 'Hell's Highway' from Son to beyond Veghel. Taylor's men suffered 2,110 casualties during Market Garden and a similar number in the two months that followed, when they were retained in the line so that 21st Army Group could turn its attention to clearing the Scheldt. Most of these losses occurred while they were performing duties far beyond what Market called upon them to do because VIII and XII Corps made such poor progress on the flanks. With supplies preferentially channelled into the salient between them, the two flanking corps had a difficult assign-ment and during the operation they were to suffer 3,874 casualties to XXX Corps's 1,480. It has been said they only 'leant' on the enemy and that they would have lost less men had they engaged the enemy more vigorously from the start. The most hotly engaged of the flanking divisions was the 15th (Scottish) and, although it did not get across the Wilhelmina canal until 21 September, it lost almost a thousand men getting there and as many fighting off counter-attacks around Best over the next ten days. If this was leaning, it was into a strong wind.

Taylor's decision to land as many men as possible in the first lift was made in the expectation that XXX Corps would soon come up and compensate for his lack of heavy weapons. This took thirty-three hours longer than expected, but on the 19th – and with astonishingly little time to get to know each other – the Americans meshed seamlessly with 15th/19th Hussars and XXX Corps artillery in a combined arms assault that made short work of the strong German position at Best. They also rescued a platoon trapped on the 17th when trying to capture the bridge, a previous effort having cost the life of Lieutenant Colonel Robert Cole, awarded the Congressional Medal of Honor for heroism in Normandy. Private First Class Joe Mann of the trapped platoon also won his nation's highest award by covering a grenade with his already badly wounded body to save the other men in his trench. As the losses later suffered by the Scottish Division testify, the German regarded the Wilhelmina crossings as crucial, and that same evening the 101st had to hold off an attack on the newly built Bailey bridge at Son by a German panzer brigade equipped with Panther tanks. Taylor called his sector 'Indian territory', and in this western the role of the US Cavalry was once again played by 15th/19th Hussars, who rolled up in time to beat back a further assault on the 20th.

101st Airborne had cut Student's army in half and he was determined to reunite it. On 22 September simultaneous attacks were launched from both sides towards Hell's Highway, but although the two German battle groups reached the road in different places on the nights of 22/23 and 24/25 September, the Americans' speed and aggressive tactics inflicted such heavy losses on them that they never realized how thinly the defenders were spread and so failed to link up as planned at Veghel, with its four vital bridges. On the 23rd the weather in England finally permitted the last of Taylor's glider-borne men and equipment to fly in and he was also joined by the seaborne 'tail' following in the tracks of XXX Corps, so in this sector at least the Allies won the reinforcement race. Although catastrophe was averted, the road was nevertheless not only cut twice but also subjected to harassing artillery fire during much of the operation. This drew British armour back from Nijmegen as well as imposing a further crucial delay on the advance of 43rd Wessex Division.

Fortunately for the Allies, the reservists and half-trained recruits who now made up the bulk of the German infantry were outclassed by the veteran US paratroopers, and German tanks advancing unsupported proved no less vulnerable than the Guards' had been to men with bazookas who were prepared to wait until the enemy closed to point-blank range. Taylor's men did not hold Hell's Highway unaided, nor were they ever intended to, but the slow progress of XXX Corps and the even slower advance of VII and XII Corps on the flanks put the fate of the entire operation mainly in their hands for a week, something that deserves more recognition than it has received. Taylor set an outstanding example and was himself wounded, but the most thought-provoking feature of this part of the battle was the manner in which the Americans and 15th/19th Hussars worked together: the contrast with the more measured approach of the Guards Armoured Division was striking.

In the sector assigned to 82nd Airborne (the 'All Americans'), the planners had permitted Brigadier General James Gavin to drop a company from Colonel Reuben Tucker's 504th Regiment at the far end of the multi-span, half-kilometre (1600-foot) long bridge over the Maas near Grave. It was to be the only major bridge captured 'with thunderclap surprise', as prescribed but not provided for by Brereton, despite being rigged for demolition. Of the four small bridges over the Maas-Waal canal, the one at Heumen was equidistant from the DZ of the 504th and the 505th, and their simultaneous approach may be the reason it was the only one captured intact. Two others were blown in the face of approaches from only one side, and the fourth and furthest was severely damaged the next morning by a stay-behind party which made good its escape to nearby Nijmegen. The soundness of disregarded airborne doctrine was again demonstrated, and another handful of gravel thrown in the working of the Allied plan.

One place very clearly marked 'here be dragons' on Browning's map was the Reichswald forest, just over the German border to the south-east of Nijmegen, from which Allied intelligence predicted the most serious counter-attack would emerge. In fact the local German commander had only a battalion of unhappy Luftwaffe clerks and another of 'stomach and ear' men previously excused military service because of physical disabilities, with no infantry training and few vehicles, support weapons or radios. But by dint of commandeering anything moving on the roads in the sector overnight, the headquarters group built up three semi-motorized battle groups of about 1,000 men each, supported by three battalions of mixed flak and field artillery, five armoured cars, 24 mortars and 130 machine guns. What their commanding officer ruefully described as 'this motley crowd' attacked before dawn on the 18th. Kershaw recounts a touching incident when a group of elderly prisoner of war camp guards, excitedly recalling their part in the great German offensive of 1918, told their young officer to leave it to them: 'Can't you see that it's up to us old boys to run the whole show again; and we will do it exactly as we did then. First of all we have got to get Tommy [they thought their opponents were British] on the run, then we've cracked it.'

Bearing in mind that these troops could only with charity be described as second rate and that they were sent to take an area held by members of the Allied infantry elite, Ryan's account renders them an eloquent tribute: 'Swarming across the German border… in overwhelming numbers, the Germans burst through the 82nd's perimeter defences and quickly overran the [landing] zones, capturing supply and ammunition dumps… All over the area troops were alerted to rush to the scene. Men on the edge of Nijmegen force-marched all the way to the drop zones to give additional support.' The attackers eventually broke when counter-attacked vigorously and when the gliders of the second lift came in among them. Although they never had a chance of taking the heights overlooking Nijmegen as ordered, their assault reinforced Allied preconceptions and thereby underlined the single most glaring contradiction in the Market Garden plan.

Browning's instructions to Gavin had emphasized that control of the high ground between Nijmegen and the Reichswald should take priority over any attempt to seize the Waal bridges, and after witnessing this attack he reaffirmed it, one of the very few operational decisions that near total communications breakdown permitted him to make. Frost and Hackett later singled it out for particular criticism, although Gavin defended it, but all three agreed that there was indeed a very clear 'either/or', and it was not between taking the great Nijmegen bridges (the road bridge was the largest in Europe) or holding the Groesbeek Heights. It was between landing the 82nd in sufficient strength to perform all three of its equally vital tasks before the Germans had time to react, or calling off the whole operation. There is room to argue whether or not the trouble the other two airborne divisions ran into should have been anticipated, but the mission parameters for the 82nd left the fate of the Waal bridges to be decided, at leisure, by the Germans. Even an extra battalion might have made all the

Sherman tanks of the Guards Armoured Division cross the mighty road bridge at Nijmegen.

difference, and this sharpened criticism of Browning's decision to fly his headquarters in with the 82nd, although it cut into the British, not the American transport allocation. The greater waste of resources came from the USAAF's refusal to heed pleas to train their glider pilots to operate as infantry once on the ground, unlike the 1,262 highly effective men of the British Glider Pilot Regiment at Arnhem. Of his own glider pilots Gavin wrote: 'Despite their individual willingness to help, I feel that they were definitely a liability to me.'

The Germans were to mount another three-pronged attack by seven battalions out of the Reichswald in the morning of the 20th, and although weather had prevented the arrival of the All Americans' air landing regiment, fortunately Guards Armoured had come up by then. A dangerous threat developed in the direction of the Heumen bridge but, with the help of the Coldstream group, this was repulsed and Gavin juggled his five perimeter defence battalions, mostly from 508th Regiment, so skilfully that the entire assault was driven back without having relieved pressure on the defenders of the Nijmegen bridges in the slightest. Elsewhere that day a battalion of the 505th and the Grenadier Guards group attacked the fiercely defended southern approaches to the road bridge, while the 504th and the Irish Guards group cleared the western suburbs of Nijmegen preparatory to launching an assault boat crossing of the Waal, an impressive day's work. During Market Garden 82nd lost 1,432 men, nearly all of them on the 20th, and when they met a few days later Dempsey, never accused of effusiveness, greeted Gavin with the words: 'I am proud to meet the commander of the greatest division in the world today.'

This was a handsome compliment but also a pointed comment to make in the hearing of Major General Allan Adair of Guards Armoured. It may partly explain, though not excuse, the tone of the after battle report written by the commander of 2nd (Armoured) Battalion, Grenadier Guards. Four of his tanks gallantly charged across the road bridge while the 504th crossed down river by boat and, pausing only to finish off the defenders of the railway bridge as they finally broke in the face of the Irish Guards group on the other side, reached the northern end of the road bridge some time after the Grenadiers had taken it: 'There is no doubt that [82nd] had done extremely well in very isolated circumstances and it was a very creditable performance by all of them, and the success of their little operation might have appeared more in the limelight had it not been overshadowed in importance by the tremendous importance of the seizing of the Main Bridge.'

Fairly or unfairly, the 'little operation' outshone even the Grenadiers' remarkable achievement. It involved the men of the 3rd Battalion of Tucker's 504th paddling canvas assault boats with which they were completely unfamiliar across 400 metres of fast flowing river in daylight under heavy machine gun, mortar and artillery fire. The two leading companies suffered 50 per cent casualties, most of them during the crossing, After this Captain Moffatt Burriss of 'I' Coy, who had a shrapnel wound in the side received when a cannon shell decapitated the helmsman of his boat, was 'so happy to be alive that I vomited'. Captain Carl Kappel of 'H' Coy dived into the river to rescue one of his men and: 'By the time I got him to the bank I was an old man and worn out.' Battalion commander Major Julian Cook chanted, 'Hail Mary – full of Grace,' in time with each stroke of the paddle all the way across, but thereafter must have prayed that She averted her eyes from what happened when his maddened men reached the shore. The naked fury of their assault, allied with German incredulity that anybody should have mounted such an operation, carried all before it.

We now know from Kershaw's meticulous work that there was at that moment no German force of any significance between the Nijmegen bridgehead and Frost's men, still holding on to the northern end of the road bridge at Arnhem. The Guards could not have known that at the time, but to the outrage of the men who had stormed across the Waal in boats they did not even send infantry forward to find out until the next morning, just too late for an unopposed advance across the last 10 kilometres (6 miles) and far too late to save Frost's command from destruction. Gavin believed that had Ridgway been in command instead of Browning he would have ordered the 82nd to make the advance regardless and there is no doubt they would have gone.

> I found Tucker at dawn so irate that he was almost unable to speak. There is no soldier in the world I admire more than the British but British infantry leaders somehow did not understand the camaraderie of airborne troops. To our men there was only one objective: to save their brother paratroopers in Arnhem. It was tragic. I knew Tucker wanted to go but I could never have allowed it. I had my hands full. Besides, Tucker and my other line officers did not appreciate some of the problems the British had at that moment.

Those problems were the same as had cost Garden momentum south of Eindhoven on the 17th, and would not normally have stopped any force under the command of Horrocks, the only British commander to rival Patton in his ability to push men further than they thought they could go. Whether because he was himself off form because of illness or because the Guards' prestige was such that he did not feel it appropriate to press them, they once again harboured through the night and part of the airborne community has never forgiven them for it. They were granted, mainly by German command errors but also by the outstanding audacity of the Allied river crossing, one last chance to redeem Market Garden, and it slipped away. There was nothing wrong with their courage – it took much to drive tanks over a huge bridge which might be expected to blow up at any moment – but it is hard to discern that sense of desperate urgency that the moment required.

Although 82nd had been dropped far from the Waal bridges, their DZ and LZ were at least on top of two of their three objectives. The British 1st Airborne Division was not so fortunate and its story is one of the progressive erosion of fighting power. Given that it would be doomed if either of the other divisions were defeated, 1st Airborne was logically given the lowest priority in the allocation of troop carriers in the first lift and was therefore more heavily dependent than the Americans on gliders. As we have seen, thirty-six of these were taken by Browning and twenty-three lost in transit, so the first British lift, already a brigade (US regiment) lighter than either of the first American lifts, was further diminished. The first wave was further weakened by leaving Brigadier 'Pip' Hicks' depleted Airlanding Brigade to guard the DZ and LZ while Brigadier Gerald Lathbury's likewise understrength 1st Parachute Brigade tackled the bridges alone.

Roy Urquhart was a newcomer to airborne operations and seems to have accepted the argument that prompt concentration would compensate for the loss of the surprise element, but his limited transport allocation – plus the certainty of having to hold out longer than the Americans – obliged him to reduce the infantry in the first lift even further by bringing in as much of his artillery as possible. Hackett's 4th Parachute Brigade was to be landed on the second day and the Polish Brigade south of the river opposite Arnhem on the third, by which time the flak around the city was supposed to have been suppressed and XXX Corps was scheduled to be across the Waal and approaching fast. But even if the weather and the ground force could be depended upon, Sosabowski was still right to protest that 'an airborne operation is not a purchase by instalments', and the brigade commanders clamoured for partial drops to be made nearer and on both sides of the bridges, to no avail.

The cards were therefore stacked against the men of 1st Airborne before the first aircraft left the ground and, although they did all that soldiers can, theirs proved to be an impossible task once the grossly underestimated German garrison stopped Lathbury's 1st and 3rd Parachute Battalions short of their first day objectives. Only part of the 2nd under Frost, marching rapidly along the bank of the Lower Rhine, reached the bridges. The railway bridge midway between Oosterbeek and Arnhem was blown up in their faces, while the central section of the pontoon bridge at Arnhem had been towed away. This left the road bridge, including its elevated approaches nearly 2 kilometres long (just over a mile), which was inadequately defended thanks to German command disorder following the killing of Kussin. Frost's leading company under Major Digby Tatham-Warter left a trail of German casualties for the rest of the battalion to follow and as night fell rushed to take up positions around the northern end of the bridge. An armoured vehicle and two

Major General Roy Urquhart of 1st Airborne Division outside his headquarters, the Hartenstein Hotel in Oosterbeek.

pillboxes on the bridge itself were destroyed with Piats and a flame-thrower, after which four trucks full of Germans blundered across the bridge and were duly dealt with. But flames from the vehicles and pill-boxes took away the cover of darkness and as a result an attack intended to secure the other side of the bridge had to be abandoned.

Here there was no question of the bridge being demolished, as II SS Corps needed it in order to send Harzer's Frundsberg (9th SS) battle group south to hold Nijmegen, in accordance with the orders given to him in person when Model arrived at his HQ following his hasty departure from Oosterbeek. Hohenstaufen (10th SS) was tasked with defending Arnhem and its commander Harmel had already sent his Reconnaissance Battalion under the dashing Captain Paul Gräbner across the bridge to contest a seemingly certain Allied landing on 'the island' between the Waal and the Lower Rhine. This was, of course, what the British brigade commanders had wanted, and the question here is whether a *coup de main* to seize the bridge would have stopped Gräbner's battalion on its way south. It seems likely that it would, because the Reconnaissance Battalion was to be destroyed by Frost's men when it returned from the island and tried to fight its way back across Arnhem bridge. Harzer was compelled to improvise rafts to get his tanks across, very slowly, further upriver and his division was thereby prevented from making a possibly decisive intervention in the fighting at Nijmegen.

If the comments made many years later by the SS division commanders are juxtaposed, they underline how crucial control of the Arnhem bridge was to them. Harmel said: 'My mission was to block the threat in the south long enough to enable the 9th SS to settle with the British Division in Oosterbeek-Arnhem,' while Harzer said: 'The Allies were stopped in the south just north of Nijmegen – that is why Arnhem turned out as it did.' Actually, that is why the last stage of the battle, the so-called 'cauldron' at Oosterbeek, turned out as it did because, as we have seen, the threat in the south was not blocked while Frost held the bridge whose successor today bears his name.

There is a danger of getting into a vicious circle of 'what ifs' here, because while it is obvious that the planners would have given the bridge a higher priority had they known it was to be the cork in the II SS Corps bottle, it is equally obvious that if they had correctly assessed the strength of the opposition 1st Airborne would encounter, they would have been obliged to reconsider the whole operation. There are no 'sure things' in war and victory tends to go to the side that makes the least mistakes. There were plenty on both sides during Market Garden but the Germans committed fewer.

The battles by Frost's men at the Arnhem bridge and by the rest of 1st Airborne and the Poles in the Oosterbeek cauldron have been well and comprehensively chronicled by others so, rather than single out a few of countless examples of heroism, I will try to convey something of the flavour of a struggle in which all the strange contradictions of men at war were uniquely concentrated. There was, almost from the start, a very high respect on both sides for the quality of their enemy, and in *Arnhem Spearhead* Private James Sims, then nineteen years old, recalled the fate of one of Gräbner's men in a burning tank: 'The paratroopers shouted to the SS man to come out, promising to spare his life, for they were impressed by his fanatical courage. The only reply was a further burst of fire. As the flames got to him we could hear his screams of agony, muffled by the steel turret, but none the less disturbing for that. They seemed to go on an awfully long time before this brave soldier died for Führer and Fatherland.'

Ryan quotes an SS squad leader and a veteran of the Eastern Front on the subject of the marksmanship Frost had inculcated among his men. 'They aimed for the head and men began to fall beside me, each one with a small, neat hole through the forehead.' Falling back, he made an accurate prediction to an artillery commander: 'The only way to get the British out is to blast the buildings down, brick by brick. Believe me, these are real men. They won't give up that bridge until we carry them out feet first.' So it proved and 'Waho Mohammed', the war cry made its own by the 2nd Battalion while fighting as line infantry in Tunisia, rang out from the little groups clinging to the northern end of the bridge. Sims described the last stand by men under Lieutenant James Woods in one of the buildings commanding the bridge as they came under fire from a German assault gun:

> The first shell burst against the White House at a range of something under a hundred yards. It hit the top storey near the roof and the entire building seemed to shake itself like a dog. We could plainly see the riflemen and airborne engineers, caution thrown to the winds, kneeling openly inside the blasted windows, pouring fire down at the Germans as though determined to take as many as possible with them to death.

Frost described the German tanks closing in on his doomed battalion: 'They looked incredibly sinister in the half light, like some prehistoric monsters, as their great guns swung from side to side breathing flame.' Usually when we describe an engagement as a 'fight to the death' there is an implicit understanding that neither side was showing much mercy, but during this battle an astonishing number of prisoners were taken by both sides in the thick of the most intense combat. Nonetheless there were those who would not surrender even after they had run out of ammunition, and one German recalled that 'a young Britisher began to dodge about to draw our fire, while another tried to come at us from the side with a knife. One man leaped at us swinging his rifle like a club.' There are few accounts of wanton killing, many of lives spared when it would have been more convenient to kill and of the wounded being tended side by side without regard to what bloodstained uniform they were wearing. Part of Frost's command eventually surrendered when flames threatened to engulf the building where wounded British and German soldiers were

stacked in conditions that beggar the imagination, and without hesitation men who minutes earlier had been trying, with total dedication, to kill each other, rushed together into the burning building to rescue their comrades.

Bearing in mind that the Germans in question were mostly members of the SS, an organization responsible for countless massacres and atrocities both before and after this battle, the experience of Private John Hall shows a less tarnished side of the coin. When bandaging another para in the front line at Oosterbeek, he looked up to find an SS trooper pointing a light machine gun at him. 'I honestly thought I was going to die there and then; we sometimes did not take prisoners, so I did not expect them to either. Perhaps he thought I was a medical orderly and spared me. I didn't ask.' Elsewhere on the shrinking perimeter, after a frenzied struggle where two of the five Arnhem Victoria Crosses were won, Sergeant Jim Drew recalled a loudhailer correctly identifying his group cornered in a cellar as South Staffords and calling on them to surrender. 'Eventually the door was kicked open, and a German threw an object on the cellar floor. We jumped to the other side, expecting a grenade to explode. After several minutes I looked and saw that it was a house brick. He was, indeed, the finest German that I had ever met.'

On the approach to the bridge several survivors recall feeling pity for a boy and a girl in Luftwaffe blue, killed serving a machine gun, but also that among the vehicles that tried to rush the bridge was a white civilian ambulance that disgorged a dozen SS men firing from the hip, who were promptly cut down. After it was over, an SS trooper who seems to have been in a fugue state shot a young Resistance fighter captured along with the rest and then a British para who objected to being looted, but immediately afterwards told Hagen in a friendly tone to get rid of anything of military significance he might be carrying, because the rear echelon troops would kill him if they found it.

As the Germans closed in on the paras at the bridge, Sims wondered out loud what it was going to be like to die. 'Don't know, kid. Never tried it,' replied one of the older men with a grin: 'It was as though my comrades grew in stature and all the small, irritating quirks of character

OPPOSITE, TOP German troops close in on Arnhem Bridge.
OPPOSITE Arnhem Bridge, looking north. The knocked-out vehicles are from SS Captain Paul Gräbner's reconnaissance battalion.

British prisoners of war, many of them wounded, march into captivity.

disappeared. Ennobled in some strange way by this physical and spiritual auto-da-fe, each man appeared concerned for his neighbour rather than himself. All seemed prepared for the end and ready to face it.'

One might suspect that in an account written long after the event an element of rose-coloured hindsight may have been at work, trying to find some posthumous dignity in an appallingly brutal brawl, but Hagen published his memoirs in 1945 and recorded much the same transcendental experience:

> The life we had led at Arnhem was nearer an animal existence than anything we could have conceived, and yet the more savage the fighting got, the more civilized the men seemed to become... There was such gentleness and friendship among them as would have made any of them almost uncomfortable back on station. Although they were fighting like tigers, and in that fight had to be completely ruthless, there was no tough behaviour or coarseness of speech. It was almost uncanny.

One reason why some of the SS officers may have been more merciful than usual is that, for many, there was genuine regret that they were fighting the British at all. Bittrich and Harmel separately expressed this sentiment to captured British officers and it is as well to remember that in Hitler's *Mein Kampf* there is a unique eulogy of the British. Of course there were also those who appreciated that the time was approaching when some rather large birds would be coming home to roost. On Sunday the 24th Colonel Graeme Warrack, 1st Division's chief medical officer, met with Major Egon Skalka, his opposite number in the Frundsberg, to arrange a truce during which the British wounded were evacuated from the Oosterbeek cauldron. To stop a battle in order to relieve your enemy of a pressing argument in favour of surrender, while giving him time to improve his defences, is a very rare event in this or any other war. After the evacuation was complete Warrack thanked Skalka, who replied: 'Can I have that in writing?' When the walking wounded from Oosterbeek arrived to join others captured earlier, Lieutenant Peter Stainforth recalled:

> I have never been so proud. They came in and the rest of us were horror-stricken. Every man had a week's growth of beard. Their battledress was torn and stained, and filthy, blood-soaked bandages poked out from all of them. The most compelling thing was their eyes – red-rimmed, deep-sunk, peering out from drawn, mud-caked faces made haggard by lack of sleep and yet they walked in undefeated. They looked fierce enough to take over the place right then and there.

When the time came, hundreds of paras either went into hiding or escaped during the early stages when they were very lightly guarded, and were sheltered and guided to safety by the Dutch. Hackett's moving memoir *I Was A Stranger* (and ye took me in) is a heartfelt tribute to a people with no reason to feel warmly towards those who had brought death and devastation down upon them, yet who risked their lives to help them through a terrible winter when most of them could barely provide for themselves and their families. The common feature of all personal accounts of this battle and its aftermath is the tremendous dignity of all involved and a kindness that transcended national boundaries. It was remarkable, undeniable and for one who was not there will forever remain inexplicable.

In uncomfortable contrast, Montgomery got the 'blame the foreigners' ball rolling with a letter to Brooke in which he accused the fanatically brave Poles, who had been thrown into the debacle on the Lower Rhine when it was well past redemption, of cowardice. His writings are often economical with the truth, but this may well have been the most extreme example. Browning followed with the charge that Sosabowski was 'quite incapable of appreciating the urgent nature of the operation… and loath to play his full part… unless everything was done for him and his brigade'. The careers of many of those involved in Market Garden suffered, but Brooke in effect rewarded Browning with a posting as Chief of Staff at South-East Asia Command. From Churchill down, the treatment of the Poles by the British was little short of shameful and stands in stark contrast to the forbearance shown by the Americans in their dealings with their own awkward junior partners.

Even as the surviving British and Polish paras withdrew across the river, Lieutenant General Courtney Hodges's First US Army to the south began a more orthodox approach to the Rhine, became engaged in the struggle to clear the Hürtgen Forest and suffered 23,000 casualties doing so. Further south, Patton ran into determined resistance and received what he admitted was 'a bloody nose' at Metz. At the same time Lieutenant General Guy Simonds's First Canadian Army struggled for over a month to clear the Scheldt Estuary and open the desperately needed port facilities at Antwerp. In December–January came the last great German offensive in the Ardennes, aimed at Antwerp, which inflicted over 40,000 casualties although suffering far more in return. In February and March, First Canadian Army attacked out of the Nijmegen salient into the Reichswald in Operation Veritable and suffered 15,000 casualties, while Ninth US Army lost 7,500 closing the other jaw of the pincer in Operation Grenade, to clear the western bank of the Rhine. Finally on 24 March came Montgomery's massive set-piece crossing of the Rhine preceded by the dropping of 6th British and 17th US Airborne in Operation Varsity – under the command of Ridgway.

All of this put Market Garden in the light of a gamble well worth taking and, despite the losses, fed retrospective 'so near but yet so far' anguish about an operation that might have ultimately saved many more lives on both sides. While it was not done as well as it could have been, most of those involved judged it better to have tried and failed than to let the opportunity slip away. Roy Urquhart spoke for most when he concluded his after battle report with the words: 'There is no doubt that all would willingly undertake another operation under similar conditions in the future. We have no regrets.'

THE BATTLE-
FIELD TODAY The operation can be properly understood only if Market and Garden are considered together rather than in isolation, and visitors should try to visit XXX Corps's route as well as the Arnhem–Oosterbeek area. They should remember, however, that roads do not always follow their 1944 courses: towns are sometimes bypassed, modern dual carriageways often replace narrower routes, and land drainage has improved, sometimes giving the impression that off-road movement was easier than was the case over half a century ago.

The route starts at Joe's Bridge, named after the charismatic commander of the armoured Irish Guards (played by Michael Caine in the film *A Bridge Too Far*), Lieutenant Colonel Joe Vandeleur. It crosses the Meuse-Escaut Canal just inside Belgium, and is now bypassed by the main road south from the little Dutch town of Valkenswaarde. About 5 kilometres (3 miles) north of the bridge the road runs between pinewoods, and on its eastern edge, just south of a small CWGC cemetery, are some of the foxholes from which determined Germans took on the Irish Guards' tanks.

The route then runs on through Valkenswaarde to Son, where a bridge was thrown across the Wilhelmina canal just west of the present structure, and a determined tank counter-attack (there is a good photograph in Kershaw's book) from the south-east came close to taking it. There is a memorial to Taylor's men in the northern end of the square at St Oedenrode, now bypassed by the main road. The bridge over the Maas at Grave, taken intact by Gavin's men, remains a formidable objective. The bunkers dominating the ground around it, which bear the scars of battle, are actually pre-war Dutch fortifications.

The road bridge in Nijmegen, captured intact but subsequently damaged, may no longer be the largest in Europe but it remains impressive. There is a good view of the crossing from the foot of a medieval fortification at its southern end. Horrocks and Browning watched Tucker's men cross the river from the roof of Nijmegen power station near the town's western edge, and although the structure which stood there in 1940 has been replaced by a new one, it stands in almost the same place (I have no head for heights, and found filming from the gallery atop the new structure unequivocally ghastly – spot the white knuckles on the programme), and it is possible to approach the river bank in the area where Tucker's men formed up for their assault.

On the far side of the river a road runs along the clearly visible dyke that divides the water meadows from the arable land to the north. It was the line of the dyke, rather than the river's edge, which was held by the Germans, and when I was there in the summer of 2000 work in progress on the dyke had unearthed a mass of ammunition boxes and similar jetsam. It is a very strong position, and standing on it, looking south towards the river, it is hard not to reckon the river crossing as anything other than a prodigious feat of arms. The railway bridge is just to the east, and light flak guns sited to defend it added their fire, so destructively, to that of the dyke's garrison. Once the Americans had crossed they swung eastwards, first taking the northern end of the railway bridge and then reaching the road bridge to meet the leading elements of the armoured Grenadiers. German accounts testify to the blind fury with which the Americans were fighting: wounded men, they maintain, were flung into the river. Despite some postwar building, and frequent traffic jams on the approaches to the road bridge, the whole area remains evocative, and the chimneys of the power station provide a useful reference point when looking south from Arnhem.

Before leaving Nijmegen it is worth driving east to the Groesbeek Heights – a gentle plateau now largely devoted to market gardening – where 82nd Airborne Division's gliders landed, a fact commemorated on a memorial. The Reichswald is visible, just across the German border to the east, and it helps put the remainder of the north-west Europe campaign into perspective if we remember that this brooding forest was not finally cleared, after grim fighting, till March 1945. Most of the 2,350 Canadians buried in the Canadian cemetery at Groesbeek were killed in the battles for the Rhineland in 1945, and there are also 265 British burials.

It is a short and poignant journey from Nijmegen to Arnhem. On reaching Arnhem it is wise to resist the temptation to look first at the John Frost's bridge, and best to view the battle in sequence by proceeding straight to the museum in the old Hartenstein hotel at Oosterbeek, which was 1st Airborne Division's headquarters and the centre of its shrinking perimeter. It is one of the best military museums I know, mixing scenes composed of life-sized models in the cellars with photographs and other exhibits in the rooms above. There is a good little bookshop, and among the guides on sale is *A Tour of the Arnhem Battlefields* by Colonel John Waddy, who fought there as a young officer and has produced the most comprehensive guide to the area. A local visit should include the DZs and LZs west and north of Wolfheze, the route taken into Arnhem by 2nd Parachute Battalion, and of course Arnhem bridge itself. The bridge fought for in 1944 replaced a structure demolished in 1940 and was itself subsequently destroyed, and though the present bridge retains its predecessors' silhouette, the buildings that hemmed it in 1944 were mostly destroyed in the fighting, and the whole feel of the area is very different.

Airborne survivors were evacuated across the river by a ferry east of Heavadorp, on the southern edge of the Oosterbeek perimeter, and a ferry there still carries passengers. Although, even now, there remains a degree of tension between some members of the airborne community and veterans of XXX Corps, a memorial on the high bluff at Westerbouwing, on the north bank of the river, testifies to the brave efforts made by the Dorsets of 43rd Wessex Division to hold open communications with 1st Airborne Division. From these heights can be seen both the church tower at Driel, used by Horrocks towards the end of the battle, and, so near yet so far, Nijmegen power station.

The Oosterbeek War Cemetery lies just north of the Hartenstein. It contains over 1,600 British burials, as well as 45 Canadians, 12 Austrians, 23 New Zealanders and 80 Poles. It is especially well remembered by the local population, whose support during and after the battle remains so highly regarded by veterans. As General Sir John Hackett, who, as a brigadier, commanded 4th Parachute Brigade, was to write: 'To see Dutch children, who were not born when all this happened, most of whose parents were not born either, laying their flowers on the quiet graves… teaches a lesson not easily forgotten.'

MARKET GARDEN: CHRONOLOGY

1944

6 Jun	Allies land in Normandy (Overlord).
13 Jun	First V-1 cruise missile hits England.
23 Jun	Russian central front offensive (Bagration).
18–20 Jul	British 21st Army Group offensive (Goodwood).
20 Jul	Attempted assassination of Hitler.
25 Jul	US 12th Army Group breakout in Normandy (Cobra).
7–11 Aug	German counter-attack at Mortain.
15 Aug	Allied landings in the French Riviera (Dragoon).
12–19 Aug	Battle of Falaise Gap.
25 Aug	Fall of Paris.
1 Sep	Eisenhower assumes operational command of Allied land forces; Montgomery made Field Marshal.
4 Sep	Second British Army captures Antwerp.
8 Sep	First V-2 rocket hits England.
12–16 Sep	Second Allied Summit Conference at Quebec (Octagon).
17–25 Sep	Operation Market Garden.
17 Sep	First lift of 1st British, 82nd and 101st US Airborne Divisions; Guards Armoured Division stopped south of Eindhoven.
18 Sep	2nd Para destroys 10th SS recce group on Arnhem bridge; 101st battle at Best; 82nd battle for the Groesbeek Heights.
19 Sep	101st and 15th/19th Hussars clear Best; Guards reach 82nd at Grave.
20 Sep	101st and 15th/19th Hussars defeat German attack at Son; 82nd and Guards defeat counter-attacks and seize bridges at Nijmegen.
21 Sep	2nd Para resistance at Arnhem bridge crushed; Germans block Nijmegen–Arnhem road at Ressen; part Polish Brigade dropped at Driel.
22 Sep	Battle of Oosterbeek 'cauldron'; Germans briefly sever Eindhoven–Grave road (Hell's Highway).
24 Sep	Germans briefly sever Hell's Highway again.
25 Sep	Survivors of 1st Airborne evacuated from Oosterbeek.
Sep–Dec	First US Army battle for the Hürtgen Forest.
Sep–Nov	First Canadian Army battle to clear the Scheldt.
28 Nov	First Allied convoy sails up the Scheldt to Antwerp.
13 Dec	Third US Army captures Metz.

16 Dec–
16 Jan 1945   German Ardennes offensive.

1945

8 Feb–9 Mar   First Canadian Army clears the Reichswald (Veritable)
                 and joins Ninth US Army (Grenade) in advance to the
                 Rhine.

7 Mar   First US Army captures bridge at Remagen.

24 Mar   Rhine crossing by British 21st Army Group includes the
                 last major airborne operation of the war (Varsity).

30 Apr   Hitler commits suicide.

8 May   VE Day.

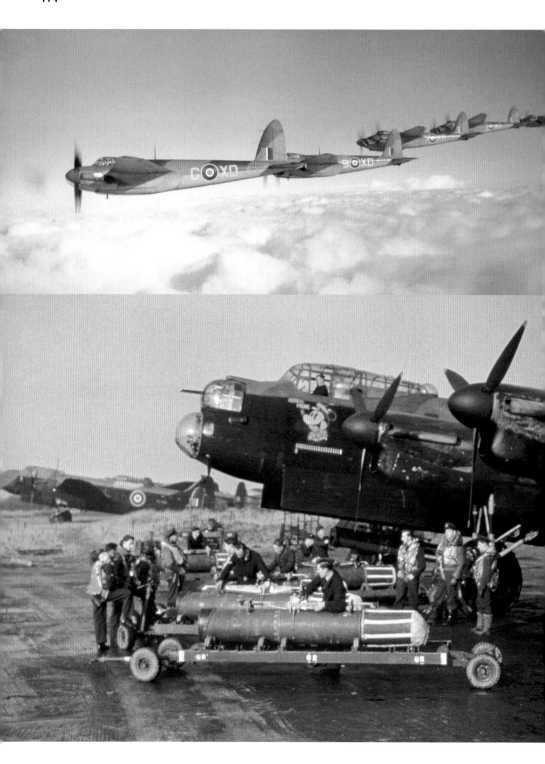

BOMBER
THE RAF OFFENSIVE AGAINST GERMANY

Until the Normandy landings of 6 June 1944 the principal offensive effort by the western Allies against Nazi Germany was conducted by RAF Bomber Command, latterly joined by Eighth USAAF. Although it did not, as its most fervent advocates hoped – and as Bomber Harris assured me personally when he visited Sandhurst to speak to the cadets in 1970 – make a land campaign unnecessary, the objective of the campaign, defined and repeatedly reaffirmed by elected authorities and enjoying wide popular support, was to inflict as much damage as possible on the Germans' ability and will to wage war.

It was, in the most brutal sense, a battle of attrition, which exchanged Allied aircraft and their crews for German cities and their populations, but Germany was an economic and military superpower and Britain was not. What was in effect a guerrilla war waged from the air became the principal means to keep hope of final victory alive at home and in occupied Europe after the Fall of France. 125,000 volunteers from all over the world, mainly from English-speaking communities but also from the nations under the Nazi heel, waged that war and kept that hope alive at the expense of their youth and, for 55,500 of them, their lives.

Many survivors have paid a high price in lost health and happiness, made worse by the denigration of their efforts by critics ranging from the

OPPOSITE, TOP De Havilland Mosquitos in formation, February 1943.
OPPOSITE The crew of a Lancaster watch their aircraft being loaded for a mine-laying mission, 1942.

morally fastidious, through those who supported the campaign until they saw what it had done and then wished to distance themselves from it, to those with a political axe to grind. Like the firestorms that were its most dreadful expression, condemnation of the bombing campaign has fed upon itself until the flames of cant and the smoke of hypocrisy have obscured its many accomplishments, not least the saving of countless Allied soldiers' lives.

Make no mistake. I do not view with equanimity the killing of tens of thousands of Germans – men, women and children – and the destruction of the homes of many more. It is impossible to contemplate the effect of a single firestorm without repugnance. And while I happen to disagree with George Bell, Bishop of Chichester, who spoke out against the bombing campaign during the war, I acknowledge that his was a stance requiring great moral courage, a commodity often rarer than physical courage. Yet the myth is that Bomber Command's campaign was somehow equivalent to the Nazi programmes of mass extermination, whereas the self-evident truth is that the physical welfare of Britain would have been better served by suing for peace in 1940, and that the decision to continue the struggle was a principled rejection of passivity in the face of rampant evil. That choice made, the rationale for the bombing campaign was set out by Churchill in an 8 July 1940 memorandum to Lord Beaverbrook, his Minister of Aircraft Production:

> The blockade is broken and Hitler has Asia and probably Africa to draw from. Should he be repulsed here or not try invasion, he will recoil eastward, and we have nothing to stop him. There's one thing that will bring him back and bring him down and that is absolutely devastating exterminating attacks by very heavy bombers from this country upon the Nazi homeland. We must be able to overwhelm them by this means, without which I do not see a way through.

Strategy demands the fusion of all the instruments at a nation's disposal – diplomatic and economic as well as military – and the most strategically valuable campaigns reap benefits that transcend their purely military utility. Churchill never seriously entertained the hope that bombing alone would bring about German defeat, but along with the guerrilla warfare of the Special Operations Executive (SOE), which he also ordered into existence at this time, it was a necessary signal of determination to potential enemies and friends alike. Hitler did indeed turn east, calculating that Britain must succumb in the face of German hegemony from the Atlantic to the Urals, but it was not the bombing that brought him back. Stalin and his supporters in the west accused Churchill of using the campaign as an excuse to delay opening a second front, so that Germany and Russia should exhaust each other, but his overriding aim – shared by so many of his generation, military and political leaders alike – was to avoid British casualties on a Great War scale.

Nonetheless the part of him that never grew up, the late Victorian schoolboy dreaming of glory as he played with lead soldiers in a lonely room in Blenheim Palace, was always secretly revolted by the realities of the war he felt compelled to wage. This emotion bubbled to the surface occasionally, as it did one evening when he saw film of the first genuinely 'devastating exterminating attack' by Bomber Command, the destruction of Hamburg aptly code named Gomorrah. 'Are we beasts?' he cried, leaping to his feet. 'Are we taking this too far?' Yet within days he was urging the Air Staff to treat Berlin the same and later still he talked of using poison gas against German cities in retaliation for the bombardment of London by V-1 cruise missiles. There was no more consistency between his head and his heart than there is in most people, but his formal verdict on the campaign, written on 15 May 1945, was unambivalent: 'I believe that the massive achievement of Bomber Command will long be remembered as an example of duty nobly done.'

The statue of the man to whom he wrote those words stands outside the church of St Clement Danes, the RAF church on the Strand, and there cannot be a more controversial monument in London, even including Haig's statue in Whitehall. It is peculiarly appropriate that the stern effigy of Marshal of the Royal Air Force Sir Arthur Harris is to be found in front of a church originally founded by the Vikings. He had much of the ruthless attitude we associate with our Norse ancestors, or perhaps the somewhat more refined Elizabethan buccaneers, and this sits ill with today's politically correct sensibilities. Harris inspired extremes of emotion even among his contemporaries, many of whom saw him as unrefined, rude, lacking in sensitivity, impatient and almost totally inflexible. Yet he was regarded with affection by his men, who identified with his earthy directness and iron sense of purpose. They nicknamed him 'Butch' and in *Lancaster Target* Flight Engineer Jack Currie described how perception of him as a distant, elemental force was a crucial ingredient in the 'two in the morning courage' that Napoleon judged the rarest of all, but which was routinely required of Bomber Command aircrew: 'It pleased us to think of him as utterly callous, indifferent to suffering, and unconcerned about our fate. There was a paradoxical comfort in serving such a dread commander: no grievance, no complaint, no criticism could possibly affect him. You might as well complain to Jupiter that the rain was wet.'

Some of the bad press Harris has received since the war can be attributed to a very belated effort by Churchill to put political space between himself and a man with whom he had dealt so closely for three years. On 28 March 1945, with reference to the destruction of Dresden by the combined efforts of the RAF and USAAF over a month earlier (something he had specifically requested), Churchill sent a draft memorandum to the Chiefs of Staff. 'It seems to me,' he wrote, 'that the moment has come when the question of bombing of German cities simply for the sake of increasing the terror [he also referred to 'mere acts of terror and wanton destruction'], though under other pretexts, should be reviewed.' Harris's cold reply, made through the Air Staff, rejected the emotive language, cited the political directives that had governed his conduct of the campaign and echoed a comment made in 1876 by Germany's 'Iron Chancellor' Otto von Bismarck: 'I do not personally regard the whole of the remaining cities of Germany as worth the bones of one British Grenadier.' Churchill reissued the memorandum with the offending phrases deleted.

It is hard to pick and choose among the horrors explicit in the term 'total war', and it is for those who wish to single out aerial bombardment for special condemnation to show how it is worse than the 'economic sanctions' they often prefer, which most affect the elderly and children. The Great War blockade of the Central Powers killed far more people through starvation and by weakening resistance to disease, and Franco-British war planning in 1939 envisaged doing the same again. And even if the highest estimate is correct and half a million civilians were killed by bombing, this still compares favourably with more than a million killed as the Allied armies fought their way into Germany.

For a fuller discussion of this issue than space permits, Horst Boog (ed.), *The Conduct of the Air War in the Second World War*, is the most illuminating single volume on the subject. While British and US authorities undoubtedly gave hostages to fortune throughout the war by semantic

Sir Arthur 'Bomber' Harris studies target photographs, flanked by
Air Vice Marshal Sandby (left) and Air Commodore Harrison.

hair splitting designed in part to deceive the public, this also reflected the
ambiguity of international law with reference to aerial bombardment.
Briefly, an attacker is required to exercise discrimination where this does
not increase the risk to his own personnel, but the ultimate responsibility
for the fate of civilians in a siege lies with the defender, who may at any
time put an end to their suffering by surrender, and whose counter measures may reduce the possibility of discrimination, for example by obliging
the attacker to bomb from a greater altitude or by night. Thus at least part
of a more complex legal argument, but USAAF General Curtis LeMay put
it more succinctly: 'As to worrying about the morality of what we were
doing – nuts. I was a soldier, soldiers fight. If we made it through the day
without exterminating too many of our own people we thought we'd had
a pretty good day.'

Harris might have expressed it slightly differently but he and the vast
majority of the men under his command shared the sentiment enthusiasti-
cally. There is an enduring myth that Bomber Command was repudiated
by the politicians at the end of the war, although Charles Messenger long
ago pointed out in *'Bomber' Harris* that Harris did receive the appropriate postwar honours and refused Prime Minister Clement Attlee's offer of

a peerage because he wanted no further part of politics, even in the House of Lords. He was denied a Bomber Command campaign medal – in addition to the Aircrew Europe Star awarded for service up to the Normandy landings and the North-West Europe Star awarded thereafter – because he specified that it should recognize the devotion of the 'erks' (ground crew) to their beloved aircraft and the hazardous nature of their work, with 1,479 men and 91 women ground crew killed. But it was judged invidious to treat them differently to those in other RAF commands, and all received the Defence Medal instead.

In the matter of how badly the campaign eroded Germany's ability to make war, critics usually cite the Summary Report of the US Strategic Bombing Survey, rushed into print in 1945 and better reflecting the prejudices of its authors than the data published two years later, as well as the views expressed by weathercock German Armaments Minister Albert Speer after twenty years in prison, which were sharply at variance with those he held earlier. Hindsight and the postwar bombing surveys, which provided the operational intelligence Harris so signally lacked while conducting the campaign, permit us to see how he might have used his force more effectively – but also reveal that area bombing substantially reduced German productivity, not least by driving the working population into air raid shelters night after night. Additionally, housing was already a serious problem in prewar Germany and bombing destroyed 3.3 million dwellings in the major cities, with evacuation and industrial relocation spreading the effects throughout the country. The proportion of the German war effort diverted to air defence was in itself considerable, including 75 per cent of the dual-purpose 88mm guns that were the bane of the Allied armour, but the primary aim of the campaign was always to make life for the average German more burdensome and less productive.

The issue of area versus precision bombing is something of a false dichotomy because the technology of the time made the heavy bombers decidedly blunt instruments, by night or day. Cloud compelled the USAAF to employ blind bombing techniques, developed by the RAF, in a large number of its daylight missions. Even in clear visibility the usefulness of the much vaunted Norden bomb sight against poorly defined targets was highly variable, as, sadly, Lieutenant General Lesley McNair and many other US soldiers discovered in Normandy when they became the casualties of their own heavies operating in the CAS role. By 1944 and with its own stabilizing automatic bomb sight (SABS), Bomber

Command was bombing as accurately by night as the USAAF was by day, but claims of precision were politically more important to the latter, not least because of the comparatively modest payloads their Flying Fortresses (B-17s) were able to carry in addition to the extra gunners and armour without which daylight operations would have been impossible. In the Far East the USAAF had an aircraft (the B-29 Superfortress) that could deliver the requisite tonnage and used it to conduct night area bombing that made the efforts of the RAF pale by comparison.

But Britain was never capable of producing a comparably over-whelming force and therein lies the main valid criticism of the war as waged by Air Chief Marshal Sir Charles Portal, Chief of the Air Staff, who seemed at times to be preoccupied with competition for resources with the other services. In November 1942, at one of the worst moments of the Battle of the Atlantic, he denounced the diversion of bombers to the 'uneconomic [maritime] role'. Better, he said, to build up 4,000 air-craft in Bomber Command to kill 900,000 and injure a further million Germans, and leave 25 million homeless. The fact that those bombers would be grounded if the Atlantic umbilical were cut was ignored, and as John Terraine acidly comments in *The Right of the Line*: 'It is at times difficult… to decide whether it is more correct to say that Bomber Command was irrelevant to the war, or the war was irrelevant to Bomber Command.' Churchill was more restrained. 'I deprecate,' he replied, 'placing unbounded confidence in one means of attack. The most that we can say is that it will be a heavy and I trust a seriously increasing annoyance.'

The Americans, no strangers to inter-service rivalry themselves, were amazed at the venomous disloyalty of senior RAF representatives towards their sister services, in which the lead was given by Portal, who effectively usurped the political functions of Air Minister Sir Archibald Sinclair and left the running of the RAF in the hands of subordinates. He had little operational experience and his main contribution in what was properly his area of activity was prejudice against long-range fighter escorts, which caused him to accentuate the stultifying division between Fighter and Bomber Commands. He was no less dogmatically opposed to the use of heavy bombers to support the armies and even as late as October 1944 could write: 'We shall sooner or later reach a stage where almost the whole heavy bomber effort has to be frittered away in small packets if the army is to attack at all.'

The official history, published in 1961 when 'Ban the Bomb' agitation was gathering strength, made much of a long and explicit correspondence between Portal and Harris in late 1944 and early 1945, in which Portal clearly had an eye on his place in the historical record. Harris was aware of it and brought the correspondence to a close with a curt comment that he was being put in a 'heads I lose tails you win… situation', and offered to resign. Portal of course backed down but he had succeeded in planting the seed which flowered into the remarkable interpretation that he and the Air Staff had second thoughts about area bombing doctrine late in the war, but were thwarted by Harris. This was not true in operational terms, for Harris did in fact make more attacks on petrol, oil and lubricants (POL) installations and to communications targets than the Americans at this time. It is still less true in the context of the war as a whole. If area bombing was an incorrect application of force in 1944–5, when Bomber Command at last had the means to smash cities, then it was even more so in 1942, when it did not. The justification for it was that Bomber Command was not capable of doing anything else for much of the war and, as Sir Maurice Dean points out in *The Royal Air Force and Two World Wars*, without an active, aggressive Bomber Command there was not, indeed never had been, much of a compelling reason for the existence of an independent RAF.

When Harris took over operational command on 22 February 1942, Portal's future was in the balance. As we have seen, after Tedder replaced Longmore as AOC-in-C Middle East, he survived only by falsifying operational data at Portal's instigation, and the same process may have been at work in the inflated claims made by Fighter Command for the ruinous cross-Channel sweeps it conducted in combination with 2 Group daylight bombers in late 1941 and early 1942. These in turn were embarked upon because night operations had been curtailed in the face of unsustainable losses and the results of a survey completed on 18 August and known as the Butt Report, after the War Cabinet official who prepared it at the instigation of Lord Cherwell, Churchill's scientific adviser and close friend. Based on 4,065 photographs taken during 100 raids in June and July by the best crews in Bomber Command (one-third of the force did not even claim to have reached the target area), the survey revealed that only one in four had dropped their bombs within 5 miles (8 kilometres) of the aiming point.

Although the Butt Report was given very limited circulation, bombing doctrine was strongly questioned in a debate in the House of

Commons on 24/25 February and Sir Stafford Cripps, Lord Privy Seal and speaking for the government, replied that the policy had been embarked upon when Britain had no allies, but now that the USSR and the USA were in the war it would be reviewed. On 19 April Mr Justice Singleton was named to conduct the review, but his terms of reference were to find 'what results are we likely to achieve from continuing our air attacks on Germany at the greatest possible strength during the next six, twelve and eighteen months respectively'. Although this brief might as well have been written by Portal, the policy decision it embodied reflected a memorandum prepared by Lord Cherwell, based on an examination of the effects of the Blitz in Britain, which concluded:

> Investigation seems to show that having one's house demolished is most damaging to morale. People seem to mind it more than having friends or even relatives killed. At Hull signs of strain were evident, though only one-tenth of the houses were demolished. On the above figures [for heavy bomber production] we should be able to do ten times as much harm to each of the fifty-eight principal German towns. There seems to be little doubt that this would break the spirit of the people.

Even if Cherwell's estimates of bomb damage and bomber production had not been grossly inaccurate, the extrapolation to 100 per cent destruction of fifty-eight cities was an absurdity on its face, all of which was promptly pointed out by Sir Henry Tizard, a scientist of comparable stature and the representative of the Ministry of Aircraft Production on the Air Council. His reward was to be buried by attacks on his integrity (there was bad blood between him and Cherwell) and even his patriotism. It was an episode that reflected little credit on the government, and the most likely explanation for it is that Cherwell belatedly realized the political damage the Butt Report had done, and sought to make amends.

Churchill badly needed a success and there was no prospect of it on any other front. Humiliating defeat followed defeat in the Far East; there was stalemate in the Mediterranean; the capital ships HMS *Ark Royal*, *Barham*, *Prince of Wales* and *Repulse* had been sunk, while the German *Scharnhorst* and *Gneisenau* had sailed up the Channel in broad daylight. Stalin seemed so cool to the idea of a formal alliance that it was feared he might make a separate peace, while the immediate effect of the US entry into the war was that its own rearmament programmes absorbed military material that might have been sent to Britain. But above all the U-boats were celebrating their second 'happy time' in the Atlantic, causing him more concern than any other threat during the entire war. Churchill once observed that 'all things are always on the move simultaneously', and now they all seemed to be moving against him. If with less reason than Portal, he had reason to be grateful to Harris for providing him with some high profile accomplishments to brandish at a barren time.

By this time Churchill may have suspected what we now know, namely that until at earliest June 1942 the human and financial cost to Britain of the bombing campaign greatly outweighed the limited damage done to Germany, and that it had not caused a single Luftwaffe squadron to be withdrawn from other theatres. But to admit this by, for example, sacking Portal, would have fatally undermined not merely Churchill's own position but also Britain's ability to influence the course of the war. This political dimension is the one most commonly overlooked in discussion of the campaign, yet it was probably definitive and helps to explain why Churchill persisted with it despite his qualms.

Procurement was the Achilles' heel of the British war effort in aircraft as well as in armoured vehicles, as shown in grossly deficient aircraft such as the Avro Manchester, the Short Stirling and the early Handley-Page Halifax, whose sole merit was that they conformed to Air Staff specifications. Harris, in a letter addressed to Air Minister Sinclair, furiously attributed the continuing production of inferior types to the corrupt influence of some manufacturers and his outrage is understandable. It was simply not true that bad designs had to remain in production because retooling delays could not be contemplated. When the need for a radar-carrying night fighter became urgent in 1940, Bristol used the wings, tail, landing gear and other systems from the Beaufort torpedo bomber to have the deadly Beaufighter in service within six months. Similarly, A. V. Roe's chief designer Roy Chadwick knew that the Manchester specified by the Air Ministry was going to be a dud, and developed an air frame that could be rapidly upgraded by the addition of extra engines to produce the incomparably superior Lancaster, thus sparing his boss from inclusion on Harris's list of domestic targets. While Chadwick found wriggle room within the specifications, Geoffrey de Havilland ran into such a barrage

---

OPPOSITE A Lancaster on a daylight raid.

A Mosquito being loaded with 500lb bombs. It could carry a remarkable 4,000 lb (1,814 kg) of bombs.

of 'Not Invented Here' flak when he proposed a true multi-role combat aircraft that he had to develop the 'plywood wonder' Mosquito as a private venture.

The Mosquito's combination of range, speed and payload was not approached by any other aircraft for the duration of the war. The prototype flew on 25 November 1940 and it entered service a year later, but by the end of the war just 7,780 of all types had been built, as opposed to 2,381 Stirlings, 6,176 Halifaxes and 7,377 Lancasters. The Lancaster, much the best of them, entered service later, cost three times as much, carried seven rather than two crew, used four rather than two Rolls Royce Merlin engines and, although it could carry three times the bomb load, could only do so for one-third the number of sorties. Yet Lancasters flew 156,192 sorties with a loss of 3,677 (2.35 per cent), while those Mosquitoes assigned to Bomber Command flew 39,795 and lost 310 (0.78 per cent). There was only a small production of 'Mozzies' in Canada, although with immense timber resources to hand and the Packard plant churning out Merlins under licence in the USA it could have been mass produced, free of charge under the Canadian Mutual Aid programme.

In 1944–5 the aircraft was finally revealed as a Main Force bomber in its own right, able to form part of the main bombing force sent against a target, and not simply part of the elite Pathfinders, or a smaller force sent against a precision target such as Amiens prison in February 1944. It was capable of carrying the same payload to Berlin as the Flying Fortress, only so high and fast that it was seldom intercepted and regularly flew two long-range sorties a day with a change of crew. Many lives would have been saved if this had been recognized earlier, or even if the advanced night fighter version had been released sooner to escort the heavy bombers.

It was of scant consolation to Harris and the aircrew under his command, but the handicaps inflicted on them by officialdom were as nothing compared to those endured by their opponents. The Nazi state was stunningly corrupt, inefficient and completely lacking the Wehrmacht's signal ability to define objectives and concentrate resources where they could be employed most effectively. Straddling this divide, in the days before he became an obese caricature figure, Reichsmarschall Hermann Göring built the Luftwaffe into the world's most powerful air force, whose strength lay not so much in a technological lead that peaked early but in the usual German advantage of fully worked out doctrine. Set out in a document entitled *Conduct of the Air War* it did not, as generally believed, reject strategic bombing in favour of CAS. It stated that attacks on enemy industries should take place either when land and naval operations had prepared the way and it could quickly affect the outcome, or when there was a stalemate and a decisive result could be achieved in no other way. Thus it did not question that strategic bombing might be able to win a war, but viewed it as something to be embarked upon only after more certain alternatives had been tried. These included the winning of air superiority over the battlefield to blind and confuse the enemy, the suppression of anti-aircraft and other artillery positions and the destruction of supply dumps and bridges deep behind enemy lines. This, of course, demanded precision.

Until (or perhaps even after) the advent of today's smart bombs the formula 'h-e-i-g-h-t spells s-a-f-e-t-y' failed to add that it also spelled inaccuracy. Like their US Navy counterparts, trainee Luftwaffe dive bomber pilots had to put ten bombs in a 50-foot (15-metre) circle to gradu-ate, a far cry from the 5-mile (8-kilometre) radius of the Butt Report. The drawback has always been that an aircraft robust enough both to do this and to survive intense ground fire will not do well in an encounter with another built for speed and agility, and that for obvious reasons dive bombing can be done only in daylight and when the target is obscured neither by cloud nor smoke. Germany was actually two years ahead of Britain in issuing specifications for a long-range heavy bomber, but the lead time was lost because of chronic problems with engines made worse by the weight of machines designed to bomb by day from medium height, or in a dive, or both. The Germans did not foresee any need to bomb by night from high altitude but then neither did the British, who became committed to it only after medium level daylight bombing, all that Bomber Command was trained and equipped to do in 1939, proved prohibitively costly.

The Germans also did not contemplate fighting an air war against an enemy whose bases could not be threatened by ground forces, whereas that was precisely the main question British bombing doctrine sought to answer. The latter was not set in stone and, as we have seen, the Desert Air Force rapidly rediscovered the value of CAS after having its forward airfields overrun. To the great good fortune of Bomber Command aircrew, there was no similar evolution in German doctrine and the Luftwaffe fought out the war very largely with the weapons systems, organization but above all the ideas of 1939. An illustrative episode was Hitler's October 1941 order to cease 'Intruder' attacks on Bomber Command aircraft over their own airfields because: 'if the [tactic] really would have been successful, the British would have copied it a long time ago, as they imitate anything that works well'. In fact it had contributed significantly to the losses that led to reduced operations in the winter of 1941–2 and it had tied down a huge force of British night fighters. When Harris, following shattering losses at Nuremberg in late March 1944, prevailed on Portal to release night fighters with up-to-date radar to offensive operations, they did indeed copy the tactic against German night fighter airfields, to devastating effect. But apart from a brief and disastrous flurry later in 1944, the Luftwaffe never again attacked the bombers when they were most vulnerable.

If British weapons procurement was often marred by bad decisions stubbornly maintained, until the appointment of Speer in 1942 the German equivalent was virtually paralysed by the original strategic sin of planning only for a short war, compounded by duplication of effort, anarchic allocation of resources, 'gold plating' – producing ever-exaggerated specifications in search of perfection – by staff officers and a

Trainee air gunners practise on the range, with a helpful flight sergeant rocking the turret for added realism.

complete absence of any mechanism to set production priorities, or at least to maintain them after they were set. As a result Germany not only lost its lead in applied technology but also produced fewer aircraft than Britain every year except 1939 and 1944, the latter because of a belated surge in fighter production to counter the bomber offensive. These were, however, tried and true types carrying an increasing burden of modifications and new equipment, not the new generation of aircraft the Luftwaffe desperately needed. It was particularly fortunate for Bomber Command that production of the specialist night fighter He 219 'Owl' was postponed on Hitler's order and only 268 entered service, because the bombers suffered quite enough from the attentions of the Me 110 and Ju 88. The former was a long-range fighter whose failure during the Battle of Britain confirmed Portal in his obdurate prejudice against the concept, while the latter was a medium bomber successfully adapted to multiple roles and produced in greater numbers (14,700 of all types) than any other.

But the outstanding British advantage was in aircrew. Thanks to the establishment of the Royal Air Force Volunteer Reserve in 1937 and to the British Empire Training Scheme set up in December 1939, the supply of aircrew kept up with aircraft availability throughout the war, despite a rate of attrition that made squadron life, as Max Hastings puts it in *Bomber Command*, 'a human conveyor belt, a magic lantern show of changing faces'. As Free French pilot Jules Roy commented: 'The missing are effaced from this earth with prodigious ease.' All volunteers first had to pass demanding physical and intelligence tests, then went to a reception centre in Regent's Park in London where they marked time listening to lectures and watching films until placed at an Initial Training Wing. Those who were found more suited to be navigators, wireless operators and gunners went to specialist training establishments while would-be pilots went to Elementary Flying Training School, where a second selection process took place. Those found to possess the necessary aptitude usually went abroad under the Empire Training Scheme, while those who did not became bomb aimers and flight engineers, also the first and second reserve pilots in bomber crews. Finally they self-selected into the crews of individual aircraft at an Operational Training Unit (OTU).

Before posting to their operational squadrons, new crews might be broken in with 'Gardening' operations to drop mines off the enemy coast, 'Bullseye' missions to draw attention away from the Main Force, and short raids across the Channel. All of these counted towards the 150 points of their two tours of duty, according to a formula in which four were awarded for sorties beyond 3 degrees east and three for shorter missions. Pilots got ahead of the rest in the accumulation of points because it was found that the more preliminary flights they made as 'second dickey' on operations, the better their chances of survival. Operational crews regarded these passengers as bearers of bad luck and there was some – rationally inexplicable – statistical basis for the belief. Many a group of 'freshers' had to find a new pilot after their chosen leader failed to return from his lonely familiarization flights, eighteen months of training gone for nought and a wrenchingly bad start for the orphaned crews.

Throughout history warriors have been intensely superstitious and given to investing talismans and omens with supernatural powers, but aircrew took this to extremes, from the good luck charms they all carried – loss of which often became a self-fulfilling prophecy – to the individual and collective rituals they all undeviatingly practised. Equally traditional was their identification with their weapon and its power, bomber engines sometimes being decorated with the shark's teeth motif more commonly associated with ground attack fighters, while 'nose art' was quite as common in Bomber Command as it was in the USAAF, if less flashy because necessarily done in the matte colours of night warfare.

Not only young men but financial contributions also came from all over the world, reflected in some squadron names: Burma, Madras Presidency, United Provinces, Hong Kong, Straits Settlements, Ceylon, Hyderabad, Jamaica, East India, Federated Malay States, Gold Coast and the enigmatic 692 (Fellowship of the Bellows), honouring the donations made by the British community living under an Axis-leaning regime in Argentina, which used a subterfuge (bellows = air force) for its fundraising activities. All fifteen Canadian squadrons had names such as Moose, Snowy Owl and Iroquois; the four Polish squadrons bore the names of provinces in their homeland; there were eight simply designated as Australian, two as New Zealand, one as Lorraine and two French, one Dutch and one Czechoslovak. Although some governments requested that their nationals should serve together – and eventually the Canadians formed their own 6 Group – the Bomber Command norm was for men of all nationalities to serve together according to personal choice and affinity, a very popular procedure and one unique to the RAF.

When Harris took over, Bomber Command had 547 aircraft in front line service, seventy-eight of them the Blenheim and Boston light day bombers of forlorn 2 Group, constantly depleted to supply other theatres. Of the 'heavies', 221 were the hard working Wellingtons, the best of the prewar designs and produced in greater numbers (11,460 in eighteen versions) than any other type. There were still 166 of the even more vulnerable Hampdens and Whitleys in service, and crews in general preferred the older types to the new two-engined Manchester and the four-engined Stirlings and Halifaxes, which had so far proved to be a serious drain on aircrew lives and morale. The Manchester in particular had a loss rate (6 per cent) over double the average for all types and was eventually withdrawn from service, while the lumbering Stirling's figures improved to

3.7 per cent only because it continued to fly in less demanding roles after crippling losses during the Battle of Berlin. Although improved Halifaxes were on the way and the arrival of the first four Lancasters provided a glimmer of light, Bomber Command was still in a very dark tunnel. Like Montgomery in Egypt, Harris's first priority was to restore the confidence of his new command, and he eliminated the two most important griev- ances by standardizing tours of duty to eliminate favouritism (although confirming them at a tough thirty missions for a first tour and twenty for the obligatory second) and by curtailing operations in bad weather. The latter immediately decreased losses due to flying accidents which, like 'unnecessary' deaths in all the services, always had a disproportionate effect on morale.

Harris also realized that his crews no less than his political masters needed to see some return on their efforts. 'I wanted my crews to be well "blooded" as they say in fox-hunting,' he wrote, 'to have a taste of success for a change' – an interesting analogy from one who often expressed con- tempt for the cavalry. This was at last possible because nine squadrons had been equipped with the long-awaited navigational aid GEE. While not as good as the *Knickebein* system fitted to Luftwaffe bombers in 1940, this at least solved the problem of bombers not even finding the target (for the six months it took the Germans to learn how to jam it). Until the intro- duction of OBOE in December 1942 there was no equivalent to the very accurate automatic bombing *X-Gerät* with which specialist German night bomber squadrons were also equipped in 1940, and concentration remained harder to achieve. Harris first experimented with new tactics, including the Shaker technique in which GEE-equipped aircraft dropped markers for others to use as an aiming point, then 'blooded' his crews with the fire bombing of the old wood-built Baltic port of Lübeck on 28/29 March and of equally historic Rostock in four raids between 23 and 28 April. These drew retaliation in the form of the so-called 'Baedeker raids' (from a well-known German tourist guide book) on Bath, Canterbury, Exeter, Norwich and York, and these in turn set the stage for Harris's first Thousand Bomber raid, against Cologne on 30/31 May.

Possibly mindful of Longmore's fate during a similar period of tran- sition in the Middle East, Harris increased the 'teeth' at the expense of the OTU, four-engine conversion and administrative 'tail', while solving the problem of incomplete aircrews by abolishing the position of co-pilot and doubling up the duties of other key crew members. He dispatched every aircraft he could squeeze out of his own and other Commands, some of them manned by instructors and crews still in training. It was good public relations but the force soon had to be broken up and returned to normal activities. He did not dispatch the same number of monthly sorties again until February 1943 and did not accumulate a front line strength of 1,000 four-engined bombers before June 1944. Because for so many it was their first operation, the raid on Cologne left an indelible imprint on the collective memory of Bomber Command, Jack Currie's reaction being representative: 'I stared at the sky in front of us. Among the groping searchlight beams, the white and yellow flak bursts formed a sparkling wall. It was hard to believe that we could pass through that unceasing barrage. Was it always like this?'

Cologne and subsequent Thousand Bomber raids on Essen and Bremen satisfied Churchill that the resources being poured into Bomber Command were not being wasted, gave the long suffering public something to cheer about and signalled Britain's allies that she was making a significant contribution to the defeat of the common enemy, although the damage was more apparent than real. The raid on Cologne demonstrated that a concentrated bomber stream could swamp air defences, but the city was well equipped with shelters and its emergency services were not overwhelmed. Of the nearly 2,000 acres of Cologne burned out during the war this raid accounted for 600, but only 460 people died and within hours trucks began pouring in with humanitarian aid. Within days thousands of glaziers and builders were at work and in a month all damage claims had been paid. Landlines, safe from British eavesdropping, soon carried the news to anxious Nazi bureaucrats in Berlin that the city was functioning normally and that the mood, as in London during the Blitz, was 'We can take it.' The results against Essen and Bremen were even poorer, local officials in the latter estimating that only eighty bombers had attacked the city and that the Thousand Bomber claim was simply propaganda, which in the broader sense it undoubtedly was.

Thereafter the story of Bomber Command was of a slow increase in the frequency of attacks and the numbers of bombers dispatched, although the rise in throw weight was of another order of magnitude: 1,047 bombers dropped 1,455 tons of bombs, two-thirds of them incendiaries, on Cologne in May 1942; in October 1944, 1,013 bombers dropped 3,574 tons of high explosive and 820 tons of incendiaries on Duisberg on the 14th and 1,005 of them followed up with 4,040 tons of high explosive and

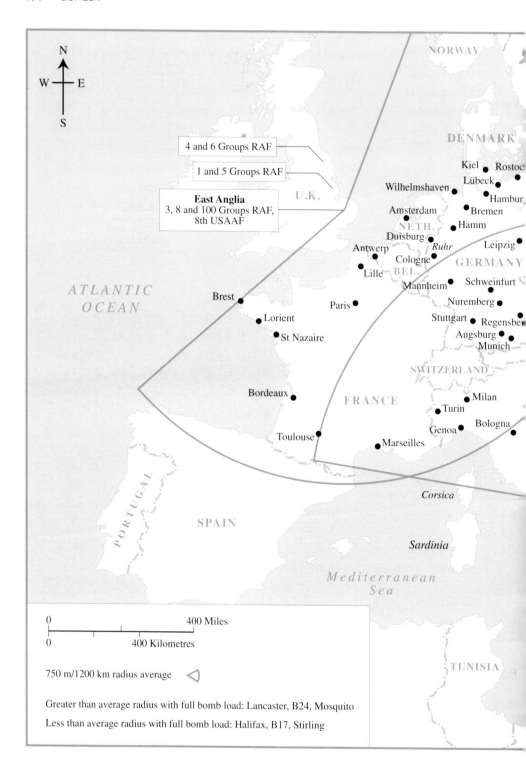

N
W ← → E
S

4 and 6 Groups RAF

1 and 5 Groups RAF

East Anglia
3, 8 and 100 Groups RAF,
8th USAAF

NORWAY

DENMARK

Kiel • Rostoc
Lübeck •
Wilhelmshaven • Hambur
Amsterdam • Bremen
NETH. • Hamm
Duisburg •
Antwerp • *Ruhr*   Leipzig •
Cologne • GERMANY
Lille BEL.
Mannheim • Schweinfurt •
Nuremberg •
Stuttgart • Regensbe
Augsburg •
Munich
SWITZERLAND

U.K.

ATLANTIC
OCEAN

Brest •
Lorient •
• St Nazaire

Paris •

Bordeaux •

FRANCE

Milan •
• Turin
Genoa • Bologna

Toulouse •
Marseilles •

Corsica

PORTUGAL

SPAIN

Sardinia

*Mediterranean
Sea*

0   400 Miles

0   400 Kilometres

750 m/1200 km radius average   ◁

Greater than average radius with full bomb load: Lancaster, B24, Mosquito

Less than average radius with full bomb load: Halifax, B17, Stirling

TUNISIA

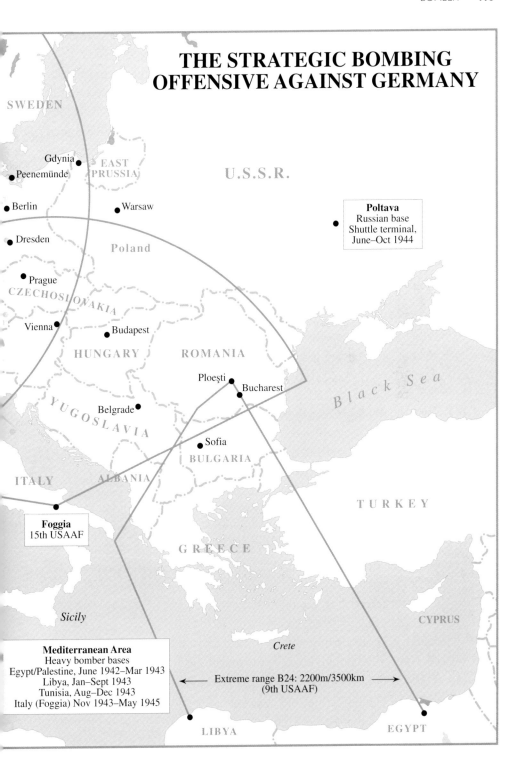

THE STRATEGIC BOMBING
OFFENSIVE AGAINST GERMANY

SWEDEN

Gdynia
Peenemünde
EAST
PRUSSIA

U.S.S.R.

Berlin

Warsaw

Poltava
Russian base
Shuttle terminal,
June–Oct 1944

Dresden

Poland

Prague

CZECHOSLOVAKIA

Vienna

Budapest

HUNGARY

ROMANIA

Black Sea

Ploeşti
Bucharest

Belgrade

YUGOSLAVIA

Sofia

BULGARIA

ITALY

ALBANIA

TURKEY

Foggia
15th USAAF

GREECE

Sicily

CYPRUS

Crete

Mediterranean Area
Heavy bomber bases
Egypt/Palestine, June 1942–Mar 1943
Libya, Jan–Sept 1943
Tunisia, Aug–Dec 1943
Italy (Foggia) Nov 1943–May 1945

← Extreme range B24: 2200m/3500km →
(9th USAAF)

LIBYA

EGYPT

500 tons of incendiaries the following night. The increase in aircraft numbers was slow because during 1942–4 losses generally exceeded 4 per cent, which meant that less than one crew in eight would survive fifty missions. A saying still current among airmen is that you start with a bag full of luck and an empty bag of experience, and the trick is to fill the bag of experience before you empty the bag of luck. Half of all Bomber Command aircrew failed to accomplish this and were lost before completing ten missions, while 'rusty' crews returning to operations for a second tour were almost as vulnerable.

During the war 10,321 aircraft (2.65 per cent) were lost in 389,809 sorties. Although 1,368 of these crashed in friendly territory and many of their crews fought on, many more that returned to base did so with battle damage and dead or wounded men on board. As the aircrew of Eighth USAAF discovered, seeing how your comrades died close up was very much more harrowing than the usually distant losses observed at night, but those that crashed on return to base left the most indelible impression. In *Tales from the Bombers*, Chaz Bowyer records bomb aimer 'Buck' Rogers's account of one such landing:

> We appeared to be undamaged apart from a few holes in the fuselage which hadn't hit anything vital, but on touching down a tyre burst and we ground-looped viciously off the runway... The noise of screeching metal and engines was frightening and I was sure I was about to die. However, the aircraft stopped very abruptly... and the next thing I knew was a babble of voices and someone dragging me to the side opening in the rear of the fuselage. Then there was a tremendous Whoof and flames burst out all around me... my next recollection is running like hell across the grass – any place to get away from that fire. I'd seen a crashed Lancaster burn on our runway some weeks before, and the screams of its crew – none of them got out – haunted me.

The upper air is an environment as intrinsically hostile as the sea and only Royal Navy submarine crews had a lower survival rate. Aircrew were three times more likely to be killed than wounded, with an even lower chance of becoming prisoners of war. Once an aircraft was fatally damaged, survival rates reflected crew members' distance from an escape hatch. The bomb aimer was the nearest followed by the other key personnel, clustered together near the nose hatch in a Halifax but fatally further away in a Stirling or a Lancaster. Pilots had to remain at the controls to give the others a chance to escape and an astonishing number of those who survived were blown clear when their aircraft exploded. Commonly, those on board were pinned inside by G forces when the aircraft went into a spin, as described by radio operator Harry Lomas in *One Wing High*: 'Having accepted that it was physically impossible to escape, I felt no urgent need for despairing frenzied effort. The end would be sudden and painless, and the fear was suddenly expunged. There came no flashbacks of my past life. All I was conscious of was a feeling of resignation and intense sadness that all was going to end like this.'

The least survivable position was the rear turret, where 'Tail End Charlie' sat uncomfortably in the front line of Harris's war, with the coldest, loneliest and most dangerous job of all. Gunners had twice the thickness of clothes as the others, eventually electrically heated because the outside air temperature fell to minus 40 degrees C and they often removed the Perspex panels around the guns to improve their chances of spotting a night fighter before it killed them, preparatory to moving in and finishing off the bomber at leisure. It was well known that isolation prompted combat refusal and in German bombers all the crew, including the gunners, were concentrated together for that reason, enjoying physical and psychological comfort in a heated cabin and in close proximity one to the other. The extra demands made on the courage and endurance of rear gunners in the heavy bombers may well have been the most ever regularly required of fighting men, and the odds against them were greatly lengthened by callous lack of consideration given to their escape route. They were outgunned by the cannon-equipped fighters, and even if they, their turret mechanism and their parachutes survived an attack that crippled the bomber, to bale out they had to retrieve their parachutes from inside the fuselage, return to the turret, rotate it and fall out backwards. Few managed it and aircraft were sometimes seen to crash with the gunners defiantly firing to the last.

Many airmen remain bitter that for most of the war they had to make do with 0.303-inch calibre machine guns, even though as early as July 1939 Air Marshal Sir Edgar Ludlow-Hewitt, then AOC-in-C Bomber Command, told the Air Ministry that: 'The gunners have no real confidence in their ability to use this equipment efficiently in war, and captains and crew have... little confidence in the ability of the gunners to defend them against destruction by enemy aircraft.' What makes this all the more painful is that there was no shortage of .5-inch guns or 20mm cannon, which as Canadian pilot Walter Thompson observes in *Lancaster to Berlin*, sat in thousands of fighters mostly 'vegetating' from 1941 to 1944. He also questions why the front turret, redundant in night operations, was retained when there was a crying need for protection in the belly of the aircraft against the upward-firing cannon (*Schräge Musik*) with which German night fighters were equipped in late 1943.

There is no doubt about the inadequacy of the .303, even in the quadruple mount rear turrets, but whether a ventral turret would have made much difference is less easy to say. There were experiments with retractable 'dustbin' type turrets in Wellingtons before the idea of a self-defending bomber formation was abandoned in 1939–40, and later some Mark II Lancasters with Bristol Hercules engines were delivered with a belly observer/gun position, but they had significantly poorer perform-ance than the Merlin equipped Marks I and III and it was usually stripped out to save the weight. In Thompson's own 6 (Canadian) Group some squadrons took the mid upper, not the front turret out of their lower flying Halifax Mark IIIs and retrofitted them with ventral bubbles as fast as they could obtain the kits from the USA, but in a *Schräge Musik* attack the night fighter would rise under the bomber, undetectable against the ground, and the belly observer/gunner had a limited field of vision if he knelt and could not fire the gun if he lay down.

Air Vice Marshal Donald Bennett, Commander of 8 (Pathfinder) Group, declared that guns should be fired only as a last resort, whereas Air Vice Marshal the Hon. Ralph Cochrane of 4 Group encouraged his men to shoot at anything they saw. Obviously the latter greatly increased 'friendly fire' incidents but Squadron Leader R. C. Rivaz, author of *Tail Gunner* (published in 1943), who died in an accident in 1945 after sur-viving countless aerial battles throughout the war, felt that hitting back was all that made the experience endurable. Nonetheless a stream of tracer did point to the bomber from which it came and gunners usually held their fire and guided their pilots with a running commentary 'patter'.

Many escaped using the violent corkscrew manoeuvre in which the pilot would bank and dive sharply at full power then climb and bank in the opposite direction, shedding speed abruptly. The less skilled could easily over bank and stall inverted but, when properly performed, the manoeuvre presented the fighter with rapid changes in deflection and the danger of overshooting into the bomber's guns. The 'aces' who ran up the big scores would be likely to move on in search of easier prey, but when one of them would not let go the contest between two good pilots could be extraordinarily prolonged. In Theo Boiten's *Nachtjagd* there is a gripping account of such a battle, in which the Lancaster pilot even stalled his aircraft wing down, only to be matched by his pursuer through aerobatics that threatened the structural integrity of both aircraft until at last the fighter pilot, whose observer refused to fly with him again after this experience, got into position for the fatal burst.

Pilot skill was the difference between life and death for a crew at all times, not only when attacked, never more so than on takeoff when loaded with tons of fuel and explosives. It was an inescapable moment of dry-mouthed tension for all on board and, unlike enemy action, it was experienced on every sortie. One pilot recalled the drill: 'Right hand on the throttles, thumb advancing port outer to stop her swinging, stick forward to get the tail up, deft use of the rudder to keep her straight, the needle creeps up to 90 knots marking the point of no return.' The flight engineer acted as co-pilot and a mistake on his part could be no less fatal, the pre-flight TMPFFGGH checklist covering his area of responsibility: trim, mixture, pitch, fuel, flaps, gills, gyro, hydraulics. Mistakes by navigators could also doom a crew by sending them over known concentrations of heavy flak or to a lingering last few hours as they flew back from a mission over the North Sea, on a course that never brought landfall. Radio operators might miss a broadcast navigational correction or a meteorological warning that made a change of course imperative, and they also had responsibility for the burden of radio counter measures (RCM) that increased steadily in complexity throughout the war.

The mid upper gunners saved more lives by giving collision warnings than they did with their guns, particularly when the aircraft were climbing to the height prescribed for the bomber stream. The ventral blind spot could also be lethal over the target when bombs might be dropped on a friendly aircraft below, horrifically frozen in time by the photoflash that went off thirty seconds after the largest bomb on board was released. This was an innovation introduced during the Battle of Berlin when the heavy 'cookies' were being jettisoned from overburdened aircraft over the North Sea by crews seeking to regain height and performance. Before that the photoflash was triggered when all bombs were gone and the time spent flying straight and level over the target so that the photographs should show where the bombs would land was one of exceptional stress. The bomb aimer, during this period commanding the aircraft, might become the object of vituperation from other crew members because it was at this stage that most aircraft were lost to radar-directed heavy flak and searchlights. The latter were capable of downing aircraft without assistance by disorienting the pilots and forcing them into fatal flying errors, but more usually when a pilot's nerve gave way he would dive to get out of the light, into the range of massed light flak guns. Being 'coned' by searchlights was a dreadful experience, as one victim described:

> Turning back was quite out of the question, we therefore flew steadily onwards and, as we did do, we found that we were skilfully handed over from one group of searchlights to another. There was nothing we could do in that nightmare situation, it was impossible to see outside our aircraft to any worthwhile degree because of the dazzle, and all sensation of speed seemed to vanish. The world had disappeared and we felt as if we were hanging motionless in space.

As aircrew discovered to their cost early in the war when they strayed over their own cities, flak gunners tended to work on the 'if it moves shoot it' principle and both sides fitted their aircraft with IFF (Identification Friend or Foe) devices. These transmitted coded signals to the anti-aircraft control centres, but like any active device they could be tracked by the enemy and many died because they left IFF on over Germany in the mistaken belief that it interfered with radar. After GEE was jammed, the airborne radar known as H_2S (from an early assessment that the idea stank) became the main navigational aid, but an example was retrieved early from a crashed bomber and the Germans developed the *Naxos* passive tracking device to home on it and on 'Fishpond', an extension of H_2S intended to detect the night fighters which it was unknowingly attracting. The Germans never managed to jam OBOE, but weather conditions often neutralized course marking techniques and obliged Main Force bombers to depend on H_2S. 'Monica', another device fitted to bombers to warn of aircraft approaching from the rear, was also

OPPOSITE Facing the rear of his Lancaster, this flight engineer checks a reading. The pilot is out of sight over his right shoulder.

captured early and the *Flensburg* receiver was developed to home on it. The salvation for many aircrew was that Fishpond and Monica mainly detected other bombers and so were often turned off, while in veteran crews the navigator, who in the words of Canadian Ron McNichol was already 'busy as a one-armed paper hanger', used even H_2S as little as possible.

For the full story of the electronic war I refer the reader to R. V. Jones's *Most Secret War*, as I also recommend Martin Middlebrook's many excellent accounts, which capture the priceless detail of individual responses to common dilemmas that men on both sides evolved, from the new crews without the experience to realize when to deviate from flawed operational orders, to the ace night fighter who became sickened after a night of slaughter and let his last potential victim escape. Based as they are on a wide range of personal correspondence and interviews with those who fought in the air and those who endured on the ground, they constitute a compelling history of the period from the spring of 1943 to the spring of 1944, a period that Harris regarded as the 'main offensive', when to him and like-minded others it still seemed possible that bombing might render a land campaign unnecessary.

The first stage was the devastation of Germany's industrial heartland in the Ruhr in forty-three major raids between 5 March and 12 July 1943, which included the famous ultra low level attack with Barnes Wallis's 'bouncing bombs' by the specialist 617 Squadron on the Mohne, Eder and Sorpe dams, with the loss of eight out of nineteen aircraft. With a loss rate of 42 per cent among the finest crews in Bomber Command, withdrawn from general operations for six weeks to prepare for it, the Dambusters raid was not likely to be repeated, but 617 Squadron was permitted to pursue precision targets. In time it employed ever larger Wallis-designed missiles, culminating in the streamlined 12,000lb 'Tallboy' and 22,000lb 'Grand Slam' earthquake bombs. These solved the problem of hitting difficult targets such as aqueducts or bridges by digging huge holes under them, into which all trace of them would disappear and over which it was impossible to rebuild them.

In Main Force operations the bomber stream was becoming more condensed to achieve maximum concentration over the target, overwhelming anti-aircraft defences and emergency services. This came together with the addition of the radar fogging chaff known as Window, released for operational use after two years during which it was withheld because of fears that the Germans might copy it – they in turn having opted not to use it during the Blitz for the same reason – in Operation Gomorrah against Hamburg, the second largest city in Germany, which confirmed that Bomber Command at last had the means to make area bombing work as Portal wished. In four raids between 24/25 July and 2/3 August, 2,592 out of 3,091 bombers dispatched dropped 8,344 tons of bombs, evenly divided between high explosive and incendiaries. On the second raid a combination of concentration around the aiming point and exceptionally dry weather produced a firestorm that was responsible for most of the approximately 45,000 people killed on the ground. Over half the dwellings in the city were destroyed and 900,000 lost their homes. Flight Lieutenant A. Forsdike was awed:

> Set in the darkness was a turbulent dome of bright red fire, lighted and ignited like the glowing heart of a vast brazier. I saw no streets, no outlines of buildings, only brighter fires which flared like yellow torches against a background of bright red ash. Above the city was a misty red haze. I looked down, fascinated but aghast, satisfied yet horrified. I had never seen a fire like that and was never to see its like again.

Gomorrah awoke the Germans to their peril in a way that the grinding campaign against the Ruhr had not. On 1 August Göring announced that air defence was to take priority and for Erhard Milch, his deputy and the Technical Director of the Air Ministry, 'It was five minutes to twelve for the Third Reich.' But this did not transcribe into greater efficiency, as shown in the response when Window temporarily blinded the German ground radar system. The Luftwaffe 'Y' service, tasked with radio listening and interpreting, already had a functional alternative based on tracking H_2S, but its parent Signals and Communications Department refused to share this information in real time with the Air Defence Organization and would release the data only as an intelligence report after a raid was over. Göring did not resolve this jurisdictional dispute until February 1944 and then only after splitting Air Defence into four geographical sections so that an integrated defence system was further away than ever. Meanwhile Air Defence had resorted to the 'Wild Boar' tactic in which single-seater fighters engaged the bombers visually over the target cities, counting on spotting them against the searchlights and fires below. Before this desperate expedient was abandoned in April 1944, 45 per cent of the Wild Boar pilots were killed.

Following Gomorrah, Harris launched the first phase of the Battle of Berlin, basically a feasibility study conducted between 23 August and 3 September, from which it was concluded that to mount a sustained offensive over such a long range the Main Force would need the long winter nights and all the peripheral support it could be given. In late September the 'spoof raid' tactic was tested, in which Mosquitoes dropping Window created the illusion of a larger force going elsewhere. In October the improved G-H navigational aid came into service as did a wide range of RCM, including the activities of the German-speaking ABC (airborne cigar, from the shape of their antenna) operators of 101 Squadron based at Ludford Magna, many of them outstandingly brave German Jews flying with false papers, who broadcast misleading instructions on the night fighters' radio frequencies. With the exception of ABC and the similar but ground-based Corona, RCM was concentrated in the new 100 Group formed in November, which also flew older model Mosquitoes equipped with the Serrate receiver that homed on the German night fighters' airborne *Lichtenstein* radar. With the nights lengthening, Harris wrote the following words to Churchill, much quoted in evidence against him ever since:

> I feel certain that Germany must collapse before this programme, which is more than half completed already, has proceeded much further. We have not got far to go. We must get the USAAF to wade in with greater force. If they will only get going according to plan and avoid such disastrous diversions as Ploesti, and getting 'nearer' to Germany from the plains of Lombardy (which are further from 9/10ths of Germany than is Norfolk), we can get through with it very quickly. We can wreck Berlin from end to end if the USAAF will come in on it. It will cost us between 400–500 aircraft. It will cost Germany the war.

He was almost right about the distances but, as we have seen, Fifteenth USAAF was at that moment building its bases around Foggia in southern Italy, not Lombardy. He was also right about the raid by Ninth USAAF

Dead civilians await identification and cremation after Operation Gomorrah, the attack on Hamburg in July–August 1943.

from North Africa on the oil production and petrol refinery facilities at Ploesti, from which fifty-four of 178 Liberator bombers failed to return while the complex itself, although much damaged, was soon producing at a higher volume than before because of that bugbear of the industrial bombing campaign, the enemy's surplus capacity. Eighth USAAF had participated in Gomorrah, but there was no chance that it would undertake further deep raids into Germany after the staggering losses and severe morale problems that followed attacks on Schweinfurt and Regensberg in August and Schweinfurt again in October. Thus when Harris sent his Main Force, defined in this memorandum as inadequate for the task, to attack a vast, well spread out, cloud-shrouded and amorphous target not only out of OBOE and G-H range but also lacking the clear H_2S signature that doomed Hamburg, he joined the serried ranks of obsessive pounders who trample across the pages of military history. In the end, 6,427 acres were burned out, but there was no repetition of the city-killing Hamburg firestorm and 625 aircraft were shot down.

Most of the German night fighter pilots were cannon fodder – literally in the case of the Wild Boars, many of whom fell to their own flak – and the majority of bombers were downed by a hard core of *Experten* such as Heinz-Wolfgang Schnaufer (121), Helmut Lent (102) and Prince Heinrich zu Sayn-Wittgenstein (83) who were given the best equipment and preferential treatment by the ground controllers in the 'Tame Boar' tactic of guided interception. Wittgenstein ran up his total in 170 sorties and, flying the latest Ju 88 with *Schräge Musik* and the new SN-2 radar that solved the Window problem, he shot down six bombers on 1/2 January and was killed by a Lancaster rear gunner when trying for his sixth during the night of 21/22 January. On one hand, Hitler's refusal to give air defence the priority his airmen wanted saved Bomber Command from losses that might have led to a curtailment of operations, as they did during the winter of 1941–2. On the other, the slow response of the Luftwaffe seduced Harris into believing Berlin could be destroyed at acceptable cost using Gomorrah tactics – until the *Experten* with their new tactics and equipment ripped into the bomber stream like sharks into a shoal of bait fish.

Until the USAF sent B-52 Stratofortresses against Hanoi during the Vietnam War a generation later, Berlin was the most heavily defended target ever attacked by heavy bombers, and losses to flak, against which skill and experience counted for nothing, remained high. Combat refusal

A Junkers Ju 88 night-fighter equipped with *Schräge Musik* upward-firing cannon.

became a problem in Bomber Command for the only time in the war, although overt rebellion remained rare for the same reason soldiers generally do not do the commonsense thing and flee – because they have more physical than moral courage and regard the possibility of death or injury with less terror than they do the certainty of disgrace. Aircrew were gentle in their judgement of those who asked to be taken off operations, partly because a man unable to control his fear might doom the rest of the team in combat but also because they knew that they themselves continued to fly only by suppressing their own imaginations. The authorities could not afford to be charitable and regarded the condition as contagious. The man would be hustled off the base immediately, stripped of his flying brevet and rank, and his papers would be stamped LMF (Lack of Moral Fibre). The view was that the man was a volunteer, had received protracted and expensive training, enjoyed comforts and privileges denied to other servicemen and to civilians and that he was in breach of contract.

It is hard to argue with this. The military code of honour that led some station commanders to salute each aircraft formally as it took off sought not so much to control fear, which is impossible, but to discourage the sort of behaviour to which fear might give rise, and there were indeed many ways short of being declared LMF in which a crew, so long as they were all of like mind, might improve their chances of survival at the expense of operational effectiveness. Dumping bombs to improve performance was one, but the clearest indicator of morale problems was the number of aircraft that aborted a mission with mechanical malfunctions, some of which could be deliberately induced. These early returns climbed steadily during the Battle of Berlin and were highest in squadrons flying the inferior aircraft types that suffered the greatest losses, to the point that they were belatedly taken out of front line service. Even the later model Halifaxes were sent out with lighter, all-incendiary loads, leaving the Lancasters to carry the main weight of the attack.

Given that the Battle of Berlin stands as a blot on his record, what then of the alternative targets Harris sneeringly described as 'panaceas'? On the night before the Nuremberg raid, the last and most disastrous area bombing raid of the pre-invasion period, 617 Squadron carried out an attack on an aero-engine factory at Lyon employing low level marking, which devastated the plant with little collateral damage – but 617 was a specialist unit of veterans led by the nerveless Wing Commander Leonard Cheshire, the supreme practitioner of precision bombing in the RAF. More representative was another raid on the railway marshalling yard at Vaires near Paris, where 105 Stirlings and older Halifaxes bombed very accurately on target indicators dropped by eight OBOE-equipped Mosquitoes, killing over 1,200 men of 10th SS Panzer Division, next to whose train French railway workers, warned of the raid, had placed another loaded with sea mines. This points not so much to a missed opportunity as to one that emerged too late to affect the development of the bombing campaign. If there had been a network of agents on the ground in occupied Europe earlier in the war, proper damage assessment and perhaps even target marking by radio beacon might have taken Bomber Command in a different direction.

Overall, it is hard to disagree with Harris's contention that heavy bombers were not, at this stage of their development, a cost-effective means of disabling industrial and communications targets, especially in the occupied countries where care had to be taken to avoid civilian casualties. As it was, tens of thousands of French men, women and children were killed in the months during which the heavy bombers were under the operational command of Eisenhower, devoted first to bombing equally heavily all over northern France in order not to draw attention to Normandy, and later trying to lay down 'carpets' of bombs for the land forces to advance over. Even in the extremely low level precision raids made by expert crews in Mosquitoes against unarguably righteous targets such as the Gestapo headquarters in occupied cities, or prisons where Resistance fighters awaited execution, it was never possible to guarantee that some slight error or enemy action would not send a bomb or a crashing aircraft into a nearby school or hospital.

With respect to the destruction of the French transport network, Bomber Command's principal contribution to the success of Overlord, the two Special Operations squadrons based at Tempsford may well have been the most cost-effective units in the whole of Bomber Command. In *SOE in France*, M. R. D. Foot points out that teams of saboteurs with 3,000lb of explosive inflicted as much critical damage on French industry and transport as the thousands of tons of bombs dropped by the strategic air forces, which flew 195,200 sorties during the nine weeks prior to D-Day and lost 1,953 aircraft. Key railway junctions, canals, tunnels, bridges, viaducts and even dams could be repaired surprisingly quickly and, unless rebombed regularly, no permanent harm would be done to the enemy's ability to make war. While a pound of plastic explosive placed by hand at the right place could derail a train and block a crucial junction at precisely the moment required, weather might prevent a bombing force from finding the target at all. Still, the expertise acquired by Bomber Command in night operations over Germany did pay off handsomely for the invasion during the night before D-Day, when three 100 Group squadrons flew over the invasion fleet jamming German radar and radio communications and 111 of the best crews in Bomber Command flew precise circuits over the Channel dropping Window in a timed pattern to create a huge 'spoof' armada moving towards the Pas de Calais.

Harris was surprised and delighted by the level of precision the Main Force showed itself to be capable of, but remained convinced that its proper function was the one for which it had been called into being. Bomber Command was at last powerful enough to smash cities and, once released from operational secondment to the ground forces, Harris proceeded to do so, although devoting far more attention to POL and communications targets than most chroniclers have recognized. Since this is the point where Portal's effort to adjust the historical record was so successful in blurring lines of responsibility, let us examine the origins of the two 'devastating exterminating attacks' we have already mentioned, Duisberg and Dresden. On 13 October Harris received a formal directive that stated: 'In order to demonstrate to the enemy in Germany generally the overwhelming superiority of the Allied Air Forces in this theatre... the intention is to apply within the shortest practical period the maximum effort of the Royal Air Force Bomber Command and the VIIIth United States Bomber Command against objectives in the densely populated Ruhr.'

Operation Hurricane, the destruction of Duisberg, followed, and Bomber Command was by now powerful enough to smash Brunswick as well in the night of 14/15 October. Responsibility for Dresden also lies at the highest levels. Even as Portal was creating his paper alibi in correspondence with Harris, the Air Staff were developing plans for Operation Thunderclap, a series of heavy raids in eastern Germany designed to paralyse German civil administration in the path of the Russians. Berlin, Chemnitz, Dresden and Leipzig were chosen because they were known to be packed with refugees from the east. These operations had been requested by the Russians at Yalta a week earlier and had the full backing of Churchill, who pressed for their prompt implementation. The Dresden firestorm on the night of 13/14 February was as great as the one that had torn the heart out of Hamburg twenty months previously and probably killed more people. It was followed up with daylight raids by the USAAF the next day, again on the 15th and on 2 March.

This was the use of air power in the European theatre most repugnant to modern sensibilities, something skilfully played upon by David Irving in *The Destruction of Dresden*, part of his lonely campaign to show that the Nazis were not much worse than anyone else. But they were, and it was because their death grip on Germany did not slacken even at this late stage that Harris had no qualms about using his sledgehammer to crush a declining supply of worthwhile nuts. In his reply to Churchill's attempt to distance himself he wrote: 'Attacks on cities, like any other act of war, are intolerable unless they are strategically justified. But they are strategically justified in so far as they tend to shorten the war and so preserve the lives of Allied soldiers. To my mind we have absolutely no right to give them up unless it is certain that they will not have this effect.'

It was not only Harris who felt that the Germans, by fighting on beyond the point where there was any hope of averting defeat, had forfeited any claim to mercy. The men on the ground became less inclined to

OPPOSITE This evocative photograph, taken after the end of the war, shows the devastated city of Dresden.

spare civilian habitation and to take prisoners; the men at sea were out-raged at the bitter-enders of the U-boat force; and fighter pilots were ordered to machine gun Luftwaffe pilots in their parachutes. It was a time of half-angry and half-fearful disgust, as one might feel when killing a rabid dog. The thoughts of Harry Lomas on VE Day, as he flew first over Rotterdam, its heart burned out by the Luftwaffe in the unprovoked attack of 1940, and then over the devastation of the Ruhr, captured the climate of the time:

> In the skies above this and other ruined cities, more than 55,000 of the aircrew of Bomber Command had perished in the six years of war. In a sense, everything around us was their memorial. They had been told what had to be done, and had done it well. Had their efforts achieved the results their leaders hoped and predicted? Surely nobody could have envisaged the endurance and resilience of the German people, in the face of the continual destruction of their cities on such a scale. If then one granted them a measure of grudging admiration, what of sympathy for their present plight? None whatsoever.

THE BATTLE-FIELD TODAY War cemeteries in which Bomber Command aircrew are buried include: Becklingen in north Germany with 895; Berlin with 2,937; Durnbach in Bavaria with 2,652; a plot in the Hamburg main cemetery with 731 (including Sergeant James Ward VC RNZAF); Hannover with 1,841; Kiel with 865 (among them the last fifteen killed on 2/3 May 1945); Leopold War Cemetery at Limburg in Belgium (with Captain Edwin Swales VC DFC SAAF); the Reichswald near Cleve – the largest with 3,971; Rheinberg in the Ruhr with 2,895 (including Squadron Leader R. A. M. Palmer VC RAFVR, who died on his 110th mission); Sage near Oldenburg with 713.

Many are buried in village cemeteries near where they fell, including: Heverlee in Belgium (with three RAF VCs: Flying Officer D. E. Garland, Sergeant T. Gray and Flying Officer L. T. Manser); Meharicourt near Amiens (Pilot Officer Andrew Mynarski VC RCAF); Senantes in northern France (Squadron Leader I. W. Bazalgette VC DFC RAFVR); and the Catholic cemetery at Steenbergen, near Bergen-op-Zoom, where RAF Wing Commander Guy Gibson VC, DSO, DFC and his navigator Squadron Leader J. B. Warwick DFC are the only Allied servicemen buried. In England, the Runnymede Memorial, three miles east of Windsor, honours 20,000 airmen and airwomen of Britain and the Commonwealth whose remains were never found.

The bomber offensive has no battlefield in the conventional sense, though it still marks the landscape of both Britain and continental Europe. The majority of the airfields used by Bomber Command and the USAAF have long been abandoned. Some have wholly reverted to agricultural use, but for many the process remains tantalizingly incomplete, with nature only gradually reclaiming runway and perimeter track, hangars sheltering farm machinery, chickens or wooden pallets, and other buildings converted to a variety of uses. I find them unutterably poignant places. Many can still be seen, especially in the Midlands and East Anglia. The Airfield Research Group, which is concerned with airfields across the UK, both military and civil, publishes a journal, *Airfield Review*, three times a year. Tracing airfields has become increasingly popular: for instance, the North Kesteven Airfield Trail (guide leaflets available from the Tourist Information Centre in Sleaford) encompasses numerous active and former RAF airfields, several of them used by Bomber Command.

The Battle of Britain Memorial Flight, at RAF Conningsby, near Tattershall, flies the Lancaster *City of Lincoln*, and the Lincolnshire Aviation Heritage Centre, at nearby East Kirkby, one of 5 Group's air-fields, has another Lancaster in admirable condition. I spent several days filming in it, and had not appreciated just how cramped it is inside such an apparently large aircraft. Getting across the main spar, which intersects the fuselage, is no easy task even in comfortable clothing and with the air-craft level, while reaching the rear gunner's confined seat (no place for the claustrophobic) involves sliding along a narrow board. Both the Imperial War Museum's outstation at Duxford, near Cambridge (a Second World War fighter base) and the Royal Air Force Museum at Hendon are worth visiting by those with an interest in the machinery of air power.

The horrific impact of Bomber Command on Germany, which shocked so many Allied soldiers who first saw it in 1945, is, though part-ly effaced by time, still visible. In Berlin it is deliberately commemorated by the ruined Kaiser Wilhelm Memorial Church, and less deliberately, but no less sharply, by the wooded Teufelsberg – Devil's Hill – made from the rubble of bombed buildings, whose sheer scale gives an indication of the level of destruction. The Germans built huge concrete flak towers in Berlin, Vienna and Berlin to mount anti-aircraft guns above the level of the city, with smaller towers nearby to house radar to direct their guns. Some survive in both Hamburg and Vienna, while in Berlin the Humboldtsthain tower, last of the city's three gun towers, has managed to shrug off direct hits from bombs during the during the war, the bombardment of Russian artillery at its end, and postwar demolition attempts. Although part of it has been destroyed, and the remainder is half-buried by Teufelsberg-like rubble, it still stands among the trees, dour and imposing, a memorial to attackers and defenders alike.

Dresden's 'Stone Bell' Frauenkirche, Georg Bähr's magnificent example of German Baroque (built 1726–43) was destroyed, like so much else in the Saxon capital, during the raid in February 1945. It is currently being restored according to the original plans and using numbered stones from the ruined original where possible. The restoration was delayed because Dresden was in impoverished East Germany, but is now scheduled to be completed in time for Dresden's 800th anniversary in 2006. At the invitation of the people of Dresden, the British contribution to the rebuilding consisted of funding and manufacturing the orb and cross which will stand on the pinnacle of the rebuilt church. Money was raised by the Dresden Trust, which launched its appeal in 1993; the orb and cross were delivered in February 2000 and form a powerful and, let us hope, enduring symbol of reconciliation.

BOMBER: CHRONOLOGY

(Losses including crashes in UK/Total sorties/Total tonnage dropped)

1939

Bomber Command: 49/333/31

14 & 18 Dec	Raids on shipping near Wilhelmshaven (17/34 Wellingtons).

1940

Bomber Command: 810/20,809/13,033

3 Apr	Portal appointed AOC-in-C Bomber Command.
12 Apr	Last major daylight raid for Wellingtons and Hampdens.
10 May–25 Jun	Fall of France (145 mostly light bombers lost).
15 May	Cabinet releases Bomber Command to attack targets in Germany.
Jun–Oct	Battle of Britain. Raids on German invasion preparations.
24–6 Aug	Luftwaffe bombs London in error. Retaliatory raid on Berlin.
Sep–May 1941	The Blitz: 43,000+ killed. (600/4,000 Luftwaffe, most to accidents.)
5 Oct	Portal appointed Chief of Air Staff.
14/15 Nov	Fire bombing of Coventry: 380 killed.
16/17 Dec	First area bombing raid, against Mannheim: 34 killed.

1941

Bomber Command: 1,631/30,608/31,704

Feb–Mar	First Manchester, Stirling and Halifax operations.
Mar–Jul	Offensive against U-boat building yards and ports.
11/12 Aug	First operational use of GEE navigation aid.
18 Aug	Butt Report reveals extreme bombing inaccuracy.
29/30 Aug	First flight in support of SOE operations by 138 Squadron.
13 Nov	High losses (526 aircraft since July) lead to curtailment of operations.

1942

Bomber Command: 2,032/35,050/45,561
Eighth USAAF: 47/1,453/1,561

14 Feb	Area bombing directive.

22 Feb	Harris appointed AOC-in-C Bomber Command.
3/4 Mar	Billancourt raid: 367 French killed. First Lancaster operations.
28/29 Mar	Fire bombing of Lübeck: 320 killed (12/257).
30 Mar	Lord Cherwell 'de-housing' memorandum.
23–27 Apr	Four raids on Rostock: 320 killed (15/523).
Apr–Jun	Luftwaffe retaliates with 'Baedeker' raids.
30/31 May	1,000 bomber raid on Cologne: 460 killed (43/1,047); first Bomber Command Mosquito operations (photo reconnaissance).
25/26 Jun	1,000 bomber raid on Bremen: 85 killed (50/1,016).
20 Dec	First operations of OBOE Mosquitoes.

1943

Bomber Command: 3,028/64,528/148,457
Eighth USAAF: 1,144/27,362/44,185

2/3 Feb	Germans recover intact H_2S radar set.
5 Mar–24 Jul	Battle of the Ruhr (310/6,037 of 1,038/24,355 total in this period).
16/17 May	Dams Raid by 617 Squadron: 1,294 killed (8/19).
10 Jun	UK/US combined bombing directive (Pointblank).
Jun–Jan 1944	Bomber Command conducts only night operations.
24 Jul–3 Aug	Gomorrah. Destruction of Hamburg: approx 45,000 killed, 1.2 million flee. (RAF 87/3,095 in four raids, USAAF 39/337 in two.)
1 Aug	Ninth USAAF raid on Ploesti (54/178).
17 Aug	Eighth USAAF raids on Schweinfurt and Regensburg (60/376).
17/18 Aug	Bomber Command raid on Peenemünde (38/596).
14 Oct	Eighth USAAF raid on Schweinfurt (60/291).
Nov–Mar 1944	Battle of Berlin: 10,305 killed. (625/10,813 in 19 raids, of a total 1,117/29,459 in raids on Germany during this period.)

1944

Bomber Command: 3,291/157,448/459,663
Eighth USAAF: 3,891/210,544/389,119

23–28 Jan	Big Week. Intensive attack on German aircraft industry.
30/31 Mar	Bomber Command raid on Nuremberg (95/795).
14 Apr	Eisenhower assumes operational control of the Strategic Air Forces.

Jun–Sep	Transport and V-weapons sites precision bombing raids.
14 Sep	Strategic Air Forces revert to control of Chiefs of Staff.
14–15 Oct	Hurricane. Destruction of Duisberg: civilian casualties unknown. (RAF 21/2,018 in two raids, USAAF 5/1,251 in one.)

1945
Bomber Command: 711/62,804/181,740
Eighth USAAF: 1,123/94,185/188,573

13/14 Feb	Thunderclap. Destruction of Dresden: 45,000+ killed (6/805). USAAF day raids on 14, 15 Feb and 3 Mar.
12 Mar	Largest raid of the war on Dortmund (2/1,107).
Apr–May	Manna: 6,672 tons of food dropped for the Dutch; Exodus: repatriation of 75,000 British POWs.
2/3 May	Last raid, on Kiel (3/231).

FURTHER READING

This is in no sense a formal bibliography, but simply lists books which, in my subjective view, deserve reading.

INTRODUCTION

Addison, Paul, and Calder, Angus (eds), *Time to Kill*, London, 1997
Anderson, Charles, *The Grunts*, Novato, California, 1983
Bidwell, Shelford, and Dominick Graham, *Fire-Power*, London, 1982
Browning, Christopher, *Ordinary Men: Reserve Police Battalion 101 and the Final Solution in Poland*, New York, 1993
Carver, Michael, *Dilemmas of the Desert War*, Bloomington, 1986
Cole, Sir David, *Rough Road to Rome*, London, 1983
Douglas, Keith, *Alamein to Zem Zem*, London, 1992
Dupuy, Trevor, *A Genius for War*, New York, 1977
Fraser, George MacDonald, *Quartered Safe Out Here*, London, 1992
Fussell, Paul, *The Great War and Modern Memory*, Oxford, 1975
Manstein, Erich von, *Lost Victories*, London, 1958
Nimitz, Chester, and Potter, E. B., *The Great Sea War*, London, 1960
Overy, Richard, *Why the Allies Won*, London, 1995
Ponting, Clive, *1940: Myth and Reality*, London, 2000
Smith, E. B., *Even the Brave Falter*, London, 1978
Van Creveld, Martin, *Fighting Power*, London, 1983

ALAMEIN

Bennett, Ralph, *Behind the Battle*, London, 1994
Bowlby, Alex, *Recollections of Rifleman Bowlby*, London 1969
Caccia Dominioni, Paolo, *Alamein 1933–1962 – An Italian Story*, London, 1966
Carver, Michael, *El Alamein*, London, 1962
Cooper, Artemis, *Cairo in the War 1939–45*, London, 1989
Kennedy Shaw, W. B., *Long Range Desert Group*, London, 1945
Lloyd Owen, David, *Providence Their Guide: A Personal Account of the Long Range Desert Group 1940–45*, London, 1980
Macksey, Kenneth, *For Want of a Nail*, London, 1989
McKee, Alexander, *El Alamein – Ultra and the Three Battles*, London, 1991
Roach, Peter, *The 8.15 to War*, London, 1982
Townshend Bickers, R., *The Desert Air War 1939–1945*, London, 1991

CASSINO

Bond, Harold, *Return to Cassino*, London, 1964
Brutton, Philip, *Ensign in Italy*, London, 1992
Buckley, Christopher, *Road to Rome*, London, 1945
D'Este, Carlo, *Fatal Decision*, London, 1991
Ellis, John, *Cassino: The Hollow Victory*, London, 1984

Horsfall, John, *Fling Our Banner to the Wind*, London, 1978
Lamb, Richard, *War in Italy*, New York, 1993
Lewis, Norman, *Naples '44*, London, 1978
Majdalany, Fred, *The Monastery*, London, 1945
Majdalany, Fred, *Cassino, Portrait of a Battle*, London, 1957
Senger und Etterlin, General Fridolin von, *Neither Fear Nor Hope*,
    London, 1963
White, M. B., *Purple Heart Valley*, New York, 1944

ARNHEM
Bennett, Ralph, *Ultra in the West*, London, 1979
Golden, Lewis, *Echoes from Arnhem*, London, 1984
Hackett, General Sir John, *I Was a Stranger*, London, 1977
Hagen, Louis, *Arnhem Lift*, London, 1945
Harclerode, Peter, *Arnhem – A Tragedy of Errors*, London, 1994
Kershaw, Robert, *It Never Snows in September*, Ramsbury, 1990
Middlebrook, Martin, *Arnhem 1944*, London, 1994
Powell, Geoffrey, *The Devil's Birthday*, London, 1984
Ryan, Cornelius, *A Bridge Too Far*, London, 1974
Sims, James, *Arnhem Spearhead*, London, 1978

BOMBER
Boiten, Theo, *Nachtjagd: The Nightfighter versus the Bomber War over
    the Third Reich*, Ramsbury, 1997
Boog, Horst (ed.), *The Conduct of the Air War in the Second World War*,
    Oxford, 1992
Bowyer, Chaz, *Tales from the Bombers*, London, 1985
Currie, Jack, *Lancaster Target*, Cheshire, 1981
Dean, Sir Maurice, *The Royal Air Force and Two World Wars*, London,
    1979
Foot, M. R. D., *SOE in France*, London, 1966
Frankland, Noble, and Webster, Charles, *The Strategic Air Offensive
    against Germany 1939–45*, 4 vols, London, 1961
Hastings, Max, *Bomber Command*, London, 1979
Jones, Geoffrey, *Night Flight*, London, 1981
Jones, R. V., *Most Secret War*, London, 1978
Lomas, Harry, *One Wing High*, Shrewsbury, 1995
Messenger, Charles, *'Bomber' Harris and the Strategic Bombing
    Offensive*, London, 1984
Middlebrook, Martin, and Everitt, Chris, *The Bomber Command War
    Diaries*, London, 1985
[See also Middlebrook's books on *Nuremberg* (1973), *Hamburg* (1980)
    and *Berlin* (1988)]
Rivaz, Squadron Leader R. C., *Tail Gunner* [1943], reprint Stroud, 1996
Terraine, John, *The Right of the Line*, London, 1985
Thompson, Walter, *Lancaster to Berlin*, Wilmslow, 1997

INDEX

PICTURE CREDITS

BBC Worldwide would like to thank the following for providing photographs and permission to reproduce
copyright material. While every effort has been made to trace and acknowledge all copyright holders,
we would like to apologise for any errors or omissions.
Key: t top, b bottom
Abbreviations: IWM Imperial War Museum, PNMP Peter Newark's Military Pictures,
PRO Public Record Office

3 Popperphoto; 5, 7t Popperfoto; 7b Topham; 10 AKG London; 13 PNMP; 15 PNMP; 16 Popperfoto;
17 Popperfoto; 23 PNMP; 27 Bettmann/Corbis; 30 PRO; 42 Corbis; 44t Topham; 44b Popperfoto; 49
Popperfoto; 51 PNMP; 53t PNMP; 53b AKG London; 58 PNMP; 65 Topham; 68 IWM; 73 Hulton Getty;
77 IWM; 79 Topham; 81 IWM; 90t David Lees/ Corbis; 90b IWM; 94 Corbis; 97 Popperfoto; 99
Popperfoto; 104 PNMP; 114 Topham; 117t Topham; 117b IWM; 121 AKG; 127 Topham; 132 Popperfoto;
135 AKG; 141 AKG; 147 PNMP; 148 Popperfoto; 157 Corbis/Hulton-Deutsch Collection; 161 IWM;
164t PNMP; 164b IWM; 166 PNMP; 174t Popperfoto; 174b Popperfoto; 179 Popperfoto; 185 PNMP;
186 Popperfoto; 189 Hulton-Deutsch Collection/Corbis; 201 IWM; 205 PNMP; 207 PRO; 211 AKG.